This work analyzes the centrality of law in nineteenth-century historical and institutional economics and serves as a prehistory to the new institutional economics of the late twentieth century. Starting around 1830 the "new science of law" aimed to explain the working rules of human society by using the methodologically individualist terms of economic discourse. By this definition, the college of the new science included members of the German and English historical schools, notably Wilhelm Roscher, Karl Knies, Gustav Schmoller, and Karl Bücher, early American institutionalists such as John R. Commons, and others such as Émile de Laveleye, Max Weber, Adolph Wagner, Carl Menger, and Achille Loria.

The new science typically employed the concept of an invariant *homo oeconomicus*, which had the effect of reducing law's diversity to diversity in the economic or transactional environment. A special premium was attached to covering laws that could account for the longitudinal and cross-sectional diversity of social experience. On the other hand, practitioners of the new science stood readier than contemporary "new" institutionalists to admit the possibilities of altruistic values, bounded rationality, and institutional inertia into their research program. Professor Pearson shows further that the positive analysis of law tended to push normative discussion up from the level of specific laws to that of society's political organization. Finally, the analysis suggests that the professionalization of the social sciences – and the new science's own imprecision – condemned the research program to oblivion in the twentieth century. Nonetheless, institutional economics is currently developing greater resemblances to the now-forgotten new science.

**Origins of Law and Economics**

*Historical Perspectives on Modern Economics*
*General Editor: Craufurd D. Goodwin, Duke University*

This series contains original works that challenge and enlighten historians of economics. For the profession as a whole it promotes better understanding of the origin and content of modern economics.

# Origins of Law and Economics

The Economists' New Science of Law, 1830–1930

HEATH PEARSON

*Koç University, Istanbul*

CAMBRIDGE
UNIVERSITY PRESS

PUBLISHED BY THE PRESS SYNDICATE OF THE UNIVERSITY OF CAMBRIDGE
The Pitt Building, Trumpington Street CB2 1RP, United Kingdom

CAMBRIDGE UNIVERSITY PRESS
The Pitt Building, Trumpington Street CB2 1RP
40 West 20th Street, New York, NY 10011-4211, USA
10 Stamford Road, Oakleigh, Melbourne 3166, Australia

First published 1997

Printed in the United States of America

Typeset in Times Roman

*Library of Congress Cataloging-in-Publication Data*

Pearson, Heath Dorset, 1961–
    Origins of law and economics : the economists' new science of law,
    1830–1930 / by Heath Dorset Pearson.
        p.      cm. – (Historical perspectives on modern economics)
    Includes bibliographical references and index.
    ISBN 0 521 58143 5 hardback
    1. Economics – Political aspects – History.   2. Economic man –
    History.   3. Institutional economics – History.   4. Law and
    economics – History.   I. Title.   II. Series.
    HB73.P43   1997
    330.1 – DC20                                                    96-35178
                                                                         CIP

*A catalog record for this book is available from
the British Library*

ISBN 0 521 58143 5 hardback

# Contents

# Preface

This study is to serve in two capacities: first, as a prehistory to the "new institutional economics" of the late twentieth century; second, as an effort to synthesize, or at least analyze, one central aspect of the highly diverse literature of nineteenth-century "historical" and "institutional" economics. That aspect is the centrality of law.

The "new science" is identified as a research program within political economy. Its aim was to *explain,* using the *methodologically individualist* terms characteristic of economic discourse, the *working rules* of human society, with a special premium attaching to the sort of covering laws that could account for the longitudinal and cross-sectional diversity of social experience. By this definition, the college of the new science included members of the German and English Historical Schools (notably Wilhelm Roscher, Karl Knies, Gustav Schmoller, Adolph Wagner, and Karl Bücher), early American institutionalists (notably John R. Commons), and many others (notably Émile de Laveleye, Carl Menger, Achille Loria, and Max Weber).

The origins of the new science are traced to the growing prestige of determinism and the evolutionary concept in nineteenth-century social thought. The economic approach to law was developed first and most fully in the German universities, where the two disciplines had long been associated in the curriculum of *Staatswissenschaft,* or the "science of state."

It is difficult to capture the essence of the new science in a simple formula. On the one hand, its analytical center of gravity strongly resembled that of today's "new institutional economics." It made free use of the conception of an invariant *homo oeconomicus,* which had the effect of reducing law's diversity to diversity in the economic or transactional environment. But on the other hand, practitioners of the new science stood readier than our "new institutionalists" to admit the possibilities of nonpecuniary or even altruistic values, of bounded rationality, and of institutional inertia.

This study includes a digression of sorts, on the normative dimension of this ferment in the positive analysis of law. In particular, it shows that the determinist turn tended to push normative discussion "up," from the level of specific laws to the level of society's political organization. In this sense the new science prepared the ground for an early version of "constitutional economics."

The study concludes with an explanation of how the professionalization of the social sciences – and the new science's own rhetorical excess and imprecision – condemned this research program to oblivion after about 1930. In an epilogue, it is suggested that the "new institutional economics" is now developing in the direction of greater resemblance to the now-forgotten new science of law.

I have tried to structure this book so that it will meet the needs of readers who have much, little, or very little time to devote to it. For those in the greatest hurry, the introduction and conclusion of each chapter, along with the general introduction, will supply the gist of my argument. The text of each chapter aims to provide a compressed tour of the arguments propounded in the literature under scrutiny. The footnotes, which contain the bulk of documentation and supporting materials, are recommended to readers who are unusually curious and/or healthily skeptical.

My own motives in wading through these sources have been curiosity, skepticism, ambition, and some degree of masochism. In satisfaction of these urges I have been aided immeasurably by those scholars who have read and commented on the entire manuscript, including Richard Adelstein, Knut Borchardt, Jan de Vries, Gerald Feldman, Charles Hanson, Benjamin Ward, and two anonymous referees. I am grateful also for the financial support of the Center for German and European Studies at UC Berkeley, for the careful editing of Diana Gillooly, and for the moral support of mentors, friends, and family – categories which very much overlap.

# Introduction

How novel is the "new institutional economics"? Are there historical precursors to "constitutional economics"? What were the core assumptions of nineteenth-century European "historical economics," and what was its relation to early twentieth-century American "institutionalism"? How, and to what extent, did materialist and humanist impulses commingle in early social evolutionism? How did economists and jurists view one another during the decades leading up to the contemporary "law and economics" movement? If these questions pique the reader's interest, read on.

By design or default, the legal order has not traditionally been included in the locus of economic explanation. To the extent that law is accorded attention at all, it is held to be an (exogenous) cause of economic outcomes, not an (endogenous) outcome of economic causes. We may illustrate with the classic example of private property and free contract. The canonical Principles of Economics text simply assumes these institutions as a point of departure. The question why people – and economies – behave differently under regimes of private and common property is also uncontroversially economic, if somewhat more recondite; but the question why private property emerges in one society, and not in another, has generally gone unexplored. As Paul Samuelson put it in his influential *Foundations of Economic Analysis* (1947: 8), the "governmental and institutional framework" should be set aside, along with tastes and technology, as "matters which economists have traditionally chosen not to consider within their province."

The best argument for such neglect goes to simplicity, and to the principle of comparative advantage in the division of intellectual labor. Economists of the "new institutional" persuasion, by contrast, have typically

1

hypothesized that social norms are equilibria endogenous to the social system and have attempted to use neoclassical tools – primarily methodological individualism and the theory of rational choice – to make sense of rules in all their variety across time and space. Two recent developments have further complicated this picture. On the one hand, institutionalism has been drawn into a more critical stance vis-à-vis the assumption of boundlessly rational calculation in the service of pecuniary egoism: this is the domain of "evolutionary" social theory, centered largely on the problems of ideology and altruism. On the other hand, the generally detached and deterministic timbre of "new" institutionalism has given way, in places, to research around the expressly normative problem of the optimal political order: this is the domain of "constitutional" economics.

These divergent trends have not lost their common thread in a single research program, however. In the words of James Buchanan (1991: 19), "economists have commenced to turn some of their attention to *choices among constraints* and away from the exclusive focus on the familiar *choices within constraints.*" Economic history too, according to Douglass North (1981: 209), would best be "conceived as a theory of the evolution of constraints," at least in so far as explanation of past economic performance is the goal of inquiry. "That task," North adds, "remains to be done"; for Buchanan the undertaking seems "almost certain to become more dominant in the next century." This study will show that it was deemed an important frontier of research a century and more ago.

If the antiquity of the "new" institutional economics has gone unremarked or unappreciated, the nineteenth-century precursors themselves deserve much of the blame. Their books were often long, tendentious, and methodologically lax. But the historians of economic thought, whose task is to bring order where it does not already exist, are also at fault. The authors who will be the focus of this study are remembered, insofar as they are remembered at all, primarily for their dissent from Classical orthodoxy: against universalism, against utilitarianism, against laissez-faire, against theory *tout court.* It is hard not to sympathize with the complaints of Gide and Rist, authors of one of the first general histories of economic thought, whose treatment of historical economics remains one of the most sensitive.

> Generally speaking, it is not a difficult task to give an exposition of the critical ideas of the school, as we find them set forth in several books and articles, but it is by no means easy to delineate the conceptions underlying the positive work. Though implicit in all their writings these conceptions are nowhere explicitly stated; whenever they have tried to define them it has always been, as their disciples willingly admit, in a vague and contradictory fashion. To add further to the difficulty, each author defines

them after his own fashion, but claims that his definition represents the ideas of the whole school. ([1909] 1948: 385)
The problem is real enough, but pointing out difficulties is no substitute for solving them, or at least resolving them into meaningful antinomies.

Most histories of economic thought have been content to outline the negative program of the historical-institutional schools, that is, to explain what it was they *held false*. The most knowledgeable treatments, however, have not failed to note the missed opportunity of a thematic overview of what the heterodox economists actually believed. "It is unfortunate," wrote John F. Bell (1953: 346–7), "that so few of the many publications have been translated and that the language barrier is so formidable to many. Perhaps in time someone will do a thorough study of the works of the lesser known authors." Again, in 1977, Knut Borchardt mused that "it appears to be high time that someone appear on the scene to initiate an appreciation of their efforts, in light of recent developments in economic science."[1] This study cannot purport to answer all these calls in full; but in demonstrating and exploring the nomothetic ambitions of these economists as regards the evolution of law, one piece of the puzzle will be put into place.

This one piece of the puzzle we have termed "the new science of law." As it is reconstructed in the pages to come, the conventional wisdom on early historical-institutional economics will be called into doubt. As against the view that the initial institutional project was basically *expository* and/or *evaluative,* we will show that it was primarily *explanatory* in intent. And against the view that institutionalist explanation, such as it was, was essentially of *teleological* and/or *holistic* complexion, we will show how far it went with causal explanation and methodological individualism. In other words, the "hard core" of the new science of law was very much in the spirit of today's neoclassical institutional economics.

This study consists of five chapters and an epilogue. Chapters 1 and 5 and the epilogue are geared to appeal to the historian's sensibilities, by contextualizing the rise, fall, and resurrection of the new science. Chapters 2, 3, and 4, on the other hand, are directed more to the economist's interests: they seek to highlight the contours, consensuses, and tensions within the new science, taken as a single research program. Those three chapters will be organized parallel to what we have called the three phases within the "new" institutional economics of the late twentieth century.

More specifically, we will proceed as follows. Chapter 1 will explore the

1. Borchardt, "Der Property-Rights-Ansatz" (1977): 150. The translation is mine, as are most translations in this study. Where an English translation already exists, I have often relied upon it: these instances are noted in the bibliography. In every such instance, page references are to the English edition.

origins of the new science of law and will give some sense of its prominence and geographic distribution by the turn of this century. Chapters 2 and 3 will impose some order on the extraordinary wealth of argumentation within the new science. Chapter 2 shows how far its practitioners carried the "materialist" conception of legal evolution, whereby institutional diversity is reduced to an invariant *homo oeconomicus* maximizing his net worth in the face of various natural, technological, and social environments. Chapter 3, by contrast, demonstrates the remarkable extent to which economists stood ready to relativize, or even abandon, *homo oeconomicus* in their models of legal evolution. Chapter 4 is something of a digression, from positive to normative economics. In particular, it addresses the following question: Given the relative determinacy of law, what scope remains for building the institutional foundations of the good society? Attempts to answer this question led practitioners of the new science to seek the optimal political constitution, much as present-day Public Choice theory has been drawn toward "constitutional" political economy. Chapter 5 is the counterpoint to chapter 1, in that it chronicles and explains the new science's fall into obscurity during the first decades of this century. The study concludes with an epilogue, followed by biographical notes on practitioners of the new science.

# 1

## A new science

The century preceding 1914 saw momentous change in the way scholars thought about society and its institutions. The primacy of the universal gave way to that of the peculiar and the evolutionary, while the causal efficacy of Ideas was derogated in favor of Matter. This study explores one important aspect of that phenomenon, namely, the increasing conviction on the part of economists that their worldly science had something germane to contribute to the understanding of law.

Why should not the production and distribution of rights be subject to economic analysis? After all, exchange in the marketplace – the economist's undisputed domain – entails above all the exchange of rights and obligations and may or may not involve the physical transfer of goods. Departing from this simple insight, one may sensibly deduce a natural affinity between the concerns of economics and the data of civil law. Indeed, most contemporary economists will assent to the proposition that economic concepts help to explain the regime of rights and obligations under which an economy operates. Economists untutored in the history of their discipline might well argue that the connection is intrinsic and must always have been patent; others would gainsay this, on the basis of a conventional intellectual history that begins with Ronald Coase's 1937 article "The Nature of the Firm," goes on to the work of Alchian, Demsetz, Posner, North, and many others, and culminates in what is known today as the "law and economics" movement. This chapter will correct both these notions: in truth, the economic analysis of rights is older than the twentieth century, but it is nevertheless younger than economics as a whole. In the eight decades preceding 1914, as political economy matured to great prestige as a science of commodities, the economic approach to law was very much a "new science."

This new science attempted to endogenize economic rights and obligations to the social process. In plain English, this means that a group of scholars attempted to solve a shared problem on the basis of a few shared assumptions. The problem they addressed may best be posed as a question: Why do economic rights take the form they do, and why do they change over time and differ across space? This concern led them into engagement with all the legal provisions that impinge on the production and consumption of goods and services, including contract law, human servitude, and especially the right of property. Their shared assumption was that any adequate solutions to the problem must recognize rules, like other economic variables, to be artifacts of purposive, rational human action.

## I     A hostile environment

Let us begin with the youth of this science. The problem we have identified was not accepted as important by many economists until the mid-nineteenth century. Indeed, many treatises dispense with it to this day. In light of our suggestion that law is a "natural" concern of political economy, this retardation itself requires some explanation. The best explanation is that early economists gave priority to the investigation of other questions, and that those prior concerns militated against effective engagement with the problem of explaining law. We will identify three such research agendas, each of which centered on an interesting question of its own.

### 1     What regularities underlie the modern economy?

A hallmark of political economy in its formative period was the effort to make positive sense of quotidian phenomena like rent, wages, and the accumulation of capital. In practice, the more economists had to say about the economic ramifications of the system of rights under which they lived, the less they cared to dwell on the origins of that system. The leading light of this school was David Ricardo, whose *Principles of Political Economy and Taxation* (1817) made no pretense of explaining the legal rules by which the economy operates. This fact should not be considered so much a defect in the Ricardian system, a taint of "commodity fetishism," as a logical corollary to his chosen research agenda. To be viable an explanatory model must draw lines between values assumed to be variable and those set constant; the division will be informed by scholarly interest and by the need to appear reasonable. Now as the Classical project's central problem was the dynamic of the "progressive" economy, it was not unreasonable that the fundamental institutions of modern society should be taken as parametric. These economists' very silence on matters of rights makes it difficult to get a sense of their reasoning, but we can gain some insight from those who did raise the issue, only to dismiss it. Consider the Frenchman Jean-Baptiste Say, who assured students that "it is not necessary, in order to study the nature and progress of social wealth, to know of property's origins, or of its legitimacy."[1] Or the German professor Karl Heinrich Rau:

> The division of *resources* . . . is different in each country, according to prior events and locational circumstance. That must be explained with reference to the history of each nation, but then presented by means of statistics. Economic theory is not concerned with the causes of these basic relations of possession, but rather with their effects, indeed principally with their influence on the division of the gross annual income.[2]

Or the American Samuel P. Newman: "It belongs not to the science of Political Economy, to investigate the principles on which the right of property is founded, or to state the methods, by which it is most fully and effectually secured. In all the reasonings of this science, it is supposed that this right exists and is respected."[3] Even such rationalizations as these were more the exception than the rule. For most Classicists, including Ricardo himself, this simplification was implicit, and justified (much as the fiction of partial equilibrium is today rationalized) as an aid to clear thought.

## 2  *Which is the just system of rights?*

The second explanation for the retardation of institutional analysis pertains to those economists who did concern themselves with the nature of rights but did not consider them to be primarily social artifacts. The essential factor deciding who would and would not pioneer the new science stems from an ambiguity in the word *right* (as well as *Recht, droit, diritto,* etc.), specifically its use in discussions of both fact and value. Depending on the context, to speak of rights may mean speaking of the actual legal privileges granted to a person in a specific society, or alternatively it may mean applying some ethical criterion to argue what those privileges *should be.* Logic does not dictate that scholars who gave priority to the normative discourse of rights should not also have participated fully in the social science of positive rights; in practice, however, this tended to be the case. Economists whose primary aim was to discover the ideal system of rights typically remained all but silent on the social foundations of empirical law.

1. Say, *Cours complet d'économie politique pratique* ([1828–9] 1840): vol. 2, ch. 4.
2. Rau, *Grundsätze der Volkswirthschaftslehre* ([1826] 1847): §140.
3. Newman, *Elements of Political Economy* (1835): 33.

Early economists tended to approach law just as did jurists and moral philosophers. It was believed that absolute principles of right were either self-evident to the student of humanity, or else accessible through the power of right reason. In either case, the royal road to insight was supposed to be clear thought, not observation. The economists' desire to transcend the phenomenal world led them beyond even the abstractions of social contract theory, to the Lockean conception of rights as prior – temporally as well as ontologically – to man's association with man. For Physiocrats like P. S. Dupont de Nemours, "the *rights* of each man, anterior to convention, are freedom to provide for his subsistence and well-being, *property* in his own person, and property in the objects acquired by the labor of his person."[4] Adam Smith is a more problematic figure in this study. His gestures toward legal realism will be taken up below; but for now suffice it to note that his treatment of rights in *The Wealth of Nations* (1776) centered on a categorical assertion that "the property which every man has in his own labor, as it is the original foundation of all other property, so it is the most sacred and inviolable."[5] This line of reasoning was taken up eagerly by academic system builders of the nineteenth century, presumably not least because it allowed them to subcontract a part of their intellectual project to more established and prestigious disciplines.[6] For example, Say argued in 1828 that

4. Dupont de Nemours, *De l'origine et des progrès d'une science nouvelle* ([1768] 1846): 342. The other main Physiocratic texts addressing rights are: François Quesnay, "*Le droit naturel*" (1765–6); Le Mercier de la Rivière, *L'Ordre naturel et essentiel des sociétés politiques* (1767); and Gustave Le Trosne, *De l'Ordre social* (1777). See also Léon Cheinisse, *Les idées politiques des Physiocrates* (1914); John A. Mourant, *The Physiocratic Conception of Natural Law* (1943).
5. Smith, *An Inquiry into the Nature and Causes of the Wealth of Nations* ([1776] 1976): 1:136. As such he remained broadly consistent with his stipulation, at the outset of his Glasgow lectures on jurisprudence, that "the end proposed by justice is the maintaining of men in what are called their perfect rights" ([1762–4] 1978: 5). Smith's links to the tradition of natural law, and his commitment to strict justice, have not been lost on all historians. See especially Istvan Hont and Michael Ignatieff, "Needs and Justice in the *Wealth of Nations:* An Introductory Essay" (1983): 26–44; and Terence Hutchison, *Before Adam Smith* (1990): 193–5.
6. Say's last and most voluminous work reduced the foundation of property rights to a simple syllogism: "If the state of nature is for man the one in which he obtains his greatest development, if he attains this development only in the state of society, and if the state of society can survive only with property, then the right of property is therefore a natural one: it derives therefore from the very nature of man" ([1828–9] 1840: 239). This was also the position of Gustave de Molinari, for whom property – "the relation of justice existing between value and its creators" – was the province of jurisprudence. The role of political econ-

speculative philosophy may busy itself seeking the true foundations of the right of property. The jurist may establish the rules that preside over the transmission of things possessed; political science may show which are the surest guarantees of this right. But political economy regards property solely as the strongest encouragement to the production of wealth; it cares little about how it is established and guaranteed.[7]

The categorical nature of natural rights appealed also to laissez-faire publicists like Frédéric Bastiat, who termed the right to property "a necessary consequence of man's constitution," valid prior to the social contract.[8] Or in the terms of the Spanish liberal Santiago Diego Madrazo, the right of property was very nearly an ontological necessity, in no way contingent upon positive law: "It is anterior because it existed at the very moment of society's birth, and superior because human law cannot abolish it or

---

omy, on the other hand, was merely to demonstrate the social utility of natural justice (Molinari [1855] 1863: 1:107–9; 1891: 244–5). Léon Faucher's article "Propriété" in the *Dictionnaire de l'économie politique* (1853) simply relied on extensive quotes from noneconomists, notably Charles Comte and Louis Adolphe Thiers.

In Italy, Gerolamo Boccardo argued that property was no social convention, but rather "the legitimate corollary of this sacred principle . . . : that each must be able to enjoy freely the fruits of his own labor" [*Trattato teoretico-pratico di economia politica* (1853): 1:§47]. Francesco Trinchera broached the subject as a digression in the fields of jurisprudence and politics, and he closed it with the purpose of "returning to our own science" [*Corso di economia politica* (1854): 1:62–81]. In Madrid, Manuel Colmeiro taught that "the institution of property owes its origin not to law, but to primitive occupation or to labor" [*Principios de economía política* ([1859] 1873): ch. 9]. Or again, "Jurisprudence teaches us what is, political economy what should be" (ch. 6).

This position spread as far afield as the German university at Grosswardein (in present-day Romania), where Gyula Kautz taught that the "social regime of rights" [*die sociale Rechtsordnung*] was rooted in "the eternal laws of human nature" [*Die National-Oekonomik als Wissenschaft* (1858): 58–60].

7. Say [1828–9] 1840: 238. This division of labor was posited also in his *Traité d'économie politique* (1803) and his *Catéchisme d'économie politique* (1815).
8. Bastiat, "Propriété et loi" ([1848] 1878): 277; and similarly Henri Baudrillart's tract *La propriété* (1867): 12–41, and Charles Le Hardy de Beaulieu's *La propriété et sa rente dans leurs rapports avec l'économie politique et le droit publique* (1868).
   The great system builder Léon Walras started out with just such a publicistic effort, in his first book *L'économie politique et la justice* (1860). "It is man's right and his duty," Walras wrote in defense of individual property, "to subordinate the accomplishment of blind destinies to the accomplishment of his own, free destiny" (134, 140–3).

change its nature."[9] Socialist treatises also sought the cachet of formal jurisprudence. Locke's labor theory of property was readily appropriated by champions of the working class;[10] and even Pierre-Joseph Proudhon, who rejected the natural right of property as a bald pretext for larceny, offered in its place a model of economic rights that was no less deductive and absolute.[11]

But why should this Platonic science of transcendent rights hinder the development of a separate science, one to explain rights as they appeared in society? Two reasons are suggested by the rhetoric of these texts. To begin with, idealist jurisprudence lent itself to pat answers and just-so stories about the origins of actual rights, stories which stifled the scientific project by denying its underlying problematic. An early example of this is

9. Madrazo, *Lecciones de economía política* (1874–6): 2:17.
10. J.-C.-L. Simonde de Sismondi insisted that "the ownership of one's own person, and of the fruits of one's labor, is prior to the law." Similarly, "power over slaves is not a right, but only robbery which, in certain countries, and under certain circumstances, the law does not punish" ([1819] 1991: 153–4).

   Consider also "Ricardian socialists" like the American Langdon Byllesby, who took as his benchmark the "natural equality of rights" [*Observations on the Sources and Effects of Unequal Wealth* (1826), cited in Dorfman 1946–59: 2:639]; and the Briton Thomas Hodgskin, who taught that "a man's right to the free use of his own mind and limbs, and to appropriate whatever he creates by his own labor, is the result of natural laws" [*Popular Political Economy* (1827): 237].

   In 1848, J. S. Mill held that the "essence" of the right of property was "that equitable principle, of proportion between remuneration and exertion" – in other words the venerable labor theory – and proposed to ask, as a natural lawyer would, "to what extent the forms in which the institution has existed in different states of society, or still exists, are necessary consequences of its principle, or are recommended by the reasons on which it is grounded" [*Principles of Political Economy* (1848): book II, ch. 1, §3; ch. 2, §2]. Even as late as 1898, Mill was taken to task by Henry George for stressing insufficiently property's exclusive origins in labor [*The Science of Political Economy:* book IV].
11. "The producer himself is entitled to only that portion of his product, which is expressed by a fraction whose denominator is equal to the number of individuals of which society is composed" [Proudhon, *Qu'est-ce que la propriété?* ([1840] 1890): 149]. But as the whole labor pool was argued to contribute to each product, and each producer was assumed to be an equal contributor to that labor pool, the result is the same. In sum, equality of opportunity of subsistence is the natural economic right, and under conditions of material scarcity it suggests that each person should enjoy equal rights of possession in all natural resources; and since production is by its nature cooperative, the only real title it should yield is that of each labor unit to a proportional share of the social product.

the German cameralist account of the economic authority of the absolutist state. Although cameralism was above all a practical science, its leading
texts were scholarly efforts that eschewed the ad hoc voluntarism that underpinned other mercantilist tracts; instead, they were immersed in the
tradition of natural constitutional law pioneered by Samuel Pufendorf and
Christian Wolff.[12] This tradition postulated a primal contract, by means
of which individuals in a presocial state had once surrendered to the sovereign their de facto possessions, in exchange for enforceable de jure rights
against depredation by one another. Henceforth it fell to that sovereign,
guided by his chancellors, to guarantee, regulate, or even abrogate each
subject's tenure as he deemed conducive to the good of the state. Society
itself was in no way responsible for the adjustment of rights to needs:
legislation was a "natural right of kings," if we may call it such, and stood
no more scientific scrutiny than the proverbial deus ex machina.[13]

Liberal prophets of progress, on the other hand, attached themselves to
fashionable notions of cultural evolution, going so far even as to endow
institutions with the power of self-realization in history. According to
Léon Faucher, author of the entry "Property" in the *Dictionnaire de l'économie politique* (1853), the right of property was not only a universal fact,
"it is at the same time an increasing fact"; the right of inheritance, too, was
"the invincible consequence of human nature and society." Grammatically,
Faucher avoided making rights the object of transitive verbs, as one would
expect for a social artifact, rather treating them as the subject of reflexive
verbs [*la propriété s'accroît, s'étende,* etc.].[14] The same trope appeared in

12. The marriage in cameralism of natural law and absolutism has been much
    remarked by scholars most familiar with the literature. The best exposition is
    still that of Louise Sommer, *Die österreichischen Kameralisten in dogmen-
    geschichtlicher Darstellung* (1920–5). See also Volker Hentschel, "Zweckset-
    zungen und Zielvorstellungen in den Wirtschafts-und Soziallehren des 18. und
    19. Jahrhunderts" (1982): 114–15; Rüdiger vom Brüch, "Zur Historisierung
    der Staatswissenschaften: von der Kameralistik zur historischen Schule der
    Nationalökonomie" (1985): 131–3; Keith Tribe, *Governing Economy* (1988):
    29; Jutta Brückner, *Staatswissenschaften, Kameralismus und Natturrecht*
    (1977); Gustav Schmoller, *Grundriß der Allgemeinen Volkswirtschaftslehre*
    (1901–4), 1:83. Mack Walker's assertion (1978: 237) that cameralists were un-
    willing to recur to natural law stands outside this consensus.
13. See Tribe 1988: 21–4; Brückner 1977: 229–31. According to Louise Sommer,
    "Natural law, ostensibly the polar opposite of the police-state ideal [*des Pol-
    izeistaatsgedankens*], is weakened and fitted to absolutism in typically German
    fashion, so that it becomes the very seed-bed of that doctrine" (1920–5:
    2:162–3).
14. Faucher 1853: 464. A translation of this piece served, thirty-six years after
    Faucher's death, as the entry "Property" in the *Cyclopaedia of Political Sci-
    ence, Political Economy, and of the Political History of the United States* (1890).

the Italian prose of Gerolamo Boccardo, who discerned in the process of civilization that "property, *individuating itself* [*individualizzandosi*], assumes forms more appropriate to its nature"; while for the Spaniard Manuel Colmeiro, communal tenure "gradually disappears in step with the progress of civilization," thus "abandoning the field" to individual property.[15]

At the other end of the ideological spectrum, detractors of liberal capitalism developed their own metahistories to substitute for social-scientific analysis. Proudhon explained the prevalence of property by means of a Hegelian version of the Tree of Knowledge and the Fall of Man. Primitive communism was undermined by man's "terrible faculty of reasoning logically or illogically," which had led him to the false conclusion that community was not the expression of equality, but its negation, a form of slavery. Property was instituted as an act of emancipation, and only too late was it recognized to be in fact the vehicle of slavery.[16] Karl Marx's *Economic and Philosophical Manuscripts* (1844, first published 1932) discussed property in terms reminiscent of Proudhon, whom Marx still held in high regard.[17] Property, like all economic phenomena, expressed "a necessary course of development." It resulted from and reproduced the negation of an essential unity, just as its abolition would restore that principle in a higher form. But whereas Proudhon's principle was interpersonal equality, Marx's was the individual's self-fulfillment in the act of labor. Private property, in Marx's terms, "is thus the product, the result, the necessary consequence, of *alienated labor,* of the external relation of the worker to nature and to himself" ([1844] 1975: 270–80).

The second ramification of the formal ethics of rights was that, once a "higher" realm of pure reason had been posited, the realm of experience

15. Boccardo 1853: 1:§59; Colmeiro [1859] 1873: ch. 9.
16. In explicitly Hegelian terms, "communism – the first expression of the social nature – is the first term of social development – the *thesis*; property, the reverse of communism, is the second term – the *antithesis.* When we have discovered the third term, the *synthesis,* we shall have the required solution" (Proudhon [1840]: 258–9). As for idealist philosophy in general, so for Proudhon in particular, property was of interest as a unitary concept in relation to a higher principle. For Hegel the principle was individuality, and property its affirmation; for Proudhon that principle was equality, property its negation.
17. Proudhon was mentioned only in passing in the 1844 *Manuscripts,* but he was referred to in glowing terms in both 1843 and 1845. Proudhon's work was for Marx and Engels "the first resolute, ruthless, and at the same time scientific investigation of the basis of political economy, *private property*" [*Die heilige Familie* ([1845] 1975): book IV, ch. 4]. See also Gregory, "What Marx and Engels Knew of French Socialism" (1983).

came to appear "lesser" by comparison. The fact is that the defense of things sacred tended, in almost every case, to inhibit explanation of things profane. An illuminating parallel may be drawn with the better known career of value theory. In its search for generality and precision, Classical economics had tended to attach greater importance to the explanation of (natural) value than to (merely phenomenal) price. Only in the last decades of the nineteenth century, as the theory of exchange finally cast off the moorings of ethical certainty, was price theory allowed to develop freely and to resolve at last the Paradox of Value, which had played on value/price discrepancies. The positive science of rights faced similar difficulties. The least discreet economists of the old school sometimes argued that there was no counterpart to the Paradox of Value in the study of rights, that for all practical purposes the laws of man were in uniform compliance with the constitution of nature.[18] But even more telling was the widespread belief that worldly legal provisions, idiosyncratic and inconstant as they were, did not deserve the same consideration as truly natural rights. It was commonly argued, from Physiocracy onward, that basic economic rights like property had preceded the advent of civil society, and that while it was within the state's coercive power to guarantee, abridge, or usurp rights, no power could actually *create* rights.[19] When

18. "The obvious *utility* of securing to each individual the produce which has been raised by his industry," J. R. M'Culloch argued, "has undoubtedly formed the irresistible reason which has induced every people emerging from barbarism to establish this right [of property]" [*The Principles of Political Economy* (1825): 75]. We may also cite Johann Schön, by whose lights "it is impossible to conceive of a *society* in which existed neither capital nor property in land" [*Neue Untersuchungen der Nationalökonomie und der natürlichen Volkswirthschaftsordnung* (1835): 83–5]; or Antoine Cherbuliez's claim that appropriation was "an absolute condition of civil society," which had therefore been instituted "wherever men of the most diverse races have commenced to live in regular society" [*Simples notions de l'ordre sociale à l'usage de tout le monde* (1848): 26–27; and *Précis de la science économique* (1862): 2:212]; or Kautz, who placed property among the "basic rules of humanity" [*menschheitliche Grundordnungen*], rules which were observable in all communities at all moments of world history, "with very few, hardly noteworthy exceptions" (1858: 65).

19. A partial list would include Smith [1776] 1976: 2:231–2 (also Smith [1762–4] 1978: 324, 404–5; Ludwig von Jakob, *Grundsätze der National-Oekonomie oder Theorie des National-Reichthums* ([1805] 1825): §§566–73; Heinrich von Storch, *Cours d'économie politique* ([1815] 1823): 3:105–13; Johann F. G. Eiselen, *Handbuch des Systems der Staatswissenschaften* (1828): Introduction, 92–3, 128, 164; Henry C. Carey, *Principles of Political Economy* (1837–40): 2:9–12 and ch. 3; Francis Lieber, *Manual of Political Ethics* [(1838–9), cited in Dorfman 1946–59: 2:869]; Bastiat [1848] 1878: 276 (where he coined the

these economists did touch on the interface between interests, politics, and rights, it was often brusquely and with distaste. For instance, Smith dismissed medieval innovations like primogeniture and entail – institutions which latter-day social scientists would seek to comprehend as adaptations to peculiar conditions – as violations of the "natural laws of succession" discovered by the Romans.[20] Clément Garnier recognized that the universal desire for property was not everywhere realized in equal measure; but that diversity he ascribed simply to political dysfunctions of undisclosed etiology and moved on.[21] Boccardo, likewise, considered it an adequate explanation to note that where the "natural" perfection of property had failed to appear, it was because rogue elements – "sultan and pasha," in his terms – had thwarted it (1852: 135–6). A passage from Proudhon epitomizes the economists' impatience with the actual profusion of human institutions:

> It is a rule of jurisprudence that the fact does not substantiate the right. . . . Of what consequence is it to us that the Indian race was divided into four classes; that, on the banks of the Nile and the Ganges, blood and position formerly determined the distribution of the land; that the Greeks and Romans placed property under the protection of the gods; that they accompanied with religious ceremonies the work of partitioning the land and appraising their goods? The variety of the forms of privilege does not sanction injustice. ([1840] 1890: 80)

It would be a precondition of the new science to transcend this prejudice of the sacred and the profane.

### 3    Which is the expedient system of rights?

This question too led to an ethical science of rights, but one of a different nature. It could be answered not by axiomatic reason, but only by the intensive scrutiny of social needs. We may call it, conveniently if perhaps anachronistically, utilitarian.

No survey of the ethical impulses coursing through Classical economics can ignore the utilitarian revolution. Utilitarianism, scourge of just the

epigram, "It is not due to laws that we have property, but rather because of property that we have laws"); Baudrillart, "Du principe de propriété" (1855): 335; Trinchera 1854: 64, 68–9; Kautz 1858: 59–60; Walras 1860: 137, 143; and Le Hardy de Beaulieu 1868: 22–3, 29–30.

20. Smith [1776] 1976: 1:407–8; see also Smith [1762–4] 1978: 70–1.

21. "Either the state has excessive rights over [private property], or else the social organization permits spoliation" [Garnier, *Élements de l'économie politique* ([1846] 1856): §406].

sort of metaphysical pretensions that have filled these last pages, was more warmly received in economics than in other disciplines, and certainly more so than in jurisprudence. Indeed, the utilitarian principle of eudaemonist social engineering had been articulated long *avant la lettre* in political economy, notably in German cameralism. Utilitarian economists made a show of contradicting many of the tenets that we have associated with an aversion to institutional analysis. They scorned the ideal of a "pure" jurisprudence keeping its splendid isolation from the world and pointed to the indispensability of factual understanding in any system of applied ethics; for utilitarians "real" rights were positive rights, and positive rights were the creation of human will. This view of rights took hold first of all in discussions of land tenure, beginning with cameralist debates over agrarian reform[22] and continuing in the work of Sartorius,[23] Sismondi,[24] and Schüz;[25] ultimately it came to call in question the "naturalness" of all rights, with exception typically made for self-ownership. In view of this, it is not surprising that the rudiments of a social science of rights are scattered throughout utilitarian writings.

But no more than rudiments are evident in much of this literature, and none at all in most of the rest.[26] It is our contention that this was to be

22. See Harald Winkel, "Zur theoretischen Begründung der Bodenmobilisierung in der Volkswirtschaftslehre" (1976).
23. According to Sartorius, individuals do have a natural right to the "forms" they inscribe on material objects, but the rest of society has an equally original and peremptory claim to the material that now bears that form. The stage is set for intractable strife, unless the state is introduced as an authoritative third party. "The state must put an end to this eternal contention and lay down arbitrary decrees [*willkürliche Vorschriften*]," he insisted, "as public laws that express intelligence and reflection; it must reconcile, so far as is possible, the claims of the one and the claims of the rest" ["Von der Mitwirkung der obersten Gewalt im Staate zur Beförderung des National-Reichthums" (1806): 199–205].
24. As Sismondi put it, property in land "is a gift of society and in no way a natural right which preexisted. . . . The ownership of land is, indeed, not based on a principle of justice but on a principle of public utility" [*Nouveaux principes d'économie politique* ([1819] 1991): esp. 138–9].
25. Schüz, *Ueber den Einfluß der Vertheilung des Grundeigenthums auf das Volks- und Staatsleben* ([1836] 1976): esp. 153–4.
26. Examples of the first sort are Sismondi 1819; J. S. Mill 1848; J. Dupuit, "Le principe de la propriété" (1861); John R. Commons, *The Distribution of Wealth* (1893); and Richard T. Ely, *Property and Contract in Their Relations to the Distribution of Wealth* (1914). Examples of the second: Henry Fawcett, *Manual of Political Economy* (1863); T. E. Cliffe Leslie, "Political economy and the Tenure of Land" (1866); and the contributions by Leslie and Émile

expected: for these economists, reformist zeal precluded detached exploration of the structures of public choice. In other words, political economy
was brandished as an instrument of political freedom, not as a prism of
social determinacy. Cameralists were silent on the determination of rights,
as befitted their judicial activism. Sismondi ([1819] 1991: 132) insisted that
"the division of rights to property is born from special circumstances,
from chance schemes, often from passions or vanity," and referred often
to the process of institutional innovation as "invention." Henry Fawcett
made worthy statements about the relativity of property rights,[27] but in
the end he, too, dismissed the suggestion that it was the economist's business to explain them: "It would be impossible to describe the origin of all
the different kinds of property, and the rights connected therewith, without writing the history of each country; . . . it does not pertain to political
economy to discuss the origin of the laws of inheritance, or of landed
tenure" (1863: 98–9). Likewise according to John Stuart Mill, a positive
science of the rules by which income was distributed would have to be

> part of the general theory of human progress, a far larger and
> more difficult subject of inquiry than political economy. We have
> here to consider, not the causes, but the consequences of the
> rules according to which wealth may be distributed. Those, at
> least, are as little arbitrary, and have as much the character of
> physical laws, as the laws of production.

The economist, in short, was supposed to be ill equipped to understand
the determination of rights. Moreover, when treating questions of applied
ethics, it was important that he not even try. "In considering the institution
of property as a question in social philosophy," Mill concluded, "we must
leave out of consideration its actual origin in any of the existing nations
of Europe" (1848: book II, ch. 1, §§1–2).

Similarly Léon Walras, once he had abandoned the categorical defense
of natural rights and accepted its status as a social artifact, determined
that rights were a normative problem, and that it was best not to risk
confusing it with positive science:

de Laveleye in a collection published under the auspices of the Cobden Club,
*Systems of Land Tenure in Various Countries* (1870). This collection is particularly illuminating in that the two articles showing genuine interest in the social
determination of agrarian rights were both written by noneconomists (C.
Wren-Hoskyns and George Campbell), while the aforementioned economists
treated the laws of land tenure as exogenous and, by extension, amenable to
radical legislative reform.

27. "A great portion of the laws of every nation concern property; such laws vary
greatly in different countries and at different times, and property has rights in
one age of a nation's existence which it has not in another" (1863: 98).

What mode of appropriation does reason commend as compatible with the requirements of moral personality? This is the problem of property. . . . It is entirely beside the point to find fault with the natural conditions of appropriation or to list the different ways in which men have distributed social wealth in different places and at different times throughout history. . . . Appropriation being in essence a moral phenomenon, the theory of property must be in essence a moral science. [*Éléments d'économie politique pure* ([1874, 1926] 1954): §§35–8]

Finally, we note this same tendency in the economic thought associated with American Progressivism, for example in the legal reasonings of John R. Commons,[28] Henry Carter Adams,[29] and Richard T. Ely. Ely, in his 995-page *Property and Contract* (1914), followed the utilitarian mainstream in allowing that "changes in private property and in all the fundamentals are very largely the result of other economic changes"; but again like the others he readily set that insight aside, the better to consider what might be the most ethically sound system of rights.[30]

Thus from seventeenth-century Germany to twentieth-century America, doctors of consequentialist ethics were averse on principle to the new, explanatory science, even as they occasionally contributed to it in practice. They may have been deterred by a lingering attachment to ideal Platonic forms, or more likely by a reluctance to surrender willingly any degrees of

28. In *The Distribution of Wealth* (1893: 59), Commons argued that "the English economists have taken the laws of private property for granted, assuming that they are fixed and immutable in the nature of things, and therefore needed no investigation. But such laws are changeable – they differ for different peoples and places, and they have profound influence upon the production and distribution of wealth." Nevertheless, economists engaged in the study of rights were not to interest themselves principally in elucidating this point, since "our special interest lies in their influence on distribution" (73).

29. Adams's 1896 presidential address to the American Economic Association bore the significant title "Economics and Jurisprudence." But the link that he strove to establish between the disciplines was far from one of explaining law by appeal to economic principles. Instead his task was an advocatory one, reflecting his conviction that property rights should be redefined in the law to reflect new economic circumstances ([1896] 1954: 137–40).

30. Ely (1914): 1:62, 2:ch. 22. "The origin of property," Ely opined, "suggests two lines of inquiry: we may examine (a) into the historical origin, or (b) into the logical and philosophical justification of property, the philosophical foundation of property, the ideas upon which property rests. . . . What we have in mind now and here is chiefly an examination into the logical and philosophical foundation of the right of private property; this has some connection with the historical origin, but the two lines of inquiry differ to a considerable extent" (2:531).

reformist freedom. Whatever the intellectual or ideological reason, their writings left little doubt that economists were not called to expound, or even to recognize, the determinism of social structures.

## II     The new science, 1830–1914

Economists did not invent the social science of rights; indeed, by the early nineteenth century their young discipline was already trailing the vanguard of research into this problem. But by 1914 economics was leading the way in institutional analysis, so much so that other disciplines like law, sociology, and even history were drawing on its stores of data and insight.

It is notoriously difficult to account adequately for sea changes in scholarly interest: the old saying *chacun à son gout* applies to science as well as to aesthetics. Moreover, this period does not encompass a "paradigm shift," if by that term is meant that after a certain date all investigation should have been structured by a single set of assumptions. Well beyond 1914 the place of law in economic theory was unsettled, and indeed it has remained so to this day. All caveats aside, though, we may stylize a change in the air of economic thought, as part of the broader reaction against metaphysical reason. The new fashion in social thought was *evolutionism:* the idea, on the one hand, of *structure,* the intuition that society did not afford much purchase to the lever of unaided human will; the perception, on the other hand, of the social structure's inexorable *mutability.*[31] One need only imagine the impact of evolutionist thought on the three questions identified above as obstacles to the new science. The first one, concerning the dynamic of industrial society, must have seemed increasingly parochial as the conviction set in that capitalism was but an exceptional condition of modernity. The problem of greater import from this perspective was to identify the elemental forces which had brought the modern institutional order into being and which in time would presumably usher it out. The latter two questions, each normative in intent, were transformed by the revaluation of *fact* as prior to *value,* and the desire to cleanse reformism of the stigma of Utopia and replace it with the nimbus of Science. For evolutionists, a political agenda could not be steered by good intentions and clear thought alone; these criteria were not jettisoned, but it was believed that their application had to take cognizance of forces operating beyond human writ. Above all, the apparently greater causal

31. A good treatment of this intellectual sea change is J. W. Burrow's *Evolution and Society* (1966).

efficacy of matter as opposed to mind lent a particular authority to the findings of economists, who had made of man's baser nature their métier.

The roots of legal realism are deep in Western culture, reaching all the way back to Renaissance humanism. In his histories, Machiavelli had noted the fact of institutional evolution, had dwelled on the problem of why certain generations succeeded in forging strong constitutions while others failed, and had revived the notion of a life cycle of polities to systematize his findings. Similarly though in a different vein, the great seventeenth-century theorists of the social contract, Grotius and Pufendorf, also relativized the social constitution, arguing that purposive individuals had once come together to achieve through the exchange of rights what they could not achieve alone. Enlightened thinkers of the eighteenth century took up these notions, extended and refined them. As early as 1740, David Hume was arguing that rights were never "natural," in the sense of existing prior to and independent of human purpose, but were instead the creatures of utility. In 1748, Baron Montesquieu's *Spirit of the Laws* expounded the environmental relativity of institutions. As various historians have shown, the greater achievement of fitting institutional diversity into an evolutionary framework was also initiated around this time, by Frenchmen and especially by Scots. Turgot, Goguet, Kames, Dalrymple, Smith, Ferguson, Gibbon, and Millar all contributed to this movement, which Millar dubbed "a new science of civil society."[32]

But Classical political economy was curiously impenetrable to this first bloom of legal science. Adam Smith is a telling example of this phenomenon. As a leading figure in both the Scottish Enlightenment and political economy, one would expect him to be, at the very least, a conduit for the introduction of historical materialism into the Classicists' treatment of rights. This was not the case, however. The positivist timbre of Smith's *Lectures on Jurisprudence* (delivered 1762–4, published in 1896 and 1978) resonated only faintly in his economic treatise. Those earlier lectures had been fairly formal exercises in Roman and natural law,[33] but that format

---

32. Among them Roy Pascal, "Property and Society: The Scottish Historical School of the Eighteenth Century" (1938); Duncan Forbes, "Scientific Whiggism: Adam Smith and John Millar" (1954); Ronald L. Meek, "Smith, Turgot and the 'Four Stages' Theory" (1971); David E. R. Gay, "Adam Smith and Property Rights Analysis" (1975); Peter G. Stein, *Legal Evolution: The Story of an Idea* (1980).

33. To be fair, we must acknowledge some real ambiguity in these lectures. In the later series (delivered ca. 1763–4), he distinguished property, as an "acquired" right dependent on the state of "civil government," from truly natural rights like that to liberty and personal security. But in the analogous place in the

did not stop him from voicing such hypotheses as that private property in livestock, dwellings, and arable lands had all arisen as social adaptations to advancing material culture (21–3, 459–60); that the rise and fall of feudal institutions had to be understood in the context of historical circumstance (186–9, 417–18, 470–1); that the gradual articulation of "manners" (by which he meant the internalization of moral principles and social norms of a higher order) had transformed certain rights;[34] and various other curiosities.[35] The *Wealth of Nations,* by comparison, contains very few references to the social determination of rights.[36] It is only by comparison with latter-day Classicism that the same book seems a mine of institutional insight. In the end one can debate whether the greater disruption was caused by Smith's failure to transpose the enlightened realism of the *Lectures in Jurisprudence* to his political economy, or by later economists' neglect of such tidbits as were to be found in *The Wealth of Nations.* Whatever the reason, by 1800 the Franco-Scottish avenue of the new science's penetration into political economy had fallen derelict.

But another avenue, one less familiar to historians of economic thought, remained open and did ultimately contribute to the fusion of legal and economic study. This is the story of the German *Staatswissenschaft* tradition, and its first protagonist is Hermann Conring (1601–81). Conring's

> first lecture series (1762–3), he admitted only that property's status as a natural right was "not altogether plain," and then went on to lecture in great detail on property's roots in the Roman legal concepts of occupation, tradition, accession, prescription, and succession. It is hard to choose between these: the later lectures may be favored as closer in time to his efforts in political economy, and the fact that they were published eighty years before the earlier ones has entrenched their view in the literature; but the earlier lectures are in general far more detailed. Most likely, Smith himself was ambivalent, and this ambivalence was carried into *The Wealth of Nations.*

34. E.g., the improvement of manners increased the role of the "secondary" sources of property right (by which he meant all except occupation and accession), especially testamentary succession, which Smith portrayed as a person's ability to bestow gifts even after he has ceased to be a person. Being driven by sympathy with the dead and piety toward their wishes, testamentary freedom constituted "a considerable refinement in humanity, and never was practiced in a rude nation" ([1762–3] 1978: 63–5, 466–7).

35. E.g., Smith relativized the rules of accession to coastal properties according to the geographic peculiarities of each country ([1762–3] 1978: 29), and he explained easements as instruments adapted to economize on transactions (470).

36. Most notable are his accounts of the dissolution of feudal relations and of the geographic heterogeneity of slavery, both in book III, "Of the Different Progress of Opulence in Different Nations."

student years in Leiden exposed him to a sort of liberal humanism unknown in Germany, and his lifelong allegiance to Aristotelian politics dis-
tanced him from the deductive rationalism of most seventeenth-century
German scholarship. More concretely, Conring was the first scholar to
dispute the conventional belief that the Holy Roman Empire had adopted
Roman law at one go in the twelfth century, arguing instead for a later
and more piecemeal reception that had allowed an organic system of common law to develop and adapt to German peculiarities. As a result of all
this and more, Conring has been credited by posterity with founding the
German conception of legal history, the German tradition of "statistics"
(meaning the comparative study of political systems), and even historical
*Staatswissenschaft* as a whole.[37]

   In light of his credentials, it is perhaps not surprising that so many
figures of the eighteenth-century German Enlightenment have been
judged beholden to Conring. A later herald of Enlightenment, Christian
Thomasius (1655–1728), called also for political observation and legal his-
toricization, and made of Halle an early center of such inquiry. But ultimately, the real center of Enlightened social science in Germany was to
be the new university at Göttingen, where the endeavors of *Staatsrecht,
Staatenkunde,* and *Statistik* first assumed a consistently modern face. The
Göttingen *Aufklärer* felt a guarded attraction to both the meticulosity of
conventional historiography and the Cartesian sweep of the rationalists,
taking care to sustain the achievements of each while avoiding their excesses. *Staatswissenschaft* as practiced in Göttingen was encyclopedic,
comparative, and historical, distinguished as readily from the vocational
emphasis of cameralist instruction as from the strict ratiocination of traditional jurisprudence. Scholars like Achenwall, Schlözer, Spittler, and
Heeren held Montesquieu in particular esteem, and like him they understood the recognition of national diversity to be a precondition of valid
generalization.[38] Göttingen historicism also inspired jurists like Gustav

37. "The teacher of *Staatswissenschaft,*" wrote Conring, "must know the history
    of every age; and if he wishes to teach, he must prove everything by means of
    history" (quoted in Roscher 1874: 256).
38. On the development of *Staatswissenschaft* in the eighteenth century and its
    implications for historical economics, see Roscher 1874: 703; Carl Menger,
    *Untersuchungen über die Methode der Sozialwissenschaften und der politischen
    Ökonomie insbesondere* ([1883] 1985): book IV; Gottfried Eisermann, *Die
    Grundlagen des Historismus in der deutschen Nationalökonomie* (1956): 10–11,
    87–9; Brückner 1977; Volker Hentschel, "Die Staatswissenschaften an den
    deutschen Universitäten im 18. und frühen 19. Jahrhundert" (1978); Bruch
    1985; Norbert Waszek, "Die Staatswissenschaften an der Universität Berlin
    im 19. Jahrhundert" (1988); Woodruff Smith, *Politics and the Sciences of Cul-*

Hugo (1764–1844), who introduced Gibbon to a German audience,[39] and Carl Friedrich von Eichhorn (1781–1854).

Arguing to similar effect from a different quarter of the German Enlightenment, one that was less academic, less ecumenical, and rather less liberal, was Justus Möser (1720–94). Despite Möser's lack of theoretical apparatus, his sense for social history would cause him to be hailed as "the greatest economist of eighteenth-century Germany" and the father of the historical school of economics.[40] Together these scholars forged a tradition that was at once more empirical and less scholastic than the norm, a tradition that suffused economics with humanist and Enlightenment advances in law, politics, and historiography.[41]

*ture in Germany* (1991): 29 ff; Hans Maier, *Politische Wissenschaft in Deutschland* (1985): 66.

On the central role of Göttingen, see also Notker Hammerstein, *Jus und Historie* (1972); Hans Peter Reill, *The German Enlightenment and the Rise of Historicism* (1975); Georg Iggers, "The European Context of Eighteenth-Century German Enlightenment Historiography" (1986).

39. On Hugo's diverse social-scientific inspirations, which included not only Conring but also Bodin, Montesquieu, and Hume, see Donald Kelley's *The Human Measure* (1990): 239–42.

40. This in the most authoritative history of economic thought to appear in the nineteenth century, Roscher 1874: 500–1. See also the appreciative comments in Remer, *Die geistigen Grundlagen der historischen Schule der Nationalökonomie* (1935): 70–5, and Eisermann 1956: 12–14.

41. As Eduard Baumstark exclaimed in 1835, exhorting young economists to follow their example: "What solidity, what a practical core did not the great Spittler give his lectures of politics, and how vibrant, how spirited does [politics] not now look in that raiment! What strength have not A. Smith and A. Ferguson breathed in this way into their immortal works!" [*Kameralistische Encyclopädie* (1835): viii–ix].

Neither the exegetic jurisprudence of the Pandects, nor the metaphysics of Kant, Fichte, Hegel, and Müller, would suit the positivist pretensions of the new science. A shared evolutionism has made the Hegelian connection irresistible to many students of historical economics (e.g., Eisermann 1956: 80–1 and passim). But against this supposition must be weighed the silence of the economists (who were otherwise keen claimants of intellectual mantles) themselves, and the critical comments of those economists who did address classical German philosophy: e.g., Knies [1853] 1883: 368–9; Roscher 1874: 642, 925; Wagner [1876] 1892–4: 2:§43; Gustav Cohn, *Grundlegung der Nationalökonomie* (1885): 158; Schmoller 1901–4: 1:§132. See also Woodruff Smith 1991: 27–8.

As the least rationalistic and the most economically oriented of this group, Müller has been located by some scholars at the center of a "Romantic" school of economics that in due course influenced the later "historical" school. In fact Müller was agreeably critical of Classical abstraction, but his

Still, its inroads into German economic discourse were modest and scattered before midcentury. We find it in Georg Hanssen's "Views on the Ancient Agrarian System" (1835–7), in which that young docent sought the hidden rationale in recently discovered Danish-German laws of settlement; in *The National System of Political Economy* (1841) by Friedrich List, who briefly held a chair in *Staatswissenschaft,* who occasionally published under the pseudonym "Justus Möser," and whose sweeping institutional history reflected his reading of Machiavelli;[42] and especially in the early economics lectures of Wilhelm Roscher. Roscher, a young professor of history and *Staatswissenschaft* at Göttingen, carried with him his forebears' respect for historical specificity as well as their sense of cyclical pattern in the organization and fortune of nations. In contrast to the many other introductions to the discipline, his lectures stressed the historical and geographic diversity of agrarian institutions, the evolution of labor from slavery to serfdom to wages, and the possible principles underlying all this institutional variety. Private property was contradistinguished to communism, and each was found prevalent under specific social conditions.[43]

neglect at the hands of later economists was near total; and when we consider that his theory of property featured such notions as that one might rightfully possess only in so far as one was in turn possessed (by the state, or by the possessions themselves), and that property resided in the last resort with God himself, such neglect is understandable. See Müller, "Welches sind die Erfordernisse eines zureichenden Staatswirtschaftlichen Systems?" ([ca. 1808] 1931): 3; Eisermann 1956: 102. It is worth noting that Friedrich List, supposed by some to have been Müller's conduit to posterity, explicitly denied any such connection ([1841] 1930: 463).

42. List, *Das nationale System der politischen Ökonomie* ([1841] 1930): chs. 1–10 and 28. Regarding his use of the pseudonym, see the statement in *Schriften/ Reden/Briefe* (1930): 5:216.

It might well be argued that List's principal service to the new science was in underlining the centrality of good law to a nation's "productive forces," and hence to its success. "History teaches," List wrote, "that individuals create the larger part of their productive powers from social institutions and circumstances." All this depends primarily on "whether public institutions and laws produce religiosity, morality, intelligence, security of person and property, freedom and right" ([1841] 1930: 171–6). List's institutional orientation (not to mention his liberalism!) are often overlooked by the received view of him; but it became common coin among practitioners of the new science. Cf. Schmoller "Über einige Grundfragen des Rechts und der Volkswirtschaft" ([1874–5] 1898): 48, 70; Schmoller 1901–4: 1:§123; Philippovich, *Grundriß der politischen Oekonomie* ([1893] 1920): 99.

43. Roscher, *Grundriß zu Vorlesungen über die Staatswirthschaft. Nach geschichtlicher Methode* (1843): 7–8, 38–49.

German economists therefore enjoyed a head start in developing the explanatory science of rights, but only a head start. Over the course of the nineteenth century, European intellectual assumptions evolved in such a way that economic inquiry as a whole was prompted to develop in the same direction.

The new science appears to have been stimulated especially in the aftermath of 1848. As a year of political revolution, 1848 was justly viewed as a failure; but its ideological ramifications spread quite far indeed. Most notably, for our purposes, it was at this moment that a modern liberal establishment first confronted the barricades of working-class radicalism. It will be recalled from the discussion above that, in the preceding decades of relative social quiet, champions of the liberal order had relied primarily on arguments to natural right. The liberal economy survived 1848, but the upheaval underscored the longer term successes of radical jurisprudence and drove home to all a lesson that would not soon be forgotten: namely, that a scholastic edifice founded on the Rights of Man could as easily harbor the foes of bourgeois liberty as its friends. As a result, henceforth the most perspicacious (or perhaps merely the least convinced?) liberal economists emphasized less the intrinsic justice of private property, and correspondingly more its social utility. But unlike the utilitarian economists of the pre-1848 era, these newer, more conservative utilitarians were concerned to show the social value of the status quo, or of something not far from it. A science of the function of extant rights, particularly one that showed the gradual perfection of those rights through an evolutionary process, would not be just inoffensive to this group: it would be a positive boon.

Roscher's contribution of about 1851, titled "Essentials of an Economic Explanation of Private Property," was palpably concerned to reaffirm the normalcy of the liberal order, but it did so in a rather novel way. Roscher identified three categories of explanation traditionally applied to the phenomenon of property: the juristic, the political, and the economic. While each of these approaches was found wanting in some regard, only the juristic approach was dismissed on principle. Property right by first occupation, enshrined in Roman law, for Roscher "explains only the slightest part of property relations, and bases it on a quite random fact at that."[44] The explanatory apparatus developed here and in his 1843 lectures were then incorporated into chapters on liberty, bondage, and property in *The Foundations of Economics* (1854), the textbook that would secure Roscher's reputation through its twenty-sixth edition, in 1922. "In instances

44. Roscher, *Grundzüge einer nationalökonomischen Erklärung des Privateigenthums* (ca. 1851): 113.

without number," Roscher taught in that work, "jurisprudence gives us but the superficial How; only economics adds the deeper Why."[45]

Karl Knies's *Political Economy from the Standpoint of Historical Method* (1853) stressed even more forcefully the relativity of property rights, calling it a juristic sophism to allege "that each and every nation has *conceived* of private property rights at all times as unlimited, and that every standard of property that in practice diverges from it must be viewed always as merely a limitation of the *actual* right." Instead Knies stressed the relativity of property as "a historical phenomenon, distinct according to epoch and nation," and instanced brief explanations of the institutional peculiarities of ancient Greece, Rome, and Germany. Knies's historical perspective demonstrated that legal (and particularly agrarian) relations were labile, but at the same time it validated the liberal hypothesis that the modern order was much the more beneficent.[46] Gustav Schmoller's verdict on this book, that it might almost be called the "prolegomenon to a whole scientific epoch" and a "confession of faith for the whole German school," underscores its import for the future of law and economics.

The ramifications of 1848 were clearer still in France, where the liberals' victory over the radical left had been especially close-fought, bloody, and not altogether decisive. In 1855 the Société d'Économie Politique met to debate a strategically important question for the defense of the liberal order: "Is the right of property better founded on the principle of social utility than on the principle of justice and individual right?" Of the nine participants whose comments were entered into the minutes, seven rejected the proposition, believing that socialist challenges had to be met on the high ground of natural law. The two dissenters, J. Dupuit and J.-G. Courcelle-Seneuil, offered at one level the standard utilitarian riposte, based on a reading of the word "founded" [*fondé*] to mean "justified." But when they held the floor, the discussion of "foundation" turned subtly toward "explanation." Dupuit called attention to the striking national diversity of property regimes, even among modern peoples, and claimed

45. Roscher, *Grundlagen der Nationalökonomie* ([1854] 1906): §16. In his preface to the jurist Dankwardt's *Nationalökonomisch-civilistische Studien* (1862: viii), Roscher made this same point with a telling analogy: political economy had developed into an indispensible auxiliary science for legal scholars, he argued, much as chemistry and physics had become for medical practitioners.

46. Knies, *Die politische Oekonomie vom Standpuncte der geschichtlichen Methode* ([1853] 1883): 181–97. Similarly did Albert Schäffle's *Das gesellschaftliche System der menschlichen Wirthschaft* ([1858] 1873: §§279, 321]) contend that on the one hand the supposed sacredness of private property was contradicted by history, while on the other hand economic progress was in fact tending to spread it ever wider.

that the deeper regularity was that "laws, however different, serve the common end of social utility." Courcelle-Seneuil elaborated on this principle, arguing that throughout history legislators had been motivated by the "quasi-physiological" imperatives of economic growth and social development, and that this had led, in the fullness of time, to the regime of private property known to modern man. "To ground the right of property on a law of social physiology," he concluded, "is to give it, I believe, a basis more solid than that of interpersonal justice. In any case it is the only *economic* basis, since all other arguments in favor of the right of property are drawn from moral and juridical, but not economic considerations."[47] Dupuit and Courcelle-Seneuil failed to carry the day in 1855, but they did not abandon their cause. Dupuit returned to the theme in an 1861 contribution to the *Journal des Économistes* where, on the authority of Pascal, Montesquieu, Bentham, and others, he reiterated his conviction that property rights were the consequence of laws, not their cause. In addition he offered a brief conjectural history of property in land, to illustrate his point that its true origin was "social consent, a human convention."[48] Following broadly Mill's *Principles,* Courcelle-Seneuil's own treatise of 1858 agreed that property was but an arrangement of human volition, and that it was therefore absurd to speak of "actual" rights violating "true" rights. Where he diverged from Mill, however, was in constructing the division of intellectual labor in such a way that it became the responsibility of economists to develop a positive science of property rights, as the "force" underpinning the distribution of wealth: "Law and ethics research the ideals according to which this force should be directed. The inquiries of political economy have a very different end: they consist in researching the origin of this force, in studying the laws of its development."[49] Ultimately Courcelle-Seneuil would call for a social science of law that was cleansed of "the subjective conceptions of priests, philosophers and jurists," one that followed instead the empirical and nomological method of physicians and chemists.[50]

47. Société d'Économie Politique, "Des fondements du droit de propriété" (1855): 144–6, 151–2.
48. Dupuit, "Du principe de propriété" (1861): 322–9. Dupuit's revisions were still so heterodox as to be prefaced by an editorial disclaimer.
49. Courcelle-Seneuil, *Traité théorique et pratique d'économie politique* ([1858] 1891): vol. 1, book 2, ch. 1, § 1. He took the occasion also to confront the tendency of jurists and economists to confuse the rational and the real: "One can argue that a certain proposed change will modify the existing system of property for better or worse; but it is ridiculous to affirm that it will destroy property."
50. Courcelle-Seneuil, Translator's introduction to Maine's *L'Ancien droit* (1874): xiii–xvi. This attitude is evident also in his "Conjectures sur l'histoire du droit

By the time of Marx's first published contribution to political economy in 1859, then, economists were already familiar with the notion that rights were contingent on social conditions. To be fair, we should note that Marx's position on the explanation of rights had begun to evolve soon after his 1844 manuscripts, as the influence of Proudhon's moralism and Ludwig Feuerbach's humanism yielded to the more thoroughgoing materialism of the Scottish Enlightenment and the Saint-Simonians and to the empirical nous of Friedrich Engels.[51] Already in *The German Ideology* (1845–6), Marx and Engels had subjected property rights to a materialist conception of history, articulating for the first time the stage theory of property that would inform their later work, an evolutionary sequence of tribal, ancient, feudal, and capitalist relations.[52] In *The Poverty of Philosophy* (1847), Marx's book-length rebuttal of Proudhon, his commitment to legal realism was reiterated.[53] By the time of his 1859 debut he had been immersed in the study of political economy for fourteen years; and although there remained little novelty in his comments there about political economy as "the anatomy of civil society," and about the dependence of "relations of production" on the "forces of production," they did capture the movement that was afoot.[54] The general currency of Marx's ideas is indicated by the fact that simultaneously, at the opposite end of the ideological spectrum, the German "Manchestrian" Karl Braun was arguing

de propriété" (1878) and his contribution "Propriété (Droit de)" to the *Nouveau dictionnaire d'économie politique* (1892).

51. As the Saint-Simonian epigones had put it in their influential summary of the doctrine, "Property is a social institution, subject, as are all other social institutions, to the law of progress. Property may thus at various epochs be understood, defined and regulated in different ways." This, they felt, set them apart from the political economists' ahistorical and undifferentiated conception of property [Bazard et al. ([1829] 1958): 86, 116–22].

    It has also been suggested (Levine 1987) that Marx's institutional historicism was informed by his reading of Linguet, Niebuhr, Hugo, and Pfister.

52. Marx and Engels, *Die deutsche Ideologie* ([1845–6] 1976): esp. 32–4, 90–2, 365. "It must not be forgotten," they warned, "that law has just as little an independent history as religion."

53. "In each historical epoch, property has developed differently and under a set of entirely different social relations. Thus to define bourgeois property is nothing else than to give an exposition of all the social relations of bourgeois production. To try to give a definition of property as of an independent relation, a category apart, an abstract and eternal idea, can be nothing but an illusion of metaphysics or jurisprudence" [Marx, *Das Elend der Philosophie* ([1847] 1976): ch. II, §4]. In light of the foregoing we can assent to Pejovich's (1982) claim that Marx had anticipated the modern "property rights school," but not to his suggestion that Marx was the first economist to do so.

54. Marx, *Zur Kritik der politischen Ökonomie* ([1859] 1987): 263–4.

identically that jurists and moral philosophers would never succeed in devising a comparative history of property and inheritance without the insights that economic science could alone contribute.[55]

The decades after 1870 were the golden age of the new science of rights, in explanation of which we may adduce the conjuncture of three collateral developments. First, in the legal profession, and especially in Germany, evolutionism and comparativism had also been growing from strength to strength and were increasingly realistic in their outlook. In fact this process had begun long before 1870, but it had been slowed and obscured by the towering figure of Friedrich Carl von Savigny (1779–1861). The problem with Savigny, from our point of view, is that his work reflected the influence not only of Möser and Hugo but also of Herder and Burke. Like each of them, Savigny understood each society to be an evolving organism whose laws developed "by internal silently operating powers, not by the arbitrary will of a lawgiver."[56] But unlike the Göttingen *Aufklärer,* Savigny understood those "internal silently operating powers" as something other than the interplay of interests at large in society. In the case of developing cultures (his examples were the Roman Republic and ancient Germany), it would appear that he meant unconscious or even irrational drives of the sort that shaped national languages and cultures in general. In the case of mature peoples in full flower (like imperial Rome and contemporary Germany), the only adequate jurisprudence was the conceptual reasoning of lawyers [*Begriffsjurisprudenz*], which would keep and articulate the national tradition. For the exercise of this praetorian "jurists' law" [*Juristenrecht*], it was important only to know what the tradition was, not how it came into being. As a practical matter, Savigny called for the same sort of rationalist jurisprudence to which professional students of the Corpus Juris Civilis were accustomed; and this in turn accounts for his high standing among that cadre throughout the century.[57]

55. Braun, "Zur Fysiologie des Eigenthums und des Erbrechts" (1865): esp. 55–8, 88.
56. Savigny, *Vom Beruf unsrer Zeit für Gesetzgebung und Rechtswissenschaft* (1814), quoted in Stein (1980): 60.
57. See Ch. Zöpel, *Ökonomie und Recht* (1974): 154–66; James Q. Whitman, *The Legacy of Roman Law in the German Romantic Era* (1990): 210–37. This modern science of the Pandects was influential especially in the field of property law. Whereas the older *usus modernus* of Roman law had developed a conception of property as a divisible bundle of entitlements and had seen this conception incorporated into the Prussian (1794) and Austrian (1811) civil codes, the new interpretation resisted anything more complex than absolute and indivisible property. See Karl Kroeschell, "Zur Lehre vom 'germanischen' Eigentumsbegriff" (1977): 36–46; Walter Wilhelm, "Private Freiheit und gesellschaftliche Grenzen des Eigentums in der Theorie der Pandektenwissenschaft" (1979).

Savigny's influence among Romanists thus served to slow the development of social-scientific legal historiography in Germany. Such progress as there was owed more to the work of lesser known Romanists like the Göttingen-trained Gustav Hugo, and especially to the minority "Germanist" [*deutsch-rechtlich*] tendency within historical jurisprudence. An important date in this process was 1828, the year in which appeared seminal studies of German legal history by Jakob Grimm and Wilhelm Albrecht.[58] Over the succeeding decades Germanist scholars would develop further the theory of a peculiarly German private law,[59] and in the fullness of time they came to confirm and stimulate further the development of institutional analysis within political economy. Among the jurists who came to be recognized as toilers in the economists' own vineyard were not only Germanists like Wilhelm Arnold (who held an appointment in economics as well) and Otto von Gierke[60] but also maverick Romanists like Burkard Wilhelm Leist and especially Rudolf von Jhering, who converted from rationalist to positivist jurisprudence sometime around

58. Grimm, *Deutsche Rechtsalterthümer* (1828); Albrecht, *Die Gewere als Grundlage des älteren deutschen Sachenrechts* (1828). *Gewere,* or the characteristically Teutonic right of possession that is nowadays commonly contrasted to the Romans' more exclusive and individualist concept of *dominium,* was first featured in Albrecht's book. See Kroeschell 1977: 46–54.

59. Georg Beseler's understanding of the problem was especially significant for jurists and economists of our period. As he formulated it, a theorist of German property must either generalize from the specifically Roman codes or else, as he obviously preferred, seek an explanation grounded in German conditions.

> In the first instance, the principle that property is a *ius infinitum* is shaped into a logical necessity, and legal relations which appear to stand in the way are subject to potentially rough treatment, in order to avoid a *contradictio in adjecto.* He who prefers the second path proceeds from the view that the various institutions of a national legal tradition have not developed in order to satisfy a logical rule, but rather have emerged freely from the needs and relations of life; and he will consider it the task of science not to read into these institutions constructs derived elsewhere, but to learn from [the institutions] themselves the factors that have determined their make-up. [*Die Lehre von den Erbverträgen* (1835), quoted in Kroeschell 1977: 51]

60. The relevant texts by Arnold are *Zur Geschichte des Eigenthums in den deutschen Städten* (1861), *Recht und Wirthschaft nach geschichtlicher Ansicht: Drei Vorlesungen* (1863), and especially *Cultur und Rechtsleben* (1865). By Gierke, *Das deutsche Genossenschaftsrecht* (1873): esp. vol. 2, *Die soziale Aufgabe des Privatrechts* (1889), and *Deutsches Privatrecht* (1895–1917). See Kroeschell 1977: 56–9; Hans Peter, *Wandlungen der Eigentumsordnung und der Eigentumslehre seit dem 19. Jahrhundert* (1949): 50–4; Diehl 1941: 91.

1860.[61] The second volume of Jhering's *Spirit of Roman Law* (1865), as well as subsequent works like *The Struggle over Law* (1872), *The Purpose in Law* (1877–83), and *The Will to Possess* (1889), were welcome validation for practitioners of the new economics. By the end of the century, journals of economics and *Staatswissenschaft* were attracting submissions from jurists interested in institutional analysis,[62] while new legal periodicals were showing heightened interest in the economic way of thinking.[63]

Meanwhile in England, by midcentury the ideas of the German historical jurists had been taken up with alacrity in some intellectual circles (Stein 1980: 72–86), whence they found their way into the work that would do most to bring historical jurisprudence to the attention of economists all over Europe, Henry Sumner Maine's *Ancient Law* (1861). Maine's belief in universal progressive tendencies (especially from "status" to "contract") is well known; but his was an evolutionism free of invidious comparisons and appeals to transcendent forces of nature. On the contrary, his method was rigorously positivistic and universalistic. Once the proper homologies and analogies have been drawn, Maine predicted in 1875, "it is not unsafe to lay down that the materials for a new science will exist, a science which may prove to be as great a triumph of the Comparative Method as any which it has hitherto achieved."[64] Like the new economists, Maine

61. Hans Peter has dated Jhering's change of mind about as precisely as is possible, noting that the revised second edition of the first volume of his *Geist des römischen Rechts* (1866) included a programmatic statement missing from the original (1852) edition: "There is *no absolute property, i.e.* none free from consideration of the collectivity" (Peter 1949: 39).

    There remains some uncertainty as to the reason for Jhering's conversion. Peter (1949: 42) has argued that Ferdinand Lassalle's *Das System der erworbenen Recht* (1861) was decisive in this regard; but Erik Wolf's biography suggests, rather more convincingly, that developments in Jhering's personal life were ultimately responsible for his epiphany (1963: 641–2).

62. Examples are W. Endemann, "Die nationalökonomischen Grundsätze der kanonistischen Lehre," in the *Jahrbücher für Nationalökonomie und Statistik* (1863); Adolph Bruder, "Zur ökonomischen Charakteristik des römischen Rechts," in the *Zeitschrift für die gesamte Staatswissenschaft* (1876–7); Adolph Samter, "Der Eigenthumsbegriff," in the *Jahrbücher für Nationalökonomie und Statistik* (1878); Otto von Gierke, "Der Entwurf eines bürgerlichen Gesetzbuches und das deutsche Recht," in *Schmollers Jahrbuch für Gesetzgebung, Verwaltung und Volkswirtschaft* (1888–9); Alexander Leist, "Die moderne Privatrechtsordnung und der Kapitalismus," in the *Grundriss der Sozialökonomik* (1911). See also Schumpeter, *History of Economic Analysis* (1954): 431.

63. Jurists could refer to the *Jahrbücher der internationalen Vereinigung für vergleichende Rechtswissenschaft und Volkswirtschaftslehre* (founded 1895), to *Blätter für vergleichende Rechtswissenschaft und Volkswirtschaftslehre* (f. 1905), and to the *Archiv für Rechts- und Wirtschaftsphilosophie* (f. 1907).

64. Maine, "The Effects of Observation of India on Modern European Thought"

doubted that the categories of Roman jurisprudence could explain the actual development of law in antiquity. Reverence toward *Ancient Law* became commonplace in the economic literature on rights – not least by his French translator, Courcelle-Seneuil.

The second development was one within economic theory, the burst of microeconomic research sometimes known as the "Marginalist Revolution." Admittedly, to suggest that the new microeconomics abetted the realist theory of rights is to contravene two pieces of conventional wisdom: first, that neoclassicism entailed a step away from social reality, back toward system-building apriorism; and second, that there arose and remained irreconcilable differences between "marginalists" and "historicists" on just this account. But the evidence regarding institutional analysis does not support either of these claims, and upon reflection this cannot be too surprising. After all, the marginalist and historicist revisions were both directed in the first instance against the Classicist synthesis, not against one another. The first task of the new microeconomics was to displace interest away from "value," that transcendent quality that had never quite lost the imprint of natural law, and toward "price," a frankly social phenomenon that now counted as more than an imperfect reflection of value. The new approach to rights fit nicely this task, as its founders made clear. Two acclaimed "forerunners" of marginalism, Dupuit in Paris and Mangoldt in Freiburg, both contributed to the new science. Carl Menger of Vienna, too, stressed the social (and particularly economic) origins of private property and urged against the "pious error" of traditional legal thought, which tended to make of institutions "something *objective,* something divine standing above human wisdom and human interest."[65] We

([1875] 1876): 225. Maine was at pains to show the social roots of even the most primitive legal regimes: "The usages which a particular community is found to have adopted in its infancy and in its primitive seats are generally those which are on the whole best suited to promote its physical and moral well-being." Similarly in "progressive" societies, "social necessities and social opinion are always more or less in advance of Law" ([1861] 1963: 15–18).

Maine upbraided mainstream economists for failing to contribute to this body of knowledge:

> The best economical writers expressly decline to discuss the history of the institution [of property] itself, at most observing that its existence is for the good of the human race. Until quite recently the theories accepted concerning the early history of Property would scarcely bear a moment's examination. The popular account of it, that it had its origin in a state of nature, is merely a way of giving expression to our own ignorance. ([1875] 1876: 221)

65. Menger, *Grundsätze der Volkswirtschaftslehre* ([1871] 1981): book II, ch. 3; Menger [1883] 1985: app. 8.

have seen that Walras of Lausanne was disinclined to pursue institutional analysis himself; but his detailed description in 1874 of how property rights result from a combination of scarcity, need, and social interaction left to his successors a clear research agenda. As he concluded:

> The appropriation of scarce things or of social wealth is a phenomenon of human contrivance and not a natural phenomenon. It has its origins in the exercise of the human will and in human behavior and not in the play of natural forces. . . . Obviously, this power does not reside in each of us individually but in all of us taken collectively. We are dealing here with a human phenomenon that is shaped, not by the separate will of each individual, but by the collective activity of society as a whole. . . . To sum up, while nature makes things appropriable, mankind determines and carries out the appropriation.[66]

William Stanley Jevons of London, the third pillar of marginalism, did not comment on the nature of rights before his untimely death in 1882. Nevertheless, we find in the table of contents of his posthumous and unfinished *Principles of Economics* that he had planned a chapter to cover "The Origin of Property," but it was not among those that he would ever complete.[67] In the end, one can reasonably question whether the microeconomic revolution positively accelerated the new science; but clearly it posed no hindrance.

The third collateral development to which we draw attention is the accumulating evidence of institutional diversity, which could only have favored the development of an economic agenda to account for it. This is not to say that earlier economists were ignorant of the longitudinal and cross-sectional contingency of rights: they knew their Herodotus, Caesar, Strabo, and Tacitus, their Gibbon, Robertson, Laffitau, and Niebuhr. But the explosion of scholarship in the latter half of the nineteenth century was without precedent, and its embarrassment of riches duly spilled into the footnotes of economic treatises and monographs. Some favorite sources were the work of jurists, like G. L. von Maurer's accounts of ancient German agrarian relations, Maine's comparative study of "Aryan" institutions in India and northern Europe, and A. H. Post's study of African legal practice.[68] There developed also a fruitful relation between the

---

66. Walras [1874] 1954: §§23, 35–6. Cf. also Walras, *Études d'économie sociale* (1896): 247.
67. Jevons, *Principles of Economics. A Fragment of a Treatise on the Industrial Mechanism of Society* (1905). The chapter was to be the fiftieth of seventy-two.
68. Georg Ludwig von Maurer, *Geschichte der Markenverfassung in Deutschland* (1856); Henry Sumner Maine, *Village-Communities in the East and West* (1871); Albert Hermann Post, *Afrikanische Jurisprudenz* (1887). In addition, Post, a judge in Bremen, produced various overviews of legal evolution that

economic and historical professions. Many future economists (and all those trained in the *Staatswissenschaft* curriculum) studied history at university, and some (including Roscher, Bruno Hildebrand, and Eberhard Gothein) even held history chairs themselves. Conversely, as the century advanced, more and more professional historians developed from their end the field of economic and institutional history.[69] These historians often contributed to the leading economics journals, where their work was quickly absorbed into the mainstream of economic thought.[70] Moreover, new historical journals were showing heightened interest in the economic way of thinking.[71] To all this academic activity must be reckoned as well the remarkable output of lay scholars like Lewis Henry Morgan, Sir John Lubbock, and Frederic Seebohm, as well as the myriad reports of ethnologists, officials, and travelers in the British, French, Dutch, Russian, and German empires. It was enough to make Ricardian generalizations from contemporary England seem pretty blinkered by comparison.

Returning now to the economists' own work in the decades following 1870, we find that the explanatory science of rights was a truly cosmopolitan enterprise. The first epochal work of the period issued from Belgium,

caught the attention of German economists, including *Der Ursprung des Rechts, Prolegomena zu einer allgemeinen vergleichenden Rechtswissenschaft* (1876); *Die Anfänge der Staats- und Rechtslebens, ein Beitrag zu einer allgemeinen vergleichenden Staats- und Rechtsgeschichte* (1878); and *Die Grundlagen des Rechts und die Grundzüge seiner Entwicklungsgeschichte, Leitgedanken für den Aufbau einer allgemeinen Rechtswissenschaft auf soziologischer Basis* (1884).

69. Among the many contributions to this genre should be counted especially N. D. Fustel de Coulanges, *Histoire des institutions politiques de l'ancienne France* (1875–89); Karl Lamprecht, *Deutsches Wirtschaftsleben im Mittelalter* (1885–6); Maxim Kovalevsky, *Tableau des origines et de l'évolution de la famille et de la propriété* (1890) and *Die ökonomische Entwicklung Europas bis zum Beginn der kapitalistischen Wirtschaftsform* (1901–14); Eduard Meyer, "Die wirtschaftliche Entwicklung des Altertums" (1895); Georg Caro, *Beiträge zur älteren deutschen Wirtschafts- und Verfassungsgeschichte* (1905); Rudolf Kötzschke, *Deutsche Wirtschaftsgeschichte bis zum 17. Jahrhundert* (1908); Alfons Dopsch, *Die Wirtschaftsentwicklung der Karolingerzeit, vornehmlich in Deutschland* (1912–13).

70. One need only browse the *Jahrbücher für Nationalökonomie und Statistik* for examples, like Georg Kaufmann, "Die Entstehung der Vassalität eine Folge wirtschaftlicher Veränderung" (1874); Karl Lamprecht, "Wirtschaftsgeschichtliche Studien in Deutschland" (1884–5); Felix Rachfahl, "Zur Geschichte des Grundeigentums" (1900); and the various contributions by Georg Caro and Georg von Below.

71. Notably, *Zeitschrift für Sozial- und Wirtschaftsgeschichte* (f. 1893) and *Vierteljahrschrift für Sozial- und Wirtschaftsgeschichte* (f. 1901).

the crossroads of northern Europe, from the hand of the Liège professor Émile de Laveleye. His researches in institutional evolution were first brought to light in 1872 in the *Revue des Deux-Mondes,* then collected in book form as *Primitive Property* (1874, 4th French ed. 1891) and soon translated into English (1878) and German (1879). Laveleye's purpose in writing was avowedly reformist, to back his calls for cooperative land tenure by establishing historically "the natural right of property as proclaimed by philosophers, as well as to show that ownership has assumed very various forms, and is consequently susceptible of progressive reform."[72] For this quest Laveleye drew inspiration from the monographic studies of Maine, Maurer, and Erwin Nasse, and from the theoretical contributions of Roscher (whom he later called "the wisest of contemporary economists")[73] and J. S. Mill (from whom Laveleye received a congratulatory note on the occasion of his 1872 articles). But despite their parallel agendas, there was a subtle difference between the approaches of Mill and Laveleye, one which probably explains why only the latter proved amenable to the new science. Referring to the rules governing the distribution of wealth, Mill had argued that it was "a matter of human institution only. The things once there, mankind, individually or collectively, can do with them as they like." Laveleye, however, thought entitlements to be worth a closer look: "We should see clearly that laws are not the arbitrary product of human wishes, but the result of certain economic necessities on the one hand and of certain ideas of justice on the other, derived from moral and religious sentiment."[74] The two men were clearly drawn together by a normative program, but as regarded the boundaries of economics as a positive science they were a generation apart. This difference led Laveleye to efface the barriers that Mill and others had tried to pose between economics and neighboring disciplines. As he wrote in his theoretical treatise of 1882, "Political economy and law are interpenetrated. He who is ignorant of law will not fathom political economy, and he who is ignorant of political economy will be unable to trace the rationale of law" [*Élements d'économie politique* ([1882] 1902): 10].

Laveleye's influence was great within francophone political economy. That much is evident from the friends he won, notably among them Vilfredo Pareto in Lausanne, who agreed that

> it is probable that there is no single evolution of landed property, but rather that there are several ones that can vary according to nation and place. They must be studied separately, without preconceptions, observing present facts and collecting

72. Laveleye, *De la propriété et des ses formes primitives* ([1874] 1878): xliv.
73. Laveleye, *Éléments d'économie politique* ([1882] 1902): 10.
74. Mill 1848: book II, ch. 1, § 1; Laveleye [1874] 1878: 5.

historical documents of the past. That is the method followed by E. Laveleye, Fustel de Coulanges, Sumner Maine, etc.; it is the only good one. [*Cours d'économie politique* (1896–7): §569]

Laveleye's German admirers were especially those economists who came to be known collectively as the Younger Historical School, the same ones also who founded and sustained the Association for Social Policy (Verein für Socialpolitik, est. 1872). Adolph Wagner, professor at Berlin, was himself responsible for the single most influential sociology of law in nineteenth-century political economy. The first edition of his *Foundations of Economics* (1876) included a 330-page chapter on law and economics, which by the third edition (1892–4) had grown into a separate volume of 564 pages. Wagner's purpose in writing was "to produce an economically tenable theory of economic law in general [*des allgemeinen wirthschaftlichen Rechts*]," something that he claimed – not altogether justifiably, as we have seen – was quite lacking in the economic literature before his intervention. The development of an economic science of rights was crucial to social progress, he believed, "for not only has legal theory not solved the task on its own, it is quite *unable* to do so without the participation of economics."[75] And although Wagner's normative economics was often at odds with Laveleye's, he did share the Belgian's conviction that a thorough demonstration of the functionality of diverse historical institutions could not fail to promote the cause of institutional reform in the present.[76]

Contributing to the German success of Wagner's research program was Karl Bücher's 1879 translation of Laveleye's *Primitive Property,* to which he added several new chapters based on his own research, chapters which were in turn included in later French editions. These addenda revealed a reformist agenda much in the spirit of Laveleye and Wagner, inasmuch as they sought to undermine the absolute Roman-law conception of property – *dominium* – by demonstrating its relativity and its conventionality. In 1893 Bücher, who now held a chair at Leipzig, followed with his own magnum opus *The Emergence of the Economy,* which went through numerous editions (the last in 1926) and translations into English and Russian.[77] Meanwhile in 1883 Karl Knies, now professor of *Staatswis-*

75. Wagner, *Grundlegung der politischen Oekonomie* ([1876] 1892–4): 2:§§1, 5.

76. Wagner called private property in land, e.g., "not an *absolutely necessary, pure-economic* category of economic life, but merely an *historical* one. It is an institution of perhaps great expedience for the whole national economy, but nevertheless it is one which has not always existed, which does not exist everywhere even today, and which therefore cannot be spared a discussion of its absolute or relative dispensability for the present" ([1876] 1892–4: §173).

77. Bücher, *Das Ureigentum* (1879) and *Die Entstehung der Volkswirtschaft* ([1893] 1910).

*senschaft* at Heidelberg, reissued his 1853 volume with postscripts to each of the original chapters. These had the self-assured air of a revolution now largely accomplished, as the linking of law and economics he had called for was now being realized.

> On the one hand it has been claimed, and proofs undertaken, that legal norms and legal arrangements are, and could only be, the result of economic needs and processes. On the other hand it has been demonstrated just as certainly that economic life-processes and relations, if not quite legal relations in themselves, are nevertheless, and must always remain, the products of legal relations. . . . Economics obviously has a very important role regarding property. It will research the substance of this right as it is actually practiced and officially protected, will expound on the economic conditions and consequences of property, . . . can call for amendment of the right's substance, can research the economic substratum of the legal means of acquiring property, and so on. (Knies [1853] 1883: 127)

Gustav Schmoller, professor at Berlin and dean of German economists in the Wilhelmine era, also appreciated Laveleye's example and called for further research of a general nature:

> We must elucidate from the social-scientific and economic perspective how, in what objects, and under what circumstances the right to property arose; what sorts of social and economic effects followed from it; how it came to be shared out to the state, to other corporations, to families and to individuals; what it signifies in essence. [*Grundriß der allgemeinen Volkswirtschafts-lehre* (1901–4): §§49, 123, 132]

Still later, Werner Sombart and Max Weber agreed that the jurist's deductive and normative approach to legal order was less fruitful than the more properly economic one. "The course of economic law and policy," Sombart averred, "indicates clearly its parallelism to that of the economic powers which set its tone at any given time." Even Lorenz von Stein, professor of *Staatswissenschaft* at Berlin, modulated his characteristically obscure idealism to the timbre of the new science: "If the principle of law lies in the essence of personality, the content – of civil law at least – must be economics."[78]

In light of the foregoing comments on the revolution in microeconomics, it should come as no surprise that economists in Austria were also coming

---

78. Sombart, *Der moderne Kapitalismus* (1902): 2:27; Weber, *Wirtschaft und Gesellschaft* ([1922] 1978, composed 1910–14): II, ch. 8; Stein, *Volkswirtschafts-lehre* (1878), quoted in Diehl 1929: 19.

around to the new science. Menger, after all, the founder of the so-called Austrian School of economic thought who is also credited with original insights into the marginal principle, had as early as 1870 called for a social science of institutions. Eugen von Böhm-Bawerk, who had studied law and economics at the leading German universities before returning to take up chairs at Innsbruck and then Vienna, tended to agree: in his *Rights and Relations from the Standpoint of the Theory of Economic Goods* (1881) he termed all rights "a requirement posed by the social organization."[79] Eugen Philippovich too was living refutation of the notion that the famous *Methodenstreit* had opened an unbridgeable chasm between Austrian and north German economic thought. Philippovich split his time between Vienna and Freiburg, was claimed by both the "marginalist" and "historicist" camps, and wrote a textbook that was for a time the most widely used in German-speaking Europe. In that text he reaffirmed the new orthodoxy that "the content of law is socially determined" and hence properly the object of social science ([1893] 1920: 96–7). Richard Hildebrand used the occasion of his inauguration to the Vienna economics faculty in 1894 to deliver a lecture, "On the Problem of a General Evolutionary History of Law and Custom," in which he portrayed positive science as indispensable to such a history.[80] Hildebrand's first book-length study, *Law and Custom at the Primitive Stages of Economic Culture* (1896), was intended to furnish just this sort of empirical grounding. All told, contributors to the German-language literature of political economy – ethnic Germans, Austrians, and the many foreign students who came to study under them – would make the most significant advances in the explanatory science of rights.

Continental developments in both legal and economic scholarship had been the object of British curiosity for some time before 1870, but it was not until late in that decade that an explanation of rights entered the scientific agenda of British political economy. That it did so at all can be credited largely to the work of T. E. Cliffe Leslie, professor of law and politi-

79. Böhm-Bawerk, *Rechte und Verhältnisse vom Standpunkte der volkswirthschaftlichen Güterlehre* (1881): 43.
80. "Regarding *human* life there is ultimately only *one* scientific standpoint, that of anatomy and physiology. In former times philosophy was the link between the various disciplines. Today, now that we have become more skeptical and critical, mature and demanding in our approach to knowledge, that link can be none other than *natural science*. By that I mean not the results that the research of natural science has arrived at, but rather its spirit, i.e. the way it poses questions and its scientific method" [R. Hildebrand, *Ueber das Problem einer allgemeinen Entwicklungsgeschichte des Rechts und der Sitte* (1894): 33].

cal economy at Belfast. Reviewing Maine's *Lectures on the Early History of Institutions,* Leslie called for the application of Maine's "historical method" to political economy, and pointed to Laveleye's recently published *Primitive Property* as an important advance in that regard (Leslie 1875: 468). Two years later Leslie contributed a preface to the first English translation of that book, on which occasion he indicated familiarity with Continental institutional economists ignored even by Laveleye, like Georg Hanssen and his Danish precursor Oluf Olufsen.[81]

Leslie's methodological convictions appear to have been shaped also by the opinions of Professor J. K. Ingram of Dublin, whose tract on *The Present Position and Prospects of Political Economy* (1878) was one of the very few contributions to the discipline in that century to show clearly the influence of Auguste Comte.[82] Ingram pointed to the works of Maine and of German economists as exemplary of the historical method, "the leading idea of which is to connect the whole juristic system of any epoch with the corresponding state of society," and called for its further cultivation (1878: 26–31). Leslie responded the following year in an article, "Political Economy and Sociology," where he too identified economics as an arm of the greater Science of Society. A major task of that science was to account for human institutions, and political economy would have a special domain in the undertaking:

> The development of the positive law of a nation . . . [is] a subject demanding the economist's investigation. The primitive ownership of things in common, the evolution of the separate possession of both chattels and land, of slavery, serfdom, and free labour, the changes in the law of intestate succession, the growth of the testamentary power, and of the law of contract in its different forms, are at once jural and economic facts which the jurist regards from one point of view and the economist from another. (1879: 41, 44)

Despite these calls from across the Irish Sea, despite also Maine and the prestige of Continental jurisprudence, the economists of Great Britain were really quite slow to join the search for the roots of positive right. In publications by Jevons, Cairnes, and Sidgwick, and even by "historical economists" like W. J. Ashley and William Cunningham, one finds only halting gestures toward an endogenous theory of institutions. Things be-

---

81. Leslie, Translator's introduction to Laveleye [1874] 1878: esp. xiii. A rarity among British economists, Leslie knew German and followed developments in the German academy.
82. On Comte's conspicuous absence from most historical economics, see Gide and Rist [1909] 1948: 406–8; Schumpeter 1954: 417–18.

gan to change only in the 1890s. In his 1891 introduction to the English edition of Fustel de Coulanges's work on the medieval manor, Ashley (1891: xli) recommended that such "social antiquities" be studied also by "scholars who are economists as well as historians."

Two years later, in the wake of Alfred Marshall's *Principles of Economics* (1890), Professor J. S. Nicholson of Edinburgh criticized that text's use of history as "vague, old fashioned and excessively weak" and set to work on an alternative.[83] The result was his *Principles of Political Economy,* the first volume of which appeared in 1893. Though beholden in some respects to Mill, Nicholson doubted that property rights could be infinitely pliable under the sovereign will: to believe such a thing, he asserted, "can only lead to the neglect of the forces actually at work in the past or present." Indeed, the great diversity of institutional patterns found in the world

> do not imply that no laws are discoverable, but only that the dis-
> covery may be a matter of difficulty. At a time, however, when
> the apparent vagaries of dialects and of superstitions have been
> brought under the domain of science, it does not seem unreason-
> able to hope that the vagaries of the distribution of wealth may
> also be resolved into uniformities; and, as a matter of fact, dur-
> ing recent years great progress has been made in this direction
> by the application of the historical and comparative methods.
> (Nicholson [1893–1901] 1902–8: vol. 1, book II, ch. 2, §5)

In support of this contention Nicholson cited empirical works that had appeared since Marshall wrote, including Vinogradoff's *Villainage in England* (1892), Kovalevsky's *Modern Customs and Ancient Laws of Russia* (1891), and Fustel de Coulanges's *Origin of Property in Land* (1889), as well as works by Maine, Laveleye, and Seebohm.

It is difficult to say whether Marshall took Nicholson's criticism to heart. But in the third edition of his own text, which appeared two years later in 1895, he praised the efforts of Germans, and particularly of Wagner (whose own famous third edition had just appeared), to marry the studies of law and economics.[84] In 1899, Palgrave's *Dictionary of Political Economy* assigned the entry on "Property" to a historian, who referred readers in turn to the works of Maine, Laveleye, Fustel de Coulanges, and Seebohm, as well as to the standard works of political philosophy.[85]

Beyond the northwest European core of political economy, the new science of rights advanced more quickly than in Britain. We have already

83. Nicholson, quoted in Koot, *English Historical Economics* (1987): 156.
84. Marshall, *Principles of Economics* ([1890] 1895): app. B, §8.
85. F. C. Montague, "Property" (1899): 232–3.

noted its prominence in the universities of Austria; it found adherents too among economists in Poland and Hungary,[86] and especially in Italy.

It has been argued that Italian economic thought was particularly susceptible to the positivist idea in the nineteenth century, not least because its own tradition of *statistica* actually predated the German *Staatswissenschaft* that we have identified as the taproot of this movement.[87] Fedele Lampertico of Padua invoked both Roscher and (especially) Laveleye in his book *Property* (1876), in order to refute the common supposition that present relations of property are somehow "essential" and to replace it with a duly scientific and evolutionary understanding.[88] But the true godfather of institutional analysis in Italy was Achille Loria. Loria's 1877 law thesis, "An Expositive Essay on Landed Property in Its Relation to Law and the Economy," set the parameters of his inquiry for decades to come.[89] Between 1877 and 1882 he studied economics first in Italy, then under Wagner in Berlin and independently in the British Museum; thereafter he held chairs in political economy at Siena, Padua, and Turin, from the last of which he retired only in 1932. Loria's major work was *The Economic Theory of the Political Constitution* (1886), the much expanded second edition of which he published in French in 1893 as *The Economic Foundations of the Social Constitution,* which in its turn was translated into German (1895), Spanish (1896), English (1899), and Italian (1902). In some respects Loria represents a culmination of the ideological developments that brought the reformist ethic into harmony with an agenda to demonstrate the social logic of the very institutions to be reformed. More so than Lav-

86. Jan Stanislaw Lewinski, *The Origin of Property and the Formation of the Village Community* (1913); Akos von Navratil, "Wirtschaft und Recht" (1905). According to Navratil, professor at Kolosvár (present-day Cluj), "One of the most important facets of economic life . . . is the influence by means of which the economic phenomenon cultivates – or at least contributes to the development of – the external order of social collaboration, i.e., to the legal order" (282). "Today, by taking into account economic phenomena, pragmatic legal history is opening a most fertile field of inquiry and explanation of social formations" (289).

87. Riccardo Faucci, "Note su positivismo e pensiero economico in Italia tra otte e novecento" (1986). See also Dionisio Anzilotti's appreciation of Giandomenico Romagnosi, whom he called the first scholar to have considered "the economic element in the science of law" ([1892] 1963: 637).

88. Lampertico, *La proprietà* (1876): esp. 34–5. It is interesting to note that Lampertico's dissertation, "Italian *statistica* before Achenwall," focused on the topic just identified.

89. It is discussed in Riccardo Faucci, "Revisione del marxismo e teoria economica della proprietà in Italia, 1880–1900: Achille Loria (e gli altri)" (1976–7): 593.

eleye or Wagner, and more so even than Marx, Loria believed that the same elemental forces that had brought into being the present state of social imperfection would inexorably call forth a remedy. The present distribution of economic rights, in other words, was "by no means the product of conditions inherent in human nature, but simply the result of powerful historical causes which will eventually disappear."[90] By revealing the determinate nature of social order and social change one might not exactly speed evolution, but one could at least play a constructive role in the realization of historical necessity. Much the same reasoning is evident in Augusto Graziani's *Economic Foundation of Law,* a lecture inaugurating the Siena law faculty's 1893 academic session. As an outsider to professional jurisprudence, Graziani featured the ideas not only of Loria but also of notable jurists who had themselves argued the social determinacy of law. On the basis of this evidence he warned his audience to treat economics not as a mere handmaiden to solid jurisprudence, but as a "most fundamental element."[91]

Much as Italian economists drew inspiration from work in northwest Europe, so would their North American counterparts pattern their work on the example of Europe as a whole. As early as 1836 Theodore Sedgwick incorporated the histories of Robertson and Sismondi into his account of emancipation,[92] and Henry George's *Progress and Poverty* (1879: book VII, ch. 4) cited the authority of Maine, Nasse, and especially Laveleye in support of its historical account of property relations. An important breakthrough came around 1890, when E. R. A. Seligman of Columbia University discovered Marx, Loria, and Richard Hildebrand and used his position as editor of the *Political Science Quarterly* to disseminate their ideas to the American academic community.[93] In *The Economic Interpretation of History* (1902), Seligman asserted that

> the legal system, like the political system, conforms at bottom to the economic conditions. . . . The realization of the fact that social institutions are products of evolution, and that they thus form historical and relative categories, instead of being absolute categories, is the one great acquisition of modern economics, which differentiates it *toto caelo* from that of earlier times. ([1902] 1907: 132, 160–1)

90. Loria, *Les bases économiques de la constitution sociale* ([1893] 1910): 1.
91. Graziani, *Il fondamento economico del diritto* ([1893] 1894): 48. In his subsequent *Istituzioni di economia politica* (1904: 307–8), Graziani offered a narrative of the new science's emergence much like our own.
92. Sedgwick, *Public and Private Economy* (1836): 1:60–3.
93. See especially Seligman [1902] 1907: 56. The American "discovery" of Loria is chronicled in Benson, "Achille Loria's Influence on American Economic Thought" (1950): esp. 185–7.

Loria's name found its way also into the work of Arthur T. Hadley at Yale, who had studied under Wagner in Berlin at about the same time, and who, like Nicholson, was dissatisfied with some aspects of the Marshallian synthesis. Hadley's *Economics: An Account of the Relations between Private Property and Public Welfare* (1896) distinguished between "static" and "dynamic" problems in economics. "In a static problem," he argued, "we assume that the character and institutions of a people remain fixed while the relations between the individual members change." This was the essence of Ricardian economics, but it was not all that economics could be:

> The economist may go one step farther back and inquire how these motives and institutions have arisen; how far they are themselves capable of modification; what causes at the present day may be contributing to modify them. This is called the historical method of inquiry, and is of special importance in the study of dynamic problems.[94]

It was also the selfsame explanatory science of institutions we have witnessed develop in Europe. But it was not to find a real home in America until much later in this century: this was due partly to the strength of Progressivism, as was mentioned above, and partly to the great influence of Thorstein Veblen and his school, as will be discussed in chapter 5 below.

## III    Conclusions

This chapter has demonstrated that, by 1914, a significant subset of economists had come to believe that part of the task of their discipline was to develop a systematic explanation for the creation and distribution of economic rights and obligations. In fact the treatises mentioned so far were but the tallest trees in the forest. The better proof of the new science's vitality resides in the thick underbrush below, in the countless monographs that touched on its problem and contributed to its solution. The chapters to follow will provide a sampling of this literature, in the process of answering questions corollary to this methodological insight: What sorts of explanatory models emerged, and was there a tendency toward consensus on a single paradigm? Was this new positive science of rights associated with a distinctive normative position? Was the work in this field influential among contemporary noneconomists? And why was the new science eventually abandoned by the economists themselves, only to be rediscovered later in this century?

94. Hadley 1896: §27. See also M. L. Cross and R. B. Ekelund, "A. T. Hadley: The American Invention of the Economics of Property Rights and Public Goods" (1981).

# 2

# Toward a normal science

Two impulses jostled for primacy in the new science. On the one hand, there was an appealing parsimony and rigor (and even cynicism) in the ideal of assimilating the theory of legal evolution to the same model of human behavior – that is, rational hedonism – that dominated economic theory as a whole. On the other hand, economists had not yet reached the point of specialization where they would decline, on methodological principle, to consider any behavioral models that diverged from rational hedonism. The first of these impulses will be explored in this chapter, the second one in chapter 3.

In the present chapter our agenda will be to revise an entrenched notion in the historiography of economic thought: namely, that early institutional economics (including that which we have termed the "new science") would have no truck with such reductionist constructs as *homo oeconomicus* and the materialist conception of history. This notion has suffused discussion in the field. Indeed, the conventional distinction between the pre-Coasian and the more recent "neoclassical" vintages of institutionalism derives, at base, from the idea that only the latter version has – for better or worse – embraced the axiom of instrumental rationalism, and has fitted its stories about institutional selection to it. We will argue against this interpretation. In actuality, much of the new science did proceed from a unified, rational-egoistic theory of economic behavior, one which would cover not only the production, exchange, and consumption of goods but the transaction of rules as well. In this respect, practitioners of the new science were seeking to make of it a "normal" science.

To be sure, our contention is not an absolute novelty in the historio-graphical literature. In recent years several articles have argued that one or another nineteenth-century economist should be recognized as a precursor to the "new" institutionalism.[1] These are stories of voices crying in the wilderness, and therein alone lies our objection to them: it is not that the historians have misheard the individual voices, but that they have missed the rest of the chorus. With so many voices crying in concert, could it really have been such a wasteland?[2]

This chapter will not seek to nuance or to tease out differences among authors. Indeed, the authors of specific ideas will seldom be mentioned outside of the footnotes. The goal is to give an impression, which must surely have struck participants at the time, of science on the march.

# I    An economic theory of rules

Nineteenth-century economists gave ample indication that laws and contracts should be approached as the precipitates, intended or otherwise, of enlightened economic self-interest. To Laveleye, it was as clear as symmetry itself that "all acts of economic life take place under the influence of civil institutions, and all civil institutions are ultimately creatures of economic interest" ([1882] 1902: 11). Likewise for Weber, "economic interests are among the strongest factors influencing the creation of law" ([1922] 1978: II, ch. 1, §3), while for Wieser, "the theory of utility explains not only the actual progress of the economy, but leads moreover to the demonstration of its legal basis."[3] The survival of rules in history was, according to Commons, "contingent on their fitness to hold together in a continuing concern the overweening and unlimited selfishness of individuals pressed on by scarcity of resources."[4] And Philippovich spoke more directly to the issue of costs when he averred that "with changes in social stratification, with shifts in the size and power of individual social groups,

1. Michael Hutter, "Early Contributions to Law and Economics: Adolph Wagner's *Grundlegung*" (1982); Izhak Englard, "Victor Mataja's *Liability for Damages from an Economic Viewpoint:* A Centennial to an Ignored Economic Analysis of Tort" (1990); Melvin L. Cross and Robert B. Ekelund, "A. T. Hadley: The American Invention of the Economics of Property Rights and Public Goods" (1981); Steve Pejovich, "Karl Marx, Property Rights School and the Process of Social Change" (1982); David E. R. Gay, "Adam Smith and Property Rights Analysis" (1975); Malcolm Rutherford, "J. R. Commons's Institutional Economics" (1983).
2. The work of synthesis has already begun: Harold James, *A German Identity, 1770–1990* (1989: 60–5), and Woodruff Smith (1991: 22–7, 174) have both noted, briefly, the materialism and methodological individualism underpinning much of the German "historical" economists' oeuvre.
3. Wieser, *Theorie der gesellschaftlichen Wirtschaft* ([1914, 1923] 1928): §175.
4. Commons, *The Legal Foundations of Capitalism* (1924): 137–8.

always goes hand in hand a change in the legal order" ([1893] 1920: 97). In this section we will attempt to systematize these rather diffuse claims.

To date, there is no textbook model of the determination of rules, such as there is for the determination of prices on the competitive market. But abstracting from discussions of contemporary neoclassicists like Coase, Demsetz, Domar, North, and many others, we may sketch briefly what a general, "economic" theory might look like.

The central figure in this model is the rational actor, who seeks with her decisions to maximize the present value of her lifetime pecuniary income – roughly, her utility.[5] Straight away this assumption contradicts intuitive truths about political existence, such as that civil society is made up of "rule makers" and "rule takers," and that at any one moment only a subset of possible rules are even conceivable. But in our world of spare assumptions, everyone is a legal "entrepreneur" and any rule is possible if only there exist the makings of a deal.

By what calculus may legal outcomes actually be predicted? As with the theory of price, we could do worse than to begin with the basic constructs of *cost* and *benefit*. Obedience to rules inflicts some disamenity upon the person who obeys: otherwise they are mere pieties. Therefore a prospective rule must provide a *benefit* to some other person; and that benefit must be great enough both (1) to provide the means to ensure the compliance of the obeyer, either through compensation[6] (carrots) or by threat (sticks), and (2) to leave some residual gain which will make the "entrepreneur's" effort worthwhile. As a result, the level of prospective benefit, which varies according to circumstance, will in part determine the pattern of rules that results.

But it is not the sole determinant. The other element in the calculus is the *cost* of inducing the obeyer's compliance. On the one hand, this cost reflects the level of disamenity that the prospective obeyer will suffer; since the cost of obedience is the cost of forgone freedom of action, this amounts to what economists term the rule's "opportunity cost." It too will vary greatly according to circumstance. On the other hand, account must

5. It is heuristically useful to anthropomorphize the problem in this fashion, but not strictly necessary. The conclusions arrived at in this section may also be arrived at by positing individual behavior that is bereft of rationality, indeed of consciousness at all. So long as an evolutionary process of ("blind") selection operates in such a way that those individuals survive whose behavior mimics that of our rational actor – not an unreasonable assumption, since high lifetime income is arguably a good indicator of reproductive "fitness" – then the empirical result will be identical.

6. Be it noted that compensation need not be in tangible value. Often – as in the classic "social contract" – compensation may take the form of reciprocal conformity to rules which benefit the opposite party.

be taken of the efficacy with which the beneficiary's endowment of resources can be turned to the purpose of coercion. If transaction costs among multiple beneficiaries are relatively low, for instance, or if the transaction costs among prospective obeyers are high, or if the technology of violence favors the beneficiary, then achieving the obeyer's consent will be cheaper than otherwise.

(Note that, stock criticisms notwithstanding, this neoclassical approach to institutions does not predict the best of all possible worlds, or even mere allocative efficiency. Clearly specified rules may be a *necessary* condition in order that the private and the social rates of return on individual enterprise be brought into line; but they are not a *sufficient* condition because the model in no way presumes that the rules themselves are the result of frictionless, transparent negotiation among society's principals. Exploration of this normative dimension of institutional selection will be deferred to chapter 4.)

The model is simpler to operationalize than it is to specify. Students of the empirical world will want to know why one rule $(R_1)$ is favored over an alternative rule $(R_2)$ in a given circumstance. The answer, according to the model, will assume one or both of the following forms:

1. $R_1$ affords greater benefits than $R_2$, and/or
2. $R_1$ incurs fewer costs than $R_2$.

> (Note that the possibility is not excluded that $R_1$ is favored *despite* its lesser benefits, due to its still lesser costs, or that $R_1$ is favored *despite* its greater costs, due to its yet greater benefits.)

A theory of comparative law and institutional evolution is only a bit more complex. The answer to the question, Why is $R_1$ favored in circumstance $i$ $(C_i)$, while in circumstance $j$ $(C_j)$ $R_2$ prevails?,[7] will take one or a combination of the following forms:

1. In $C_i$ the benefits of $R_1$ are greater than in $C_j$;
2. In $C_j$ the benefits of $R_2$ are greater than in $C_i$;
3. In $C_i$ the costs of $R_1$ are lesser than in $C_j$; or
4. In $C_j$ the costs of $R_2$ are lesser than in $C_i$.[8]

Let it be stipulated at the outset that the practitioners of the new science did not achieve, and perhaps did not seek, this degree of generality. But much of their institutional analysis did converge on exactly the insight contained herein.

---

7. In this example, $i, j, \ldots, n$ may stand for different times, different places, or different sectors within a single economy.
8. Note that these propositions may be interdependent. E.g., if circumstances change such that $R_1$ becomes more beneficial, then the opportunity cost of the alternative rule $R_2$ will increase, and it will likely become more costly to negotiate and enforce.

The beauty of this way of thinking is its great simplifying power. The mysteries of human behavioral response having been exposed to the light of generalizing science, the only operative variables in the profusion of institutions are technology, relative scarcity, the number of agents and their heterogeneity, and the like. Thus did practitioners of the new science take evident pleasure in waving aside the intricacies of the soul, the better to concentrate on the economic environment. As Richard Hildebrand (1894: 17) put it, "*the fulcrum* [der Punkt des Archimedes], *upon which the entire world of law and custom may be levered, lies in the economic arena.*" Or more positivistically Loria: "Legal history shows us that instead of being the product of abstract reason, or the result of national conscious- ness, or a racial characteristic, the law is simply the necessary outcome of economic conditions."[9] Or Navratil:

> Even those legal institutions which are characterized by so-
> called *Nationaleigenthümlichkeiten* [national peculiarities] may
> be viewed in a very different light, and their nature can be far
> better understood, their worth better appreciated, once we have
> gone behind the so oft-cited national genius, and investigated
> the postulates of economic life which are of greater causality be-
> cause they are more originally operative.[10]

Superficially, statements like these suggest a kinship of spirit with Marx, whose best known pronouncement on the subject – what he called the "leading thread" of his studies – bears repetition as well:

> In the social production which men carry on they enter into
> definite relations that are indispensable and independent of their
> will; these relations of production correspond to a definite stage
> of development of their material powers of production. The sum
> total of these relations of production constitutes the economic

---

9. Loria [1893] 1910: 86. Also illuminating is Loria's assertion that "man of him- self is neither good nor bad, he is neither controlled by virtue nor by vice. A single sentiment guides him, one impulse drives him on: the instinct of self- preservation or personal egoism, which in its turn is nothing but one of the multiple manifestations of the conservation of energy" (45).

10. Navratil 1905: 289. Similar points may be found in Wagner [1876] 1892–4: 2:§§2, 14; Lampertico 1876: 36; Courcelle-Seneuil 1878: 175–6; Grazi- ani [1893] 1894: 21, 29; Loria [1893] 1910: 79, 114; Leroy-Beaulieu, *Traité théorique et pratique d'économie politique* ([1895] 1900): 545; Wittich, "Die wirtschaftliche Kultur der Deutschen zur Zeit Cäsars" (1897): 56; Lewinski 1913: 56, 67–71; Weber [1922] 1978: II, ch. 7, §3. According to Lewinski, "Such factors as race, imitation, legislation, etc., have no important part in the evolution of property." Similarly for Weber, "No national legal peculiarities, in particular, can be derived from any differences in the operation of the 'sense of justice,' at least not as far as present knowledge goes."

structure of society – the real foundation, on which rise legal
and political superstructures and to which correspond definite
forms of social consciousness. (Marx [1859] 1987: 263–4)

As this passage implies, however, the kinship was rather distant. Even
Marx's materialist side never quite freed itself of the teleological vision of
social existence, which caused him to drift into what we might call, with
license, "economics with the economic agent left out." The remainder of
this chapter will demonstrate that behind the bold strokes of broad
brushes, the new science was motivated by a methodological individualism
that bore far more in common with Darwin than with latter-day idealists.[11]
It will accomplish this by surveying economic accounts of three types of
rules: (1) property rights, (2) contract and inheritance law, and (3) hierarchy (servitude and the firm).

## II    Property rights

Property rights are rules that exclude all but a subset of persons
(or in the extreme, a single person) from enjoyment of a resource. The
"right," then, is a right of redress against trespass. Being intrinsically
costly to negotiate and enforce, property rights will be of interest only if
they promise meaningful benefits. As Lewinski put it, "Every appropriation necessitates a certain effort, consisting in separating, keeping and de-
fending the goods. It is clear that everybody will try to avoid this trouble,
in so far as by so doing he does not deprive himself of the satisfaction
of his wants" (1913: 8–9). "Men are communists," wrote Menger more
succinctly, "whenever possible under existing natural conditions" ([1871]
1981: 96–101). And Richard Hildebrand's formulation was lapidary in the
extreme: "A right which is not yet needed, will not yet develop" ([1896]
1907: 87). The point of each of these dicta was, first, that it would be
foolish to waste resources on the negotiation and enforcement of rules
that yielded no benefits (or, more precisely, no benefits exceeding those
obtainable through the resources' next best employment); and, second,
that people are not foolish.

This insight had its great historical application in the study of primitive
society, when goods were supposed to be more abundant than in any subsequent epoch of human experience. Labor being the scarcer factor of
production, it was not to be expected that people would expend it in gov-

---

11. Consult Knapp, "Darwin und die Sozialwissenschaften" (1872), Schäffle, *Bau
    und Leben des sozialen Körpers* (1875–8), or Commons, "A Sociological View
    of Sociology" (1899–1900), for a taste of how the economists wished to be
    perceived on the spectrum of scientific endeavor. Similarly, R. Hildebrand
    1894: 17; [1896] 1907: iv.

erning access to resources when perfect substitutes waited around every corner. Economists were therefore inclined to accept the likelihood that exclusive possession was not original in society, and specifically that hunter-gatherers had never recognized personal property in the fruits of their activity.[12] The propertylessness of primitive humanity, Schmoller argued, did not denote the absence of a "conception of property," as some had imagined, but followed logically from the "valuelessness" of useful goods that were nevertheless abundant (1901–4: §123). Man could survive simply by plunder of nature's abundant capital, so there was little to be gained from specifying title to the output. The game of negative liberty simply was not worth the candle of eternal vigilance.

What was true for consumption goods was doubly so for natural resources like land, and not only for hunter-gatherers. For pastoralists, and even for early agriculturalists, it made little sense to sink much labor or capital into particular parcels of the superabundant soil, since the potential gains from exclusion were so slim.[13] An example of this sort of reasoning is evident in Richard Hildebrand's skepticism toward the historians' claim that the practice of shifting cultivation that Caesar had attributed to the Germans was evidence of common property rights being enforced to assure that each lineage had its turn on the best soil. Under conditions

12. E.g., Lewinski noted that "there is not the slightest necessity for appropriating objects which in the case of loss can be replaced without any difficulty. This is the case with all goods which are a free gift of nature, and which are at our disposal in a quantity surpassing our wants" (1913: 8–10).

   The absence of property in fish and game, for Roscher, was "quite natural: their sources issue them of their own accord, inexhaustibly, and the accumulation of catch or of capital is out of the question for those subsisting by the hunt" (ca. 1851: 127). See also Roscher [1854] 1906: §83; Scheel, *Eigentum und Erbrecht* (1877): 7–9; Courcelle-Seneuil 1878: 163; Sax, *Grundlegung der theoretischen Staatswirtschaft* (1887): 124; Béchaux, *Le droit et les faits économiques* (1889): 94; Commons [1899–1900] 1965: 77; Meitzen, "Feldgemeinschaft" (1900): 831.

13. Richard Hildebrand wrote that property in land did not exist in any form before it grew scarce, because land had no value and did not even constitute an object of "acquisitory interest" [*Vermögensinteresse*]. To speak of property under such conditions, he went on, was "like saying that because one breathes, one has property in air" ([1896] 1907: 45, 86–9).

   Similarly, Lewinski argued that "so long as the nomad was sure that in his wanderings he could find the necessary pasture, it was not to his interest to take the trouble to appropriate any part of it. Pasture-land had not greater value for him than air has for us" (1913: 9). See also Roscher ca. 1851: 133–4; Laveleye [1874] 1878: 3–4; Lampertico 1876: 36–7; Scheel 1877: 9; Courcelle-Seneuil 1878: 163; Bernard, "L'évolution de la propriété foncière" (1886): 174; Brentano, *Ueber Anerbenrecht und Grundeigenthum* (1895): 15.

of abundance, Hildebrand reasoned, such an elaborate institution would have presupposed improbable degrees of benevolence and political reflection.[14] Moreover, the lack of market outlets minimized the danger that the common patrimony would be depleted opportunistically, since only with relative difficulty could surplus product be realized as durable assets.[15] And finally, even if the returns to exclusion were more than negligible, the costs of policing vast and thinly exploited resources probably would not be.[16]

Inevitably, though, the economist's greater task was to explain why property rights came to exist, not why they sometimes remained absent. The lodestone in the new science's reckoning about property rights derived from the demand side and centered on the relative scarcity of useful resources. If an article is both "rivalrous" in consumption (which means that consumption for one purpose preempts its use for other purposes) and scarce (meaning that collective satiety cannot be reached with the stocks on hand), then a property rule will benefit the person or persons who retain exclusive access. Again to quote Lewinski:

> If we lose an object which has been produced by us, we must to replace it make another one. If the commodity at our disposal exists only in a limited quantity we often cannot replace it at all, or only with great difficulty. In both cases we are exposed to an effort in comparison to which the effort of appropriation is relatively small, and for this reason economically rational. Of two evils it is the smaller one.[17]

By extension, the proprietor will also benefit from the prospect of garnering exclusive returns from any improvements he may make in the property. And if he succeeds in laying claim to more resources than he can make good use of himself, then with his rights of refusal he may extract rents from other individuals who crave their use.

Departing from this insight, some economists concluded that the rule

---

14. R. Hildebrand [1896] 1907: 94–5. He preferred to explain it as a decentralized, primitive form of soil rotation, i.e., as not a rule at all, but a spontaneous practice.

     Hildebrand's corrosive logic could even be extended to the political rules that make up a society's constitution. "It is curious that the modern citizen cannot imagine life at primitive stages of development without a 'constitution,'" he wrote, "and never even raises the question of why one would be required" ([1896] 1907: 107). Cf. also Wittich 1897: 59.

15. Roscher, *Die Nationalökonomik des Ackerbaus* ([1859] 1903): §79.

16. Roesler, *Vorlesungen über Volkswirthschaft* (1878): 89–90. See also Bagehot, "The Postulates of English Political Economy" ([1876] 1978): 244.

17. Lewinski 1913: 10. See also Turgot, *Plan d'un ouvrage sur le commerce* ([1753–54] 1913–23): 380–1; Walras [1874, 1926] 1954: §23; Cohn 1885: 412–13.

of property had been asserted by the individual against the world, even against the general will. The result might be a hostile equilibrium, what Meitzen called "a mutual demand for consideration, backed by the sword if necessary," but it was a property regime nonetheless.[18]

But if the proprietor's gain merely amounted to the loss of others, surely it would be rarer and more closely contested than was in fact the case. To explain the institution's ubiquity, economists pointed also to benefits that spilled over from proprietors to nonproprietors. As early as 1850, Roscher's readers were guided through a mathematical example of the "free rider" problem, which illustrates how a normal desire to minimize one's own sacrifice can, absent the right to exclude, result in the underproduction of valued goods. In his example of a community of 100,000 members, each member would recognize that he can expect only a 1/100,000 share in his marginal effort and would act (or shirk) accordingly.[19] Conversely, when the commons was split into freeholds, private stewardship resulted in a far greater total product of valued goods, some of which in time would find their way into the hands of those who had been denied direct access. These spillover benefits of private property were such that society as a whole – or at least some critical subset of society – had often been happy to underwrite diversions from the common pool.[20] A fiscal authority, too, would find the clear delineation of property to simplify the problem of taxation.[21] And at a minimum, property had long proved its value in repressing unproductive – and even violent – conflicts over scarce resources.[22]

Whatever the exact distribution of benefits from appropriation, its logic had found expression since the earliest days of human interaction: earliest

18. Meitzen, *Siedelung und Agrarwesen der Westgermanen und Ostgermanen* (1895): 2:193. For a sense of just how bloody-minded the "bourgeois" economists' view of the history of property could be, see also Dupuit 1861: 329; Scheel 1877: 10–11; Roesler 1878: 77; Block, *Les progrès de la science économique* (1890): 477; Hadley 1896: 30; Wittich 1897: 65; Commons [1899–1900] 1965: 15, 108; Schmoller 1901–4: §125; Colson, *Cours d'économie politique* (1901–7): 3:48.
19. The example is found in Roscher ca. 1851: 122; and Roscher [1854] 1906: §81.
20. Menger [1871] 1981: 96–101; Cossa, *Primi elementi di economia politica* ([1875] 1922): 174–5; Philippovich [1893] 1920: 103; Colson 1901–7: 3:25, 38, 56; Ely 1914: 546. As Leroy-Beaulieu put it, "It is not so much in the interest of the first occupant, . . . as in that of society, that the rule of possession has been admitted" ([1895] 1900: 553).
21. Meitzen, e.g., linked the development of private landed property in Finland to the intrusions of Swedish and Russian absolutism (1895: 2:181–92).
22. Mill 1848: II, ch. 1, §2; Lewinski 1913: 10.

and most uniformly in goods that were the artifice of human hands;[23] in livestock, the first major capital good;[24] in arable soil;[25] and ultimately even in ideas.[26] Typically, the right of disposal and the right of enjoyment were unified in a single hand. But in some cases resources fell more logically to the control of magistrates and bureaucrats who were charged with administering them in the public interest. Schools, hospitals, transport systems, and forests, for instance, were supposed to tend toward public administration, lest they fall victim to market failure.[27]

Moreover, the economic way of thinking was able to resolve the paradox that civil law should protect the possessor of a good even against its rightful proprietor, until such time as the latter could prove his legitimacy. Such protection seemed absurd, since only legitimate property was ultimately deserving of protection, and yet the provision was found in the legal traditions of many cultures. The reason found was that the provision would, at the cost of occasional (and usually temporary) protection of illegitimate possession, save the legitimate owner the great trouble of standing ready to prove his title at any moment (Graziani 1904: 32–4).

23. Schäffle [1858] 1873: §279.I.3.(c).a; Mangoldt, *Grundriß der Volkswirthschafts-lehre* ([1863] 1871): 22–3; Laveleye [1874] 1878: 3; Scheel 1877: 7–8; Sax 1887: 124; Leroy-Beaulieu [1895] 1900: 540; Schmoller 1901–4: §123. Cf. also Rachfahl, "Zur Geschichte des Grundeigentums" (1900): 3–4.

24. Schmoller 1901–4: §124; Brentano 1895: 15. According to Schmoller, private property in livestock had been a rational response to the conditions of primitive pastoral production, where "the personal strength and skill of the individual man was best suited to the care, preservation and augmentation of that property."

   Those holding property to have originated in pastoralism included Wittich 1897: 47; and R. Hildebrand [1896] 1907: 25, 97, who cited Jakob Grimm's authority.

25. In Ely's hands, the story of Plymouth Plantation became one of how an ill-considered agrarian communalism inevitably gave way to private tillage once Governor Bradford and his advisers reflected upon the cause of their penury (1914: 49). In making of private property in land a universal precondition for successful agriculture, Ely was following in the footsteps of Turgot ([1769] 1913–23: §§1–13). As we shall see, it was a minority opinion among economists of our period.

26. According to Hadley, the law of patent was devised "not primarily as a stimulus for invention or for disclosure, but for utilization and development of new methods requiring the investment of capital and the guarantees which shall make such investment possible" (1896: 134).

27. Philippovich [1893] 1920: 103–4; Meitzen 1895: 1:167; Diehl, *Theoretische Nationalökonomie* (1923–4): 2:247.

Most land had been privatized with the passing centuries, principally as a result of the "pressure" of rising population, closing frontiers, and shallowing resource pools, but also as a result of technical progress and the opening of market outlets. Taken together, these developments suggested growth on the intensive margin, that is, through ever greater infusions of (supply-elastic) labor and capital into the (inelastic) stock of land; at the same time, they threatened the soil's natural recuperative power under a regime of free access.[28] The solution, when such was achieved, was to limit access and to guarantee to investors exclusive returns: usually by outright private property,[29] but sometimes also through the incremental restriction of usufruct.[30] This line of reasoning explained why, ceteris paribus, private property emerged sooner in arable than in waste, soonest in arable that was least fertile, and soonest in the proximity of towns.[31]

To grasp the timing of property's appearance, though, it was necessary to pay heed to the variability of its costs across specific situations. As Emil Sax formulated the problem, "The equilibrium between interactive egoistic economic agents, which is expressed in property relations, is a labile one. Each shift in the relations of the interested powers disturbs it" (1887: 125). For instance, property was established in land-abundant societies like Finland sooner than would be predicted from a calculation of its gross returns, largely because the open frontier made it far less likely that anyone would seriously *resist* the appropriation of land, either.[32] The

28. What we today call the "tragedy of the commons" was known to German economists by the oft-quoted proverb *"Wes Wiese ist gemeine, der Gras is gern kleine"* ["Where the meadow is common, the grass is short"]. Vivid depictions are found in Roscher [1859] 1903: §80; and Lewinski 1913: 33–4.

29. Wirth, *Grundzüge der National-Ökonomie* ([1856–9] 1873–83): 1:422–3; Schäffle [1858] 1873: §279.I.3.(c).a; Roscher [1859] 1903: §195; Dupuit 1861: 327; Mangoldt [1863] 1871: 22–3; Laveleye [1874] 1878: 125; Lampertico 1876: 36–7, 82–3, 359; Wagner [1876] 1892–4: 2:397–8, 410–13; Courcelle-Seneuil 1878: 172; Cohn 1885: 417–19; Bernard 1886: 183; Béchaux 1889: 94; Graziani [1893] 1894: 25, 35; Philippovich [1893] 1920: 100; Leroy-Beaulieu [1895] 1900: 534–62; Brentano 1895: 16; Hadley 1896: 31, 127–9; R. Hildebrand [1896] 1907: 134; Fuchs, "Bauernbefreiung" (1898a): 299–300; Commons [1899–1900] 1965: 13; Sombart 1902: 2:122–3, 164–5, 173; Bücher, *Die Allmende in ihrer wirtschaftlichen und sozialen Bedeutung* (1902): 7; Graziani 1904: 317–20; Colson 1901–7: 3:50; Wieser, *Recht und Macht* (1910): 66–7; Ely 1914: 811–12; Diehl 1923–4: 2:241.

30. Schäffle [1858] 1873: 353; Lewinski 1913: 33–7.

31. Graziani 1904: 320–1. Meitzen also linked the relative longevity of the Great Russian *obschina* to the exceptional fertility of its soil (1895: 2:229).

32. Meitzen 1895: 2:193. See also Schmoller 1901–4: §125.

gradual perfection of weaponry was also believed to have played a role in enforcing exclusion from private territories (Roesler 1878: 90).

But right down to the present, other resources like pastures, forests, fisheries, roads, and waterways often remained as commons. This fact was explained by their lesser rivalry in use, and by potential economies of scale.[33] Further, there was little scope for their improvement through the intensive application of labor and capital: as a result, there was little in the way of second-order benefits to those who would be excluded from them under a regime of private property.[34] In addition, the problem of institutional cost reared its head here also, inasmuch as the survival of free access was linked to the relatively greater cost of policing certain resources as private property.[35]

Tillable soil was a centerpiece in the economic history of property, and consequently great interest focused on accounting for the many respects in which it diverged from the ideal type of absolute dominion over chattels. The ancient practice of intermingling privately owned strips of arable in unenclosed fields, for instance, was investigated and found not wanting in benefits: not only did it help peasants to spread their individual risks (the reason usually mooted today), but it could also – ironically, perhaps – serve to economize on transaction costs. Behind the careful division of the early German village's lands into open fields of homogeneous quality, and the subsequent division of each field into as many strips as there were legitimate claimants, economists saw not equalitarianism per se (recall that multiple and fractional shareholdings were common), but an attempt to minimize the negotiation costs of partitioning a scarce resource among political equals. Several of these authors noted that the system served further as a standardized measure, to facilitate private transaction of lots.[36]

33. Common tenure of pasture, e.g., permitted significant savings in labor, fencing, and breeding stock. See Roscher [1859] 1903: §79; Keussler, *Zur Geschichte und Kritik des bäuerlichen Gemeindebesitzes in Russland* (1876): 7; Wittich 1897: 192–3.
34. Roscher ca. 1851: 133–4; Lampertico 1876: 37, 54; Leroy-Beaulieu, *Précis d'économie politique* ([1888] 1910): 119; Philippovich [1893] 1920: 100–4; Cunningham, *Modern Civilization in Some of Its Economic Aspects* (1896): 17–18.
35. This was Keussler's argument for why forests and fisheries tended to be the last of all resources to be partitioned (1876: 7).
36. Meitzen 1895: 1:77. This view was supported by the observation that equalization of shares was practiced only within the same village polity, while lots could vary significantly between villages: "All that mattered was that the individual shares of the members of the same village were equalized without strife and doubt." The notion that lot-equalitarianism served to minimize political

Moreover, intermingling private strips made the collective defense less costly to organize, since no invader could damage one holder without damaging all others in the process (Roscher [1859] 1903: §79). Whatever its particular merits, the open-field system survived despite long-standing laws which permitted the contractual consolidation of lots, and sometimes even their unilateral enclosure.[37]

Other, more direct attenuations of strict *dominium* were also rationalized by reference to the social savings they offered. Often primitive agriculturalists were denied claims of proprietorship over land left fallow, in light of the needs of slash-and-burn shifting cultivation.[38] More draconian still was the practice, in sedentary agrarian communities, of periodic and compulsory land repartitions. This was a defining feature of the "village community" around which had centered so much historical curiosity (in Western Europe) and policy debate (in Slavic regions); and various hypotheses were adduced to explain it. It was seen as a vehicle of intracommunal class conflict;[39] or, alternatively, as a cooperative solution to achieve the proportional application of labor to land in the face of population changes,[40] or to meet new collective tax liabilities.[41] On the other hand, the practice

transactions is reflected also in Hanssen [1835–7] 1880: 2, 8–10; Wagner [1876] 1892–4: 2:§180; Inama-Sternegg 1896: 757.

37. This was Hanssen's finding for medieval Jutland ([1835–7] 1880: 45–6).

38. Bücher, "Die Wirtschaft der Naturvölker" (1908): 46; Lewinski 1913: 42–4.

39. Graziani 1904: 314, citing the historian Boris Chicherin; Weber, "Der Streit um den Charakter der altgermanischen Sozialverfassung" (1904): 464–7; Lewinski 1913: 48–54.

40. Laveleye [1874] 1878: 24–5; Schmoller 1901–4: §125; Weber 1904: 465. Besides the relatively straightforward imperatives of population growth, R. Hildebrand noted that redistribution was also a functional response to the challenges posed by social differentiation. In particular, redistribution could ensure that those patrons who enjoyed the largest dependent labor force in a given period enjoyed correspondingly ample lots of arable land ([1896] 1907: 125–37).

41. Miaskowski, *Das Problem der Grundbesitzverteilung in geschichtlicher Entwicklung* (1890): 6; Meitzen 1895: 2:230; R. Hildebrand [1896] 1907: 108, 182–9; Graziani 1904: 312–13; Weber, *Wirtschafts-Geschichte* ([1923] 1924): 34–8. This line of reasoning grew more popular as evidence accumulated to the effect that many village communities – outstandingly the Russian mir, but also those found in Germany (especially the Westphalian *Gehöferschaft*), England (the system of hides found in Domesday Book), India, Dutch Indonesia, and China – were the creatures of fiscal absolutism. The logic of this arrangement was that repartitions would ensure that each household's holding would be proportional to the labor power at its disposal. Interestingly, Graziani argued from Russian evidence that this rule was especially functional in the not

could result from a collective effort to attract new migrants into underpopulated villages.[42] Finally, it could be explained as a strategy to make the system of open fields consensually feasible,[43] and to prevent its excesses.[44] Easements and compulsory schedules were also typical of village agri-

uncommon situation where the tax burden *exceeded* the yield of the soil. In this case each family would attempt to *minimize* its holdings, and thereby its share of the burden. Therefore the allocation of land in proportion to household labor was seen as an expeditious means to avoid collective arrears.

42. Keussler used this logic in explaining why the Russian agrarian corporation was "democratic," in the sense that new and equal shares were regularly created for immigrants, while the German one appeared "aristocratic," i.e., maintaining a fixed number of shares and unwilling to admit new members on equal terms, if at all. According to Keussler, German and Russian communities alike maximized the utility of their members by optimizing their number. Specifically, calculations were based on the fact that while new households added to the group's total tax-paying and defense capacity, they would inevitably reduce the pool of land available to established members. The optimal membership was the number at which the marginal (economic) costs of admitting a new member was equal to the marginal (noneconomic) benefits of doing so. The German corporation, therefore, "granted land and permitted settlement only to the extent that it considered sufficient land to be available so that the previous usufructories would not be impaired, or to the extent that the advantage of increasing the number of arms-bearing and tax-paying members was greater than the economic disadvantage." But so also did the Russian community, naturally. The difference in practice resulted from the fact that land was more abundant in Russia than in Germany, more homogeneous, and (consequently) more fertile on the margin of cultivation. To Keussler's mind this explained why Russians, unlike Germans, not only welcomed newcomers but actually competed to entice them: living in a sparsely populated country, each new member would add palpably to the group's assets, while imposing only a vanishingly small price in terms of forgone output per household (1876: 45–56).

43. According to Roscher, minimizing political friction was also the purpose of those communities which periodically redivided the open fields, or simply rotated the shareholders' claims among lots already marked out. The prospect of future re-reckoning, they thought, had served to soften resistance to perceived inequalities in the division at hand ([1859] 1903: §17). See also Rachfahl 1900: 7.

44. According to R. Hildebrand, redivision of the arable often took place immediately after a new field had been cleared. Without a global repartition, the only way to preserve equality among the communists would be for each increment to be divided equally as well. This process, however, could press the progress of fragmentation well beyond whatever economic advantages it offered ([1896] 1907: 171).

culture and were explained as functional in the common defense,[45] as facilitating the coordination of improvements and helping to enforce "best practice,"[46] or simply as necessary corollaries of the open-field system.[47] Like the regime of free access before them, these rules were in time modified in the direction of permanent and absolute property;[48] but conversely, expropriation[49] and the vested interests of labor[50] were accorded greater legal sanction as economies expanded on the intensive margin.

45. Roscher reasoned that compulsory schedules [so-called *Flurzwang*] worked to deter aggression from without, since field work tended to occur in close proximity ([1859] 1903: §74).
46. Courcelle-Seneuil 1878: 165; Bücher 1902: 16.
47. In particular, grazing beasts on the fallow would be much impaired if the cultivated fields were in stubble at significantly different periods (Keussler 1876: 6–7). Meitzen, additionally, pointed out that the practice of limiting access to individual strips during the growing season allowed land to be cropped that would otherwise become pathways (1895: 1:71).
48. Roscher [1859] 1903: §195; Schäffle [1858] 1873: 353; Hanssen, "Die mittelalterliche Feldgemeinschaft in England" ([1870] 1880): 491–2; Laveleye [1874] 1878: 125; Wagner [1876] 1892–4: 2:416–20; Leroy-Beaulieu, *Essai sur la répartition des richesses* ([1881] 1888): 69–71; Leroy-Beaulieu [1888] 1910: 117–18; Miaskowski 1890: 8; Leroy-Beaulieu [1895] 1900: 534; Fuchs 1898a: 299–300; Lewinski 1913: 64.
49. Thus Wagner saw the law of expropriation developing in concert in the various "old, densely populated, civilized states of Europe," while Russia and the United States, which stood apart on account of their abundant natural resources, had not found any necessity to articulate such laws ([1876] 1892–4: 2:§237). See also Mangoldt [1863] 1871: 22–3.

    The mutability of water rights was noted by Colson in his discussion of the response to hydroelectric technology (1901–7: 3:32), and by Seligman (1904: 56) and Ely (1914: 546–7), when comparing the moist climate of England – home of the common law – to the aridity of the western United States.
50. According to Graziani, the recognition of a tenant's *jus in re* "derives from the necessity of assuring the cultivator against a summary dismissal, which would impede or diminish the intensity of cultivation and of production in general" ([1893] 1894: 42).

    Similarly, Loria believed prescription (which, like the closely related *usucapio* of Roman law, granted the right of property to bona fide possessors after passage of a long time without contestation) to be peculiar to Europe, due to the relatively intensive nature of that continent's agriculture, and to the consequent need to encourage the tenant to improve his holding. But in the Orient, where agriculture could proceed quite adequately without great investment by the tenant, summary eviction could be permitted and even, as in the case of the Jubilee of the ancient Jews, regularized ([1893] 1910: 91–2). See also Graziani [1893] 1894: 36, which notes additionally the fact that *usucapio*

### III    The law of contract and testament

Property may have been the first rule pursued by *homo oeconomicus,* but by no means would it be his last. Once secure title to resources had been established, people naturally wished to seal mutually beneficial transactions on their basis. The very existence of judicial rules compelling the performance of promises were explained by reference to the greater predictability they afforded,[51] as was the judge's practice of assuming certain conventions as inherent in each contract, unless stipulated otherwise.[52] The historical ascent of the law merchant over Roman quiritary law (which had hindered exchange at least as much as it facilitated it) and the primacy, in commercial law, of bona fides over the letter of contract were both linked to the gradual intensification of trade in antiquity and the Middle Ages.[53] Still later, the law of the corporation and of limited liability were instituted as adaptations to the increasing importance of the labor- and capital-intensive margins of growth.[54]

But the law was not solely facilitative of contracts. It could also further economic interests by countenancing their breach. Judges were expected to refuse to enforce contracts, if strict performance was found to be uneconomic (Graziani [1893] 1894: 41–2). And legislatures were at least as likely to bend with the wind of expediency as was the bench, as the case of perpetual leases illustrated: these solemn contracts were called into question as the economic constraints of perpetual lien began to pinch, and

spared a prospective buyer costly investigations to confirm that a given lot was really the seller's to sell.

This same principle became operative also in industry, where late antiquity saw the introduction of the Proculeian legal principle whereby the product of one party's labor and another's materials became the property of the laborer, unless otherwise stipulated (Loria [1893] 1910: 93).

51.  Graziani held that, without legal recourse to punish opportunistic behavior, contracts would become "an exceptional occurrence in social life. Therefore judicial oversight is an effect of economic necessity" ([1893] 1894: 41).

52.  Hoyt, "The Economic Functions of the Common Law" (1918): 190–1; Weber [1922] 1978: II, ch. 8, §ii. Weber maintained that such default clauses existed to save contracting the effort of covering each contingency.

53.  According to Courcelle-Seneuil, "Political economy teaches us why commercial law was introduced, has prevailed, and will prevail still more fully in the future: it is because it is simpler and more expeditious; because it occasions fewer losses of time and effort, and consequently is far more favorable to production than is most civil legislation" ([1858] 1891: 2:book 1, ch. 1, §6). See also Courcelle-Seneuil 1878: 175; Loria [1893] 1910: 84–5, 92–3; Weber [1922] 1978: II, ch. 8, §ii.

54.  Hadley 1896: 144–6; Colson 1901–7: 3:63.

then broken (by the right of redemption) quite as soon as tenants surpassed their lords in political power (Loria [1893] 1910: 101–2).

Of course, one had to account also for rules that prohibited contract. Usury was outlawed not just as a result of moral scruples, but also by cold calculation of its social costs.[55] Where military readiness was at a premium, as in the case of the early German tribes, sumptuary restrictions were often recurred to, including even blanket prohibitions on trade with the outside world. In more developed societies, feudal devices like entail, mortmain, *fidei-commissum,* and preemptive rights protected the integrity of family estates from rapacious sovereigns and spendthrift heirs;[56] but all were discarded once their advantages were overbalanced by the obstacles they posed to the redeployment of resources from the nobility to men of affairs.[57] The Indian village's caste system exacted a high economic price in that it stymied the reallocation of labor to its most valued use; but these costs were more than offset by the social savings it offered, by preventing distributive strife where magisterial authority was too weak to hold the ring (Bagehot [1876] 1978: 244–5, 249). In the Europe of old, industrial and commercial restrictions had long promoted the interests of powerful groups, and their eventual abolition was due in large part to the diffusion of capital, which made rent-seeking coalitions a practical impossibility.[58]

Constraints on personal relations were modeled according to this same

55. Bücher [1893] 1910: 115; Weber [1923] 1924: 234–5. Weber believed that tribal societies had prohibited lending at interest because it could lead to the imprisonment of debtors, and imprisonment would in turn lessen the collective's military capacity. According to Graziani, the prohibition on usury fell eventually into contradiction with the growing importance of capital as a factor of production: usury, at this point, became "incompatible with the new exigencies of industry" and was consequently dropped (1893: 12–13).

56. Schäffle [1858] 1873: §279; Wagner [1876] 1892–4: 2:420; Loria [1893] 1910: 95; Brentano 1895: 23; Wieser [1914] 1923: §75.

57. Hadley 1896: 128; Weber [1922] 1978: ch. 8, §ii. Loria ([1893] 1910: 90–1) and Meitzen (1895: 1:234) made a similar argument in explaining the relaxation, during the late Roman Republic, of traditional *mancipatio* constraints on the alienation of real estate. Such a reading was very much in keeping with Maine's *Ancient Law.*

58. Brentano, "Ethik und Volkswirtschaft in der Geschichte" ([1901] 1923): 64–74; Sombart 1902: 2:29–31; Schwiedland, "Allgemeine Volkswirtschaftslehre" (1912): 30–3. Sombart's reasoning seems to suggest a conception of what is today called "hegemonic stability," which was destroyed by the decentralizing ferment of capitalism. Wieser, conversely, held that new commercial opportunities gave the long-dormant bourgeoisie the decisive impetus to combine effectively in the defense and promotion of their common interests ([1914, 1923] 1928: §75). Compare Marx, *Das Kapital* ([1867] 1977): vol. 1, ch. 28.

logic. The practices of prostitution and concubinage (which Weber stylized as "freedom of sexual contract") were understood to be generally rare, due not so much to a lack of demand on the part of men, but rather resulting from the resistance of married women, who feared greater competition from their more attractive peers. Similarly, when women were relatively dependent on their spouses they tended to oppose the right of divorce; but where they enjoyed a greater measure of economic independence (as in America), their resistance was softened by the recognition that legitimate divorce could work in their favor as well (Weber [1922] 1978: II, ch. 8, §ii). And laws denying marriage to individuals who lacked adequate means to support a family served a more collective purpose, of ensuring that the population did not grow to outstrip the means of subsistence (Graziani [1893] 1894: 26).

Freedom of bequest was unusual in the agrarian peasant household, since the patriarch's powers were considered those of stewardship rather than arbitrary disposal. On his death, "his" assets fell incontestably to the members of his household (now under the stewardship of a new patriarch). Testamentary freedom arose at around the same time as private property itself, and with much the same purpose of exciting interested individuals to ever greater effort in the creation of values.[59] Therefore it developed first where achievement was most closely linked to individual effort, namely in towns, and over the fruits of commerce and war (Brentano 1895: 19–21). Even after the freedom of testament had been entrenched in principle, the economic interests of nonproprietors were furthered by primogeniture[60] and by restrictions on entail.[61]

## IV    Rules of hierarchy

The economic approach to rules was extended to cover also that large class of institutions which predicate the subjection of one person to

---

59. Mill 1848: book 2, ch. 2, §3; Wirth [1856–9] 1881: 1:422–3; Leroy-Beaulieu [1888] 1910: 129; Philippovich [1893] 1920: 108–9; Brentano 1895: 19–21.
60. According to Commons, primogeniture was a characteristic specific to sparsely settled regions. In light of the logistical obstacles to the common defense, security required that "each [manor] should be undivided and controlled by a single will. This was the economic basis of primogeniture" ([1899–1900] 1965: 47).
61. Graziani argued that prohibitions of *fidei-commissum* were driven by the social purpose of fomenting "the free circulation and application of wealth" (1893: 37). Weber, on the other hand, believed that they had historically served the narrower interest of the bourgeois class ([1922] 1978: II, ch. 8, §ii).

the will of another: archetypically in chattel slavery and in serfdom, but also in patriarchy, in producer cooperatives, and in the capitalist firm. Instead of surveying each of these institutions separately – after all, the point of generalizing science is to reduce specific cases to their common denominators – let us consider the general economic considerations that informed their articulation.

The analytical blade of economic choice might seem a dull instrument with which to lay open the relation of master and servant, much less the subordination of wife to husband, child to parent. But try the economists did, and not without success. J. R. Commons captured the economic theory of hierarchy at its most abstract when he applied to it the terms of Darwinian evolution: "Organization, in biology, is the means of economizing the vital forces and increasing the chances of the organism for survival. The same is true of social organization, which economizes the social forces.[62] But this could be only half the story, since economic "organization" is far from ubiquitous. The new science would therefore have to go beyond such general formulations, to explain the differentiation of tutelage from alternative patterns of labor allocation through "spot" labor markets or by coercion ad hoc.

As always, the degree of economic benefit attending tutelage was deemed an important independent variable determining its presence or absence. In primitive societies, for instance, women were especially liable to become the chattel of their menfolk for the very reason that their economic activities (principally gathering and gardening) contributed such a large share to the household's total product. Controlling women was therefore tantamount to controlling scarce, productive labor. Not only patriarchy, but also patrilocality and the exaction of bride price followed from this basic datum; and as the relative value of women as capital goods declined, so were alternatives to these draconian practices more likely entertained.[63] Conversely, hunting bands were averse to enslaving captured warriors, because men who could not be given weapons could not contribute to production, and so would be a net economic burden. Only in the pastoral and agrarian ages did conquerors begin to show interest in male slavery, as the growing division of labor opened up new, subordinate tasks that yet generated a surplus.[64] Similarly, in the later agricultural age, slavery was impractical in both northern Europe and northern North

62. Commons [1899–1900] 1965: 109. See also Wagner [1876] 1892–4: 2:41–2.
63. Brentano, "Die Volkswirthschaft und ihre konkreten Grundbedingungen" (1893): 130–45; Schmoller 1901–4: §90.
64. Roscher [1859] 1903: §§8–12; Madrazo 1874–6: 1:262; Brentano 1895: 14; Hadley 1896: 27–8; Ely, *Studies in the Evolution of Industrial Society* (1903): 47; Oppenheimer, *Der Staat* ([1907] 1914): 37–40.

America, principally because agricultural labor in those less temperate climes could hardly support its own keep, and still less provide for an idle elite.[65] And given the very extractive nature of southern American plantation agriculture, the end of the frontier and falling surpluses would in the long run have made slavery unprofitable there as well.[66]

An important wrinkle was introduced into this rather simple calculus when one went on to ask whether bondage was not merely feasible but actually the *best* way to relieve labor of its surplus value. The consensus opinion was that the answer to this question depended on the alternative opportunities available to labor. In countries where the population was sparse or the frontier ill policed, specifically, the would-be aristocrat had an especial incentive to bind the worker closely to him, lest the worker withhold his services opportunistically to better his bargain—or simply leave the enterprise for greener pastures.[67] Thus was early patriarchy linked to the practice of wife capture, which in turn was caused ultimately by the exogenous (i.e., unexplained) factor of female infanticide: by making women relatively scarce, infanticide raised the return to men who took their wives without consent or contract.[68] Thus also were efforts to bind the Russian peasants to the soil intensified in response to an incipient exodus to the east and south.[69] Once labor had grown plentiful and resources scarce, however, involuntary servitude came to appear to landowners a pointlessly costly way of squeezing economic rents from the proletarian, inasmuch as those same rents would now be forthcoming anyway from the operation of supply and demand on a free market.[70]

Rules of tutelage depended also on more purely "economic" considerations, like relative factor scarcity, the state of technology, and consumer

65. Molinari, "Esclavage" (1853a): 712; Cairnes, *The Slave Power* ([1862] 1863): 42–3, citing Tocqueville.
66. Weber [1922] 1978: II, ch. 8, §ii; [1923] 1924: 86.
67. Schäffle [1858] 1873: §270; Wagner [1876] 1892–4: 2:§26; Loria [1893] 1910: 100; Leroy-Beaulieu [1895] 1900: 526–7; Commons [1899–1900] 1965: 76–7. See also Sismondi, "Lessons of Experience on the Emancipation of Slaves" (1833): 266.
68. Commons [1899–1900] 1965: 12–13, following McLennan.
69. Simkovich, "Die Bauernbefreiung in Russland" (1909): 602–3. According to R. Hildebrand, the Russian village community also had an interest in immobilizing its labor force, since each member lost to greener pastures had the effect of increasing every remaining soul's share of the collective tax liability ([1896] 1907: 182–9).
70. Schäffle [1858] 1873: §270, quoting Lammenais; Loria [1893] 1910: 5; Commons [1899–1900] 1965: 48, 77; Page, *The End of Villainage in England* (1900): 375; Weber [1922] 1978: II, ch. 8, §ii. Roscher noted that Justus Möser had arrived at this same insight already in the 1770s (1874: 511).

preferences. The supervision of labor could be indicated if it offered technical advantages in production, specifically by facilitating coordination of the sort that would not be forthcoming by spontaneous association, or at least not forthcoming at comparable cost.[71] The very great size of Pleistocene mammals, for instance, was implicated in the regimentation of Stone Age hunting bands under a single leader (Bücher 1908: 50). Conversely, to the extent that the general environment made of man the *hunted* as well, association and strict coordination of action became even more important. Thus was the agrarian village cooperative characteristic of the forested, brigand-ridden expanses of the northern European plain, as anywhere where no state authority could be relied upon to enforce order.[72] The advent of cavalry and of Viking boats gave a similar stimulus to the development of large-scale military enterprises, constructed around the feudal bond.[73] The superiority of gang labor in the cultivation of certain crops could lead to slavery (as in the case of tropical plantation crops)[74] or to corporate labor pooling (as in the case of haying in European villages; Hanssen [1835–7] 1880: 62). The relative inaccessibility of East Elbian Germany to the continental market militated for a peculiar form of capitalist "second serfdom" [*Gutsherrschaft*], since only a large business enter-

71. Such links between economies of coordination on the one hand, and scale of enterprise on the other, were noted in Roscher [1859] 1903: §79; Bücher [1893] 1910: 98; Loria [1893] 1910: 122–3; R. Hildebrand [1896] 1907: 96; Commons [1899–1900] 1965: 30–1, 109; Schmoller 1901–4: §§89–90, 124; Graziani 1904: 310–11; Colson 1901–7: 3:48–9; Wieser [1914, 1923] 1928: §75; Ely 1914: 805–6; Weber [1922] 1978: I, ch. 2, §22.

72. Hanssen [1835–7] 1880: 6, 27–8; Laveleye [1874] 1878: 34; Wagner [1876] 1892–4: 2:402–8, 426; Béchaux 1889: 94–5; Bücher [1893] 1910: 117–20; Schmoller 1901–4: §89; Colson 1901–7: 1:55–6, 68; Weber [1922] 1978: II, chs. 3–4.

   The prevalence of independent homesteading on the North American frontier, apparently a great exception to this rule, actually confirmed it. What made America unique, according to Meitzen (1900: 831), was the relative ease with which apparently isolated settlers could call down the protection of a modern state structure, should the need arise. In this respect, American frontiersmen had precious little in common with their medieval counterparts.

73. Minghetti, *Dell'economia pubblica e delle sue attinenze colla morale e col diritto* ([1859] 1863): 481; Wittich, *Die Grundherrschaft in Nordwestdeutschland* (1896): 133; Wittich 1897: 57. In a similar vein, Weber noted that early patriarchy had been favored by the fact that large-scale military and political structures had been possible only on the basis of secure male dominance over a household, by means of which each could equip himself for action ([1922] 1978: II, chs. 3–4).

74. Cairnes [1862] 1863: 48–50. "In a community of peasant proprietors," he wrote, "each workman labours on his own account, without much reference

prise could effectively economize the costs of transaction with outside merchants.[75] And when the concentration of mineral deposits drew miners into close mutual proximity, they tended to form producer cooperatives as a means to spread their risks, as well as to control negative externalities.[76] Finally, bondage was useful in less monetized economies,[77] but its value tended to dissipate as the ease of transaction grew.[78]

But just as the value of servitude in generating economic rents had to be weighed against the variable degrees of rent forthcoming on the "free" market, so too did these technical advantages of tutelage have to be discounted to the extent that free labor offered technical efficiencies of its own. These latter efficiencies were usually associated with individual initiative: as such they were no less variable than those of supervision, and furthermore they existed in tension with them. Under very primitive conditions of production, for example, the tendency of supervision to quash

to what his fellow-workmen are doing. There is no commanding mind to whose guidance the whole labour force will yield obedience, and under whose control it may be directed by skilful combinations to the result which is desired. Nor does this system afford room for classification and economical distribution of a labour force in the same degree as the system of slavery."

Or as Otto Neurath put it, rather less generously, in describing Greek slavery, "In enterprises which required regular, mechanical activity, slaves were often more useful than free laborers, especially when they possessed that degree of stupidity which furthered the sort of work that had to be carried out in unison" [*Antike Wirtschaftsgeschichte* (1909): 47].

Meitzen (1895: 1:71–2) and Roscher ([1859] 1903: §79) both noted further the value of compulsory rotations in forcing a regime upon lazy or incompetent members.

75. According to Weber, "The Hamburg merchant being in no position to transact individually with each peasant in Brandenburg or Silesia, the transition to large-scale enterprise was only natural [*war von selbst gegeben*]" ([1923] 1924: 90).

76. Foremost among those externalities, according to Weber, was the danger that if a single miner abandoned his shaft and ceased to care for its proper drainage, it might fill with water and "drown" the shafts that were still operating ([1923] 1924: 161–2).

77. Leroy-Beaulieu, e.g., noted that slavery was so common in Africa in part because slaves were especially valuable there as a means of exchange ([1895] 1900: 526–7).

78. Roscher [1854] 1906: §70; Hanssen [1870] 1880: 507–8; Laveleye [1874] 1878: 251; Wagner [1876] 1892–4: 2:§26; Miaskowski 1890: 17; Page 1900: 332, 347. This line of reasoning harkened back to Smith's observation that the development of a money economy and the availability of "baubles" and other purchased luxuries had led the feudal barons to dissolve their circles of retainers in favor of market-oriented farming ([1776] 1976: book 3, ch. 4).

initiative was largely irrelevant, or potentially even beneficial.[79] But whenever production required a modicum of skill and enterprise, as in the use of complicated tools, the cultivation of delicate crops, or the production of higher quality goods, unfree labor was disadvantaged because it did not share in its own marginal revenue-product.[80] Hence the evolutionary intensification of production had led the masters – motivated as always by sheerest self-interest – to accept freely rules limiting their share of labor's surplus product. In Hadley's example,

> The freeman working for himself can produce so much more than the serf that there is a chance for both parties, lord and vassal, to gain by the process of emancipation. If the amount which a man produces in a day when he works for his landlord is worth a halfpenny, and the amount which he produces when he works for himself is worth one and a half pence, it is for the advantage of both the landlord and the laborer to make a contract whereby the laborer agrees to pay the landlord a penny in lieu of each day's labor previously rendered.[81]

In agriculture, this logic had led gradually down the path from ancient slavery to peculium, colonate, and serfdom, thence to sharecropping and ultimately to capitalist farming. The experience of industry was more complicated. In southern Europe industrial slavery either survived intact or not at all; in the north, however, where colder weather and more fulsome peasant purchasing power had created a vibrant decentralized market for rough manufactures, formally unfree laborers were for a long time allowed operational discretion and residual claimancy over their product, in exchange for fixed regular payments [Russian *obrok,* German *Leibzins*] to the master (Weber 1923: 122–4). In many cases, the workers were able to accumulate, or borrow, sufficient capital to purchase their manumission

79. Courcelle-Seneuil [1858] 1891: vol. 2, book 1, ch. 1, §6; Wagner [1876] 1892–4: 2:§33. See also the quote from Neurath, n. 74 supra.

   In some spheres of activity this logic retained its efficacy longer than elsewhere. Regarding haymaking, e.g., Hanssen pointed out that meadows tended toward collective sowing, reaping, and division largely because there was no real margin for productive improvement through privatization ([1835–7] 1880: 62).

80. Knies [1853] 1883: 386–7, citing Aristotle; Roscher [1854] 1906: §70; Rodbertus, "Zur Geschichte der agrarischen Entwicklung Roms" (1864); Schäffle 1875–8: 2:143; 3:91; Wagner [1876] 1892–4: 2:§§ 26, 33–7; Leroy-Beaulieu [1895] 1900: 512–13.

81. Hadley 1896: §§39–41; Sismondi 1833: 258–9. Similarly, Loria argued that, historically, peculium and testamentary rights had come to mitigate pure chattel slavery, as incentive enhancements to offset the increasing technical inefficiency of bondage ([1893] 1910: 90–4).

and become truly free agents. By this juncture, clearly, the efficiencies of discretion had come to overbalance the advantages of coordination, and tutelage accordingly withered away.[82]

But no rational choice of institutions could ignore their costs, and these too varied greatly according to the natural, social, and economic context. In the first place one had to take account of the resources that were expended in supervision itself. The importance and variability of supervision costs were implicated in the observations that slavery was unusual in the cultivation of breadgrains, which required dispersed labor;[83] that farmsteads were advantaged over village cooperatives in zones of sparse population and difficult communications;[84] that the spatial concentration of activity in Oriental "hydraulic civilizations" had made possible a fiscal despotism, whereas the decentralization of Europe's "forest civilization" had led inexorably toward tax farming;[85] and that the medieval European elite's preoccupation with distant wars had made oversight-intensive ma-

---

82. This process was remarked upon by Sedgwick 1836; List, *Le système naturel d'économie politique* ([1837] 1930): 245; Roscher [1854] 1906: §73, citing Tucker's *Progress of the United States* (1843); Molinari 1853a: 714–15; Molinari, "Servage" (1853b): 610–13; Knies [1853] 1883: 386–7; Schäffle [1858] 1873: §270; Cairnes [1862] 1863: 52–3; Mangoldt [1863] 1871: 20–1; Madrazo 1874–6: 1:264–5; Wagner [1876] 1892–4: 2:§38; Sax 1887: 133–4; Loria [1893] 1910: 3; Brentano 1895: 24–5; Leroy-Beaulieu [1895] 1900: 512–16, 529; Grünberg, "Unfreiheit" (1901): 322; Neurath 1909: 48, 73; Schwiedland 1912: 32.

83. Cairnes [1862] 1863: 43–53. According to Richard Jones, it was primarily the size of estates that determined the cost of supervision, and thereby the viability of slavery. This explained why the maturation of the Greek and Roman economies, which led to the consolidation of holdings into latifundia, had been associated with the rise of sharecropping [*Literary Remains* (1859): 204–5].

84. Roscher [1859] 1903: §75; Meitzen 1895: 1:193, 269–70; Knapp 1896: 5. For Knapp, the fact that Teutonic settlers in Norway created a family-farm system so foreign to the supposedly Ur-German *Markgenossenschaft* proved that Germanics could act "efficaciously rather than 'stereotypically'" [*zweckmäßig, statt "volksthümlich" oder "volksmäßig"*]. This assessment was seconded by the historians Rachfahl (1900: 194) and Below (1897; [1920] 1926: 29).

85. Weber [1923] 1924: 63–4. And within European feudalism, according to Oppenheimer, there were definite limits to the lord's capacity to monitor far-flung villages without recurring to costly – and politically dangerous – reliance on plenipotentiary bailiffs. Inevitably, as feudalism matured the peasants were emancipated and their dues were commuted to fixed rents ([1907] 1914: 232–6).

norial organization less feasible than had been the case in under the Pax Romana (Weber 1923: 72–7).

Still more prominent were the costs of bringing tutelary institutions into force and maintaining them: in other words, the costs of obtaining the compliance of those who would have to obey. Most straightforwardly, the cost of enforcement – and therefore the prevalence of tutelage – varied in step with the attractiveness of formal liberty. Thus clientage had come to prevail as resources grew scarcer, social differentiation progressed, and the probability increased that a household would fall into the sort of financial straits that would make of servitude a relatively attractive option.[86] Peasants were also more likely to commit themselves to the service of a lord in times of civil insecurity.[87]

On the other hand, servitude tended to dwindle whenever the laboring mass saw some prospect for a better life through escape. The viability of slavery in the ancient Greek city-states, for example, was inversely correlated to the ease of escape, which in its turn varied positively with the frequency of war, and inversely with the distance of borders (Roscher [1854] 1906: §75). The barbarian invasions of the early Christian era squeezed the Roman slaveholder by bettering the bondsman's options,[88] as did the settlement movements of the High Middle Ages lighten even the lesser burdens of serfdom (Weber 1923: 72–4). The commercial revolution of the twelfth century eroded Italy's longstanding patriarchal household-

86. Roscher [1859] 1903: §§8–12; Wagner [1876] 1892–4: 2:§§27–8; Meitzen 1895: 1:138; Leroy-Beaulieu [1895] 1900: 511; Wittich 1896: 104–5; R. Hildebrand [1896] 1907: 100–3; Wittich 1897: 48–64; Grünberg 1901: 318; Weber 1904: 457; Ely 1914: 47, 805–6. It was indubitably lost on no one that destitution had also been the cause of the Israelites' enslavement to Pharaoh (Genesis 47:13–26).

   Roscher used the example of the South Pacific to illustrate his general rule that "most peoples have the strictest servitude in the very period when the soil yields the easiest subsistence." His explanation was that in such situations, when land is abundant and population sparse, land has no value except in so far as it assured a supply of labor: therefore the straitened household's salable assets are virtually limited to its own labor power ([1854] 1906: §67).

87. Ely 1914: 47. Brodnitz invoked this thesis to help explain the growth of manorialism in England during the centuries of Danish and Norse invasion ["Die Grundherrschaft in England" (1912): 149–51]; as did Fuchs, to explain the acceleration of enserfment in East Elbian Germany during and after the Thirty-Years War [*Die Epochen der deutschen Agrargeschichte* (1898b): 11–14].

88. Molinari 1853a: 714–15. Schmoller noted that the decline of Roman slavery had actually begun much earlier, due not to military defeat, but merely to the deceleration of conquest. This constricted the supply of slaves (who had originally been a by-product of conquest, so to speak), thus raising their price to would-be owners (1901–4: §125).

economies, by affording subordinate members new alternative lifestyles;[89] and the severe demographic reversals of the fourteenth and fifteenth centuries saw off serfdom in England, in that they put the surviving tenants in a far better position to bargain with the manorial lords.[90]

The other great variable in the costs of slavery or serfdom was the efficacy with which the prospective enforcer's resources could be transformed into threats that were sufficiently effective to elicit compliance. Specifically, the viability of a tutelary regime depended on the balance of coercive power between the would-be master and the might-be bondsman. Thus the rise of servitude was associated with the movement of societies to a war footing: obviously, in the sense that military success brought suzerainty over the vanquished,[91] but also subtly, in that external conflict and the development of military technology often favored the deployment of elite corps rather than mass mobilization.[92] By contrast, repeated attempts on the part of men to establish patriarchy in primitive hoe cultures tended to founder on the sexual division of labor, which afforded them little leverage over the economically self-sufficient matriarchal structures. By this logic it was the improvement of agriculture from shifting hoe cultivation to sedentary plow culture which precipitated the decline in female status: men were required for the heavy work of clearing, tilling, and housebuilding, and this in turn soon granted the male the coercive power he craved.[93] In

89. Graziani 1904: 30–2. Laveleye generalized this connection between the late medieval spread of the money economy on the one hand, and the decline of the extended household unit of production on the other ([1874] 1878: 208–9].
90. Page 1900: 339–65. Up to the arrival of the Black Death, according to Page, the threat of escape was credible enough only to ensure that the "customs of the manor" were in some measure respected (328–39).
91. Baumstark, "Die Volkswirthschaft nach Menschenrassen" (1865): 110; Wagner [1876] 1892–4: 2:§§27–8; Knapp, "Der Ursprung der Sklaverei in den Kolonien" (1889); Leroy-Beaulieu [1895] 1900: 511; Wittich 1896: Appendix: 111; Wittich, "Die Frage der Freibauern" (1901): 256; Grünberg 1901: 318; Schmoller 1901–4: §124; Sombart 1902: 1:342; 1928: 3:325. Conversely, military reversals led to inflation of slave prices and decline of the institution: see Hadley 1896: §38; Schmoller 1901–4: §125; Neurath 1909: 140–1; Weber [1923] 1924: 74.
92. Roscher [1859] 1903: §72 n; George 1879: 372; Meitzen 1895: 1:166; Brodnitz 1912: 155–6; Weber [1923] 1924: 59–61, 72. Ironically, it was the *displacement* of noble cavalry by standing armies in the sixteenth century which helped bring into being the East Elbian "second serfdom," inasmuch as it turned the aggressive skills of the Junker class toward exploitation on the home front (Schwiedland 1912: 32).
93. Schmoller (1901–4), §90; Weber [1922] 1978: II, ch. 4, §1. Loria argued, with characteristically dubious logic, that patriarchy arose at the exact moment

ancient Germany an analogous process worked to more felicitous effect, whereby debt peons, once set to work in undesirable agricultural tasks by their pastoral betters, eventually created a separate economic sphere and with it achieved an independent political base (Meitzen 1895: 1:138–9). In historical times, the superior collective organization of peasantries in China (Weber 1923: 96), England,[94] West Elbian Germany (Miaskowski 1890: 17–19), and Switzerland[95] were associated with greater difficulty in establishing and maintaining parasitic elites.

Intraelite politics demanded cognizance as well. Walras suggested, rather too simply, that "on the day when three men had to live together in an isolated corner of the globe, two of them agreed to the subjugation of the third. . . . And in effect, here we have the very history of slavery and serfdom in ancient and modern times" (1896: 143). In practice, political coalitions were a complex variable in the shaping of institutions, and this complexity went far to explain the divergent paths to modernity traversed by the European nations. The English barons of the eleventh and succeeding centuries, for example, often found their lordly prerogatives uniquely constrained by the interest that the new, stronger monarchy took in their villains.[96] Likewise in Germany from the sixteenth century onward, serfdom was checked in the west (and, beginning in the eighteenth century, in Brandenburg-Prussia) by the rising power of territorial princes, while most East Elbian princes were far too weak vis-à-vis their Junker barons to halt the consolidation of serfdom there.[97] The lords of western

when population had grown so dense, and the average product of labor consequently so desultory, that women and children could no longer feed themselves and so had to submit to the authority of the stronger adult males ([1893] 1910: 88). Why those males should be interested in accepting the burden of feeding dependents was not stated.

When Brentano doubted the historical existence of matriarchy, he was dissenting not from the economic model of the household as a political arena, but from the notion that women had *ever* enjoyed sufficient material autonomy to resist male power ["Die Volkswirthschaft und ihre konkreten Grundbedingungen" (1893): 130–45].

94. Rogers, *The Economic Interpretation of History* (1889): 23–45; Brodnitz 1912: 156–63.
95. Colajanni, "Di alcuni studî recenti sulla proprietà colletiva" (1887): 524.
96. Brodnitz 1912: 156–63; Weber [1923] 1924: 81. See also Mangoldt [1863] 1871: 20–1.
97. Knapp, "Die Erbunterthänigkeit und die kapitalistische Wirtschaft" (1891): 345; Wittich, "Gutsherrschaft" (1898): 934; Fuchs 1898a: 297–300; 1898b: 11–14; Oppenheimer [1907] 1914: 255–6; Schwiedland 1912: 32–3; Weber [1923] 1924: 91. All over Europe, the striving central powers were likely to ally with the nascent towns against their common enemy, the overweening feudal lords (Weber [1923] 1924: 125).

Germany were further disadvantaged by the fact that there, unlike the east, the various feudal prerogatives were dispersed among different parties [typically among *Grundherren, Leibherren,* and *Gerichtsherren*], which afforded to the peasant the opportunity to play these interests against each other, to his own benefit.[98] In Russia, peasant policy was determined in large part by the balance of power between the greater lords, who favored peasant mobility because they were best positioned to attract it, and the lesser lords, who opposed it for just the same reason. For a long time this stalemate worked to the peasant's advantage; but the scales were finally tilted in favor of binding the peasants to the soil when in 1597 the emergent Muscovite state sided with the lesser nobles in order to gain their political support.[99] Despite growing disaffection among the rural masses and the intelligentsia, this alliance between the Tsarist government and the nobility lasted up to the Crimean War's aftermath, by which time the central authorities had learned an object lesson in the superiority of free-labor economies (Simkovich 1909: 603–5).

Taken together, all these considerations supported the claims of economists like Molinari, who challenged the conventional civic humanist dictum that the state of freedom in a given nation was primarily a reflection of its moral mettle. "The causes which led to the suppression of slavery in Europe pertain, as we see, principally to the economic order; Christian religion played a role also, . . . but it would be quite a superficial examination which attributes all merit of abolition to Christianity."[100] Even in an enlightened age, this was a fairly radical idea.

## V    Conclusions

This chapter has made the strongest case possible for erasing the boundary between the "old" and "new" institutional economics, with the explicit purpose of corroding certain prejudices that have grown up in the literature. It has not been evenhanded, however. As the following chapter will document, the "old" institutionalists *were* different, in the freer rein they gave to their suspicions that, after all, there might be more to the human mind than Jeremy Bentham had postulated. Whether this placed them behind the "new" institutionalism or ahead of it is a matter of legitimate debate.

---

98. Wittich 1898: 937; Fuchs 1898a: 985; Weber [1923] 1924: 80–1, 90. Oppenheimer considered this a general feature of European feudalism ([1907] 1914: 254–5).
99. Simkovich 1909: 602–3; Weber [1923] 1924: 88.
100. Molinari 1853a: 714–15. See also Schäffle [1858] 1873: 2:§270.

# 3

# Ghosts in the machine

One of the central points of this study is that the new science of law prefigured today's "new" institutional economics far more than the conventional wisdom allows. This chapter, however, must begin with a partial concession to that conventional wisdom. The fact is that the model of *homo oeconomicus* – the staple of political economy in general, and of chapter 2 in particular – was more problematic to practitioners of the new science than to their mid-twentieth-century heirs.

We have termed the scientific paradigm of the preceding chapter "normal" because it predicated a complete model of human behavior, the fulcrum of which was rational calculation in the pursuit of maximum personal net worth. To this extent, the economist's brief was to rend the veil of culture and reveal environment as the prime mover of institutional diversity. But this high degree of causal specificity was not intrinsic to the new science of law, which stood firm only on the premise of methodological individualism; nor, in the opinion of most economists who voiced one, was it quite adequate.

The materialist conception of law elicited more than a little skepticism. Schmoller, for instance, doubted that the natural and technical conditions of economic development were "solely and absolutely determinant of the organization of the economy in question" ([1874–5] 1898: 52). Wagner agreed, taking to task utilitarianism and radicalism by name: "Both extreme tendencies – that of the older economic individualism and that of socialism – tend all too often to consider economic-technical considerations the absolutely decisive point of view in problems of law, neglecting all others" ([1876] 1892–4: 2:§15). Comparable also are Knies's emphatic warnings to the effect that property rights exist *"categorically not as the result of economic urges and conditions,"* and that the theorist of property must go beyond the mere "bodily existence of man and the role of technology"; Brentano's criticism of the "Machiavellian bias" that prevents economists from perceiving obvious ethical motivation; and Weber's contention that "purely economic motives are not decisive for primitive appropriation or the primitive division of labor."[1]

Such criticism reinforces the "old" institutionalism's unfortunate reputation for unrelenting negativity. Did not these economists, and the many others who followed their lead, have any constructive suggestions upon which a new paradigm could be founded? Judging from certain programmatic statements, one could be forgiven for doubting. Sketches of institutional selection gestured freely and imprecisely to "the opinions and feelings of mankind" (Mill); to "psychic nexuses and the requirements of human culture" (Knies); to ineffable "turns of mind" (Beauregard); to "psychological and cultural-historical" factors (Wagner); to "religious and political beliefs" and "socio-psychic motives" (Commons); and to "the psychological-moral life of nations" (Schmoller).[2] This sounds the stuff of obfuscation, and it has often been judged as such.

In what follows, we will attempt to fill the vacuum created by this famous critique of orthodoxy. Our discussion will be structured around the problem of retaining the science's nomothetic unity without the utilitarian anthropology. Ideally it would be replaced with assumptions that seemed more realistic, and yet did not throw open the Pandora's box of contingency: for if the goals pursued were allowed to vary as freely as did the environment in which the pursuit took place, then the method of comparative statics would be greatly complicated, and the explanation of rules would as a consequence carry far less conviction. Three broad approaches will by stylized, in ascending order of heterodoxy vis-à-vis the utilitarian research agenda: remodeling human nature to take account of nonpecuniary motives, though without compromising its universality (section I); relaxing the assumption of uniform preferences, while retaining the assumption that those ends are rationally pursued (sections II and III); and relaxing the assumption of rationality itself (section IV). Conclusions follow in section V.

1. Knies [1853] 1883: 181, 201 (italics original); Brentano [1901] 1923: 63; Weber [1923] 1924: 40. See also Commons [1899–1900] 1965: 76 n, where Loria's predilection for geographic determinism is challenged.
2. Mill 1848, book 2, ch. 1, §1; Knies [1853] 1883: 201; Beauregard, "Droit" (1891): 741; Wagner [1876] 1892–4: 2:§24; Commons [1899–1900] 1965: 6; Schmoller [1874–5] 1898: 57.

I        **Beyond cupidity**

It is by now a commonplace in the historical literature that, during the period under consideration in this study, economists considered
human "values" more problematic, and hence more analytically important, than ever before or since. Real-world economic agents, that is,
were supposed to be motivated by more than the simple utilitarian calculus underpinning *homo oeconomicus.* But historians of economic thought
have had precious little to say about just what those multifarious values
were thought to be, even less about how economists attempted to systematize the newly fraught problem, and next to nothing about how it all fit
into the explanation of institutions.

The ideal alternative to *homo oeconomicus* would not surrender its claim
to coextensivity with humanity itself: like *h. politicus, h. hierarchicus, h.
ludens,* or any number of other species that have not yet been captured by
the taxonomy of social science, it would restore axiomatic determinacy to
the science of rules. What sorts of generalizations appealed most to these
generations of economists?

The drive to attain social status – a sort of acquisitive instinct that could
not be measured in exchange values – was an attractive possibility. Already
in the eighteenth century, Smith had argued that "the love of dominion
and authority over others" had caused slavery to appear wherever it was
economically feasible, even when it was not optimal.[3] This approach found
greater support in our period than in the generations immediately succeeding Smith. Thorstein Veblen, to cite one famous example, believed
that exclusive possession corresponded to a universal instinct to improve
one's relative standing through the accumulation of trophies: "Ownership
began and grew into a human institution on grounds unrelated to the
subsistence minimum. The dominant incentive was from the outset the
invidious distinction attaching to wealth, and, save temporarily and by
exception, no other motive has usurped the primacy at any later stage of
the development" (1898a: 364). Here and elsewhere in his writings, Veblen
stressed that the status-seeking component of human nature had not been
effaced by the passing of centuries and millennia.[4] Very early in our period, Roscher made the similar point that persons of flesh and blood will
ever be exercised by the perception of exploitation, every bit as much as
by absolute impoverishment. This, he believed, explained the correlation
of communist social movements to advancing division of labor, luxury,

3. Smith [1762–4] 1978: 187, 452; [1776] 1976: 1:411–12.
4. See especially Veblen, *The Theory of the Leisure Class* (1899): ch. 2.

and socioeconomic polarization.[5] According to Weber, law "guarantees above all positions of political, ecclesiastical or familial authority, and all sort of social privileges in general, which may well be economically conditioned, and of economic significance in various respects, but which in themselves are not economic, and which are not coveted primarily for economic reasons" ([1922] 1978: II, ch. 1, §3). This manner of reasoning accounted for a variety of specific rules that were widespread and tenacious, but which did not seem to serve pecuniary motives. For example, Lujo Brentano (1895: 23) found in the desire to maintain the luster of family names the force preserving rules of entail into the modern age, long after their economic and political rationales had atrophied. In Weber's view it was "male vanity" and the "authoritarian instincts" of husbands which had sustained many of the legal obstacles to free divorce in most societies ([1922] 1978: II, ch. 8, §ii). And for Walter Bagehot the wide prevalence of caste strictures – as well as the tendency of caste to assert itself even where it had not existed – responded to a deep-seated desire to celebrate one's difference as a mark of superiority.[6]

This concern for status was certainly self-centered, but it cannot be said that it was self-regarding, since ultimately it was one's standing in other eyes that would be the measure of success. Very different, therefore, was the occasional suggestion that the desire for personal or familial autarky was an essential factor in the delineation of rules. Philippovich, for instance, traced the primacy of private property to

> the demand for free development of individual personality, and for the assurance of the family's freedom from outside influence. Of the motives furthering private property this one is the strongest, because no social community is capable of guaranteeing the individual the sort of independence that springs from the soil of economic self-sufficiency. ([1893] 1920: 103)

Similarly, Keussler found the long evolution from common to private property to have resulted from a gradually shifting equilibrium between man's unchanging moral constitution on the one hand, which featured an "urge to control" [*Streben nach Herrschaft*] which always and everywhere had meant an inclination toward private property, and the economic logic of cooperation on the other hand. For centuries the latter's force had over-

---

5. Roscher ca. 1851: 114–15; [1854] 1906: §72. On the other hand, Wagner argued that bondsmen suffer willingly the material deprivations of their station, so long as they derive some satisfaction of a job well done ([1876] 1892–4: 2:§35).

6. "There is an intense disposition in the human mind – as you may see in any set of schoolboys – to hate what is strange in other people, and each caste supplies those adjoining it with a conspicuous supply of what is unusual" (Bagehot [1876] 1978: 248).

ridden man's inclination and dictated common proprietorship; but with population growth and increasing pressures on the resource base, the benefits of communalism diminished to the point where human nature could finally be indulged (Keussler 1876: 5–8).

Still more divergent from the model of *homo oeconomicus* was the argument that ideas of natural justice had informed the selection of legal norms through the ages. "In enquiries as to the origin of property," wrote Laveleye in his seminal study, "sufficient attention has not been given to ancient historic facts, which may be called natural as everywhere springing from an instinct of justice, which seems innate in human nature."[7] It was considerations like these which led economists like Emil Sax to elevate the principle of "mutualism" to theoretical standing equal to the better established principle of egoism (Sax 1887: 130–1).

In each of these examples, the dream persisted that universal human motivations lay behind the institutional record, with the difference that more notions could be entertained than were captured in the one-dimensional caricature of *homo oeconomicus*. But in general this approach was exceptional, for it yielded little more satisfaction to empirically minded economists than had the species of universalism it replaced. In too many instances these motives could only be understood as being themselves contingent on circumstance, evolving over time or varying across space; indeed, some of the motives that often suggested themselves, such as public spirit, could not conceivably have been held analogous to gravitational forces in the precipitation of rules. "In every age and in each society," wrote Beauregard (1891: 743) of the sources of law, "the collective conscience has conceived an ideal: but this ideal has varied according to the times and circumstance." The challenge, then, was to achieve the next best thing, a systematic account of the factors shaping the motivations that in turn shaped economic institutions. The sections to follow will explore how this challenge was met, and the determinacy of human motivation reasserted.

## II    Beyond universalism (*a*): Cross-sectional plurality of values

The simplest approach to institutional diversity was to assert that rules differed because peoples differed, and peoples differed because it was in their natures to do so: in other words, the variance of rules was a function of ingrained cultural preference. As we might expect, it was German

---

7. Laveleye [1874] 1878: xxxviii–xxxix; also Schwiedland 1912: 33. Hadley believed that the near-universality of usury laws had stemmed from common conceptions of what sorts of lending were fundamentally fair (1896: 139).

economists who took the lead in this folkish style of analysis. It was they who went the furthest in documenting the cultural correlation of economic institutions,[8] and who developed the richest vocabulary to describe cultural peculiarities (*Ideen, Sitten, Seele, Volksgeist, Lebensanschauung, Gemüthsanlage,* and the like).[9] For a few Germans, like Eduard Baumstark, Lorenz von Stein, and August Meitzen, national difference constituted the key organizing principle of their research;[10] but more typically, for Germans as for others, culture was invoked ad hoc, as part of a general explanatory scheme.

In light of the prominence of Germans on this frontier of research, it is not too surprising that the institutional ramifications of the Teutonic mind-set received the lion's share of attention in the literature. According to Stein,

> The collective character of the Germanic peoples consists in the fact that each individual strives to achieve by himself, through his own labor and his own property [*Besitz,* not *Eigentum*], his own personal development. He wants to be a free man, dependent on no power and subject to no person. The basis of his freedom is his property. It incarnates that which lies deep in his soul. (1881: 15–16)

Wagner, too, believed that "peoples of Germanic spirit" were predisposed to the "free fashioning of individual lifestyle"; Helferich called this Teutonic tropism an "inborn inclination to individual private property."[11]

In juxtaposition to this idea of Germanic individualism, however, the

---

8. E.g., Meitzen pointed out that the various European property regimes coincided more closely with national boundaries than with topographical ones (1895: 2:683 and passim). This was also the finding of Max Sering et al. regarding the patterns of inheritance law in Eastern Europe (1908, cited approvingly by Weber [1922] 1978: II, ch. 4, §2). Wittich, too, noted that the German regions where peasants enjoyed the broadest prerogatives over their land coincided with the ancient boundaries of the Saxon tribe (1898: 935).

9. Wagner's analysis of expropriation furnishes an example of this sort of reasoning. Having first noted some materialist-functionalist logic in the geographic diversity of laws of expropriation, he hastened to add that specific practices were shaped "in practice still far more by the opinions which take shape in the national conscience [*Volksbewusstsein*] regarding the necessity and permissibility of expropriation in specific instances" ([1876] 1892–4: 2:§237).

10. For Baumstark, the first task of economic anthropology was "knowledge of the *soul* [*Seele*], its powers, its life, its variation among races," and of "the genealogical specificity of the spirit [*Geist*]" (1865: 87–91). See also Meitzen 1895: 1:269–70.

11. Helferich, "Zusatz zu Kawelin" (1864): 46; Wagner [1876] 1892–4: 2:§§174–7, 186. Wagner did not, however, believe that this preference was strong enough to exact a great price in terms of forgone consumption possibilities.

literature of the new science stressed also an image of Germanic sociability, which was supposedly characterized by a vital political life in a distinctly constituted public sphere. It was generally accepted that the quintessential German pattern of agrarian property had been based on a convoluted system of claims to equal, interspersed shares [*Hufen,* cognate to the Anglo-Saxon *hide*] in the open fields, and to notional shares in meadows, pastures, and waste. As Meitzen explained, political designs lay behind this arrangement. And yet it was not equalitarian in the sense imagined by utopians: rights were associated with shares in the corporation, not with persons per se, so that a single villager might hold multiple shares, a fraction of a share, or no share at all. The important equality was rather political equality among shareholders. The point of this typically Germanic system of property rights was to nourish the public sphere through sound principles of corporate governance:

> With it was achieved the organization of a cooperative polity [*genossenschaftliches Gemeinwesen*], founded on tracts of sufficient size to feed a peasant family, which linked concretely all corporate rights and responsibilities in equal measure to this pattern of distribution, and which left it to individual generations of shareholders [*Besitzer*] to manage their interpersonal relations within this lasting association, in whatever ways its changing circumstances and needs required, or permitted.[12]

More impressionistically, Stein too understood positive, political freedom to be another key desideratum of the German psyche. This freedom he described as an edifice resting on four pillars: popular legislation, clan solidarity, kingship, and, most important for Stein as for our own purposes, a peculiar system of land tenure. The German approach to property, by assuring the citizen independent subsistence at the same time that it reserved broad rights of eminent domain to the collectivity, assured the stability of the other three principles and, through them, the constitutional order as a whole. This practice of divided sovereignty over land, which survived into the twentieth century as the *Almen* of Upper Germany, seemed also to Bücher to respond to "an Ur-Germanic instinct," a public spirit solicitous of the community's good above all else. For Knies the citizens of German towns, too, had long evinced a "wondrous righteousness," which explained why municipal taxes could there, and there alone, still be collected on an honor system.[13]

The Germanic spirit was alleged to have suffused the Middle Ages and

---

12. Meitzen 1895: 1:62–3, 121–2. Therefore we must discount Weber's claim (1904: 436–7) that Meitzen had posited simple equalitarianism [*Gleichheitsstreben*] as the essential underpinning of the German village system.
13. Stein, *Die drei Fragen des Grundbesitzes und seiner Zukunft* (1881): 17–20; Bücher 1902: 13–14; Knies 1852: 277.

thereby was credited with changing the course of European institutional history. Greek and Roman slavery, wrote Knies, had been sustained by "nationality," specifically by "the lesser moral and religious development of those heathen peoples." This incubus was exorcised from Europe by the world-historical conjunction of German *Volkscharakter* and Christian ethics, which together constituted "an obliterating act against the national political life of the ancient peoples, and against their religion founded on the political sovereignty of citizens" ([1853] 1883: 387–9). More generally, the Nordic races were by nature more vigorous than others and had therefore resisted effectively the sort of servitude upon which classical civilization rested (Molinari 1853a: 712). In the place of Roman master-servant relations, the Germans had substituted the brand of private, bilateral institutional arrangements at which they excelled: indeed the whole feudal dispensation had derived naturally from the bond of personal loyalty between warrior and chief (Minghetti [1859] 1863: 481). But ultimately, the revival of Roman law in the Renaissance reversed the fortunes of Germany's consensus-based constitution and saddled its system of property with a foreign incubus for centuries to come (Scheel 1877: 10–11).

Discussions of Celtic culture drew principally from sources on Britain and especially on Ireland, the last and most authentic exemplar of that nation. Topographic remains (which Meitzen in particular used to great effect) suggested that the quintessential Irish – and hence Celtic – agrarian institution was the *tate,* a consolidated plot of sufficient size to sustain a nuclear family. Actual proprietorship was a bit more complex, however, as it was original practice that upon a tenant's death his holding should revert to the chieftain of his clan for redistribution. This earliest system, it seemed to Meitzen, "could only have emerged from ideas and customs based on tendencies of national life as a whole," especially those bound up in the concept of the clan, in the overarching "idea of familial existence under patriarchal leadership."[14] Weber, similarly, glossed Caesar's reports to the effect that ancient "Gallic" institutions had differed from "German" ones in their greater reliance on patriarchy and clientage (1904: 451). Meitzen believed that this typically Celtic political culture had facilitated the privatization of landed property around the seventh century A.D.; we may speculate that Marshall had this same vision in mind when he suggested

---

14. Meitzen 1895: 1:178–83, 220–1. Faced with the fact that Rhenish Germany showed much less evidence of corporately owned open fields than did other German lands, Meitzen could square the circle only by arguing that since this region had once been conquered from the Celts, its exceptionality in fact confirmed the causal priority of culture.

that England had led the way in the late medieval revolution of agrarian relations due especially to its specific national "qualities."[15]

Slavic folkways were often described in terms reminiscent of the Celtic and German ones. Meitzen's conjecture as to the original Slavic property system (i.e., the one obtaining before the westward migrations of the first millennium A.D.) was admittedly close to his findings for the Celts, with the one important exception that the Slavic "way of life" [*Lebenssitte*] presupposed patriarchal property, not on the scale of the whole lineage group, but only on that of the closed, communal extended household, which now survived only in the South Slav *zadruga* (1895: 2:269–71). Its extinction in Great Russia was, according to Keussler, best ascribed to the Russian mind's unusually strong "individuation drive" [*Individualisierungstrieb*], which had led to the early fission of patriarchal households (1876: 39). But Russians could not escape altogether their Slavic heritage: "The Russian spirit knows no life beyond the community," wrote Keussler, which explained their reassociation in *contractually* organized village communities (known as *obshina* or *mir*). These were comparable to the German *Markgenossenschaft*, except that land tenure within them was not based on interspersed strips in open fields, but on integral homesteads. Helferich, too, postulated a certain cultural atavism in the Great Russian *obshina*, which he considered another emanation of their "collective principle" [*Gemeinschaftsprinzip*], a sort of patriarchal family writ large (1864: 46). The belief in Slavic cultural specificity was so tenacious that Diehl, writing all of fifty-eight years after Helferich, could explain the *obshina*'s extraordinary longevity in terms quite reminiscent, as following from "the Russian's so strongly developed collective spirit, and the striving for close, insular combination."[16]

The peoples of classical antiquity enjoyed distinctive institutions of

---

15. Meitzen 1895: 1:194–7; Marshall [1890] 1895: app. A, §10.
16. Diehl 1923–4: 2:242. We may note here in passing the influence of Baron August von Haxthausen, the traveler who supplied much putative data for professional economists, especially on Russia. Haxthausen dichotomized national cultures by their degree of gregariousness [*sozialer Trieb*], into those preferring a "homestead system" [*Hofverfassung*], like the Celtic peoples, and those favoring a "village system" [*Dorfverfassung*], including both Russians and Germans. For the latter peoples the village community was an "organic whole," and the many attenuations to which they subjected the economic rights of their members expressed, as did their actual settlements, a certain "corporate character." Peoples of the "homestead system," by contrast, were only weakly gregarious, preferring to subsist independently and structuring public endeavors around the principle of free association [*Die ländliche Verfassung Rußlands* (1866): 13–15].

their own, which suggested to some economists the operation of the Greek and Roman cultural peculiarities. In Knies's estimation, the Greek "national conception of private property" had reflected the ancient Hellenic understanding of the individual's political – and even ontological – subordination to the collective purpose. The Roman tradition in property relations was comparable to the Greek one, in the sense that the civil law had not hesitated to place the commonweal above individual prerogative; but its sources were rather different, issuing as it did from "the life-principle of this *warlike, conquering* people."[17] This republican urge survived even the republic, according to Meitzen: the "political idea" underpinning Roman popular conscience was responsible for the inexorable transmission of uniform, formal conceptions and institutions throughout the known world (1895: 1:234).

Nonwestern cultures often suffered by comparison. John Commons, for example, linked the prevalence of despotism in the Orient to the proposition that Asiatic nobilities had failed to develop the "psychic qualities" – like integrity and self-sacrifice – which had shaped the history of European institutions ([1899–1900] 1965: 46). On the other hand, certain exotic nations compared favorably with the finest European ones. Among these, American Plains Indian tribes stood out: Baumstark ascribed to them just the sort of warlike virtues that were usually reserved for the ancient Germans, especially their grim readiness to lay down their lives in the defense of their liberties. African and Australian tribesmen, by contrast, were judged uniformly willing to surrender their freedom to save their lives (1865: 93–113).

Most ethnological data on "primitive" values, however, did not fit this paradigm of cross-cultural comparison. The reason is that, in economic discourse by the middle of the nineteenth century, the evolutionary insight had attained greater currency than the essentializing method of racial and cultural distinction. It was assumed that all societies had traveled a single evolutionary road, a road so well demarcated that humanity's apparent diversity at any historical moment could be reduced to different stations occupied along the way. Primitive peoples, in other words, were now less likely to be viewed as "others," as children of Canaan, Ham, or what have you, and more likely to be seen as reflections of modern man's own past. The stage theory offered a substitute for the hypothesis of institutional vestiges, and a corrective to its bias toward national specificity. "One must beware the tendency," warned Roscher, "to discern as peculiarities of na-

---

17. Knies [1853] 1883: 182–90. Compare Braun's identification of Roman "instinct for personal power and freedom," which made them especially resistant to circumscription of their property rights (1865: 66).

tional character, which must have been forever preserved and developed, what are in fact the peculiarities of certain cultural stages."[18] It is to this reasoning that we now turn.

## III Beyond universalism (*b*): Longitudinal plurality of values

*1 Before* homo oeconomicus

Increasingly in the nineteenth century, the principles of human nature were viewed as refractory to timeless generalization. By 1903, J. S. Nicholson could affirm confidently that, when treating of early economic relations,

> it is absolutely necessary to apply the historical method. Nothing can be more fallacious than the attempts to construct the social arrangements of primitive societies by the simple plan of divesting human beings of their civilised surroundings and supposing that otherwise there would be no change in their thoughts or ideas; to suppose, for example, that primitive man actually did act just as civilised man might be supposed to act, if thrown by shipwreck on a desert island. In truth, as Sir Henry Maine (the great populariser of the historical method in this country) observes, in general, it would be safer to suppose that in primitive times men would act in quite a different manner. Recent researches on comparative superstitions have shown in a striking way how widely different are the ancient and the modern ideas of what is natural in social arrangements.[19]

But if the ancients were not like the moderns, how were they? Various traits were suggested.

To the extent that property rights developed in primitive cultures (and develop they did, wrote Bücher, to an "unbelievable" degree, especially over personal effects),[20] their primary function was often understood to be as tokens of social status. In other words, property was what today's

---

18. Roscher [1859] 1903: 318. R. Hildebrand seconded this warning against mistaking institutional variety for "*national* differences, when in fact it is rather a question only of differences in the *stage of development*" ([1896] 1907: 129). Similarly Oppenheimer: "The psychology pertains to the stage of development, not to the race!" ([1907] 1914: 103).
19. Nicholson 1903: 99–100. Or as Brentano put it, "It is not a question of any urge that is somehow intrinsic to human nature; rather, that striving [for maximum pecuniary income] evolves through historical development" ["Die klassische Nationalökonomie" ([1888] 1923): 29].
20. Bücher, "Volkswirtschaftliche Entwicklungsstufen" (1914): 7. Bücher believed that hunter-gatherers proscribed the exclusion of neighbors from food, but that otherwise individual property was recognized over all articles of daily use.

sociologists call "symbolic" capital: the point of owning things was to dispose of them in culturally meaningful ways, especially ways that advanced the disposer's standing within the group.[21] A principal function of property consisted in its alienation, in a complex system of transfers that maintained the social structure at the same time that it achieved a certain division of labor.[22]

Unlike Veblen (quoted above), Bücher and others believed that economic institutions had gradually been purged of the obsession with status. But remnants of it were still visible up to the modern age. The pleasure intrinsic to holding bonded labor, for instance, diminished only slowly and was not fully extinguished before the money economy offered alternative outlets for conspicuous consumption and the lesson was finally learned of the great opportunity costs of indulging one's passions.[23] At the extreme, Cairnes doubted whether the American Southerners of his own day, with their peculiarly retrograde ethics and theology, had yet absorbed that home truth ([1862] 1863: 156–66).

More radically, many economists denied that the writ of possessive individualism could run far back in man's evolutionary past under any guise. Solidarity, they argued, was the substrate of primitive rules. This was an epochal finding for nineteenth-century social science. It galvanized revolutionaries like Marx, who declared that for early man the goal of labor had not been the production of exchange values but the subsistence of self, family, and community;[24] at the same time, it led relative conservatives like the jurist Maine to comment that "the men who composed the primitive communities believed themselves to be kinsmen in the most literal sense of the word; and, surprising as it may seem, there are a multitude of indications that in one stage of thought they must have regarded themselves as equals" ([1875] 1876: 226–7).

If the causes of this ethic were obscure – typically it was explained, if at

21. One such good was cattle which, in Africa at least, were sought not for any intrinsic economic value, but as "tokens of wealth and objects of truly effusive admiration" (Bücher 1908: 52).
22. Bücher stressed how practices that appeared to be ad hoc or purposeless transfers (like "gift-giving, . . . *robbery, pillage, mulct, recompense and gaming*") were actually rules that were embedded in social reciprocity. Gifts, in particular, were not the sort of unrequited gesture that we like to imagine them today. Bücher believed it to be a common blunder that European travelers would mistake such pseudogifts, given purely in the expectation of immediate reciprocation, for the real thing (1908: 23, 62).
23. Fuchs 1898b: 7; Leroy-Beaulieu [1895] 1900: 526.
24. Marx, *Grundrisse der Kritik der politischen Ökonomie* (1857–8): 375.

all, by the intimacy of association in a parochial world[25] – its implications for society's institutional complexion seemed quite clear. Pareto, for example, argued that patriarchal authority in the ancient world had found a key buttress in the domestic cult, which placed the household at the center of both ritual and belief.[26] Elsewhere in the literature the greatest good was held to be tribal solidarity. From this perspective the striking collectivism of the early Germans indicated not so much their national essence, as their pertinence to a particular stage of social development, a stage applicable to pastoral-agricultural tribes the world over. It was perceived as a universal feature of transhumant peoples that they thought of their polity as a single family under patriarchal leadership.[27] Bücher called the motive force at this stage "communal sensibility: subordination and obedience, esteem of elders, renunciation of individual discretion" (1914: 11). Concern for the sustenance of this solidarity was deemed responsible for such diverse economic rules as the ritual division of labor within Stone Age tribes (Inama-Sternegg 1885: 16–17), the strict regulation of aristocratic wealth in Lycurgan Sparta (Minghetti [1859] 1863: 477), and the widespread practice of periodic redivisions within open fields.[28]

In these salad days of the national life cycle, rules that granted economic power always presupposed some reciprocal considerations. This was so in the republics of antiquity, where proprietorship was supposed to carry with it the burden of political activity and office.[29] It was also true in the High Middle Ages: appearances notwithstanding, George (1879: 377) saw in the feudal system "the triumph of the idea of the common right to land, changing an absolute tenure into a conditional tenure, and imposing peculiar obligations in return for the privilege of receiving rent." According to George this reciprocity had to be imposed upon the lordly class; for others, the manorial nexus was a system of obligations accepted by all.[30]

The money economy posed poignant threats to the community's integrity, and so special rules were devised to parry its thrusts. Strict controls of lending at interest, and especially the stigma of antisociability which was attached to moneylending, reflected this ethic. "What the legal prohi-

25. Schmoller 1901–4: §106; Roscher [1859] 1903: §79.
26. Pareto 1896–7: §559, citing Fustel de Coulanges's findings in *La cité antique.*
27. Roscher [1859] 1903: §14; Schmoller 1901–4: 238.
28. Laveleye [1874] 1878: 116 and passim; Bücher 1879; Schmoller 1901–4: §126. See also Maine [1875] 1876: 227.
29. According to Roesler, in this era "the state vouchsafes property only to those who can use it as citizens, and to those to whom can be confided the exercise of civil power [*potestas*] in the land" (1878: 92–3).
30. Roesler 1878: 109–10; Brentano [1888] 1923: 29; Knapp 1891: 343, 349–50; Bücher [1893] 1910: 109.

bition of usury expresses," wrote Sombart, "is none other than a recognition of the economic principle of livelihood [*Bedarfsdeckung*] through production, as befitted an economic life organized around handicraft." As such, it was an expression of "popular opinion."[31] To this same collective ideal was ascribed also the stringent guild and market laws of the medieval town,[32] as well as, on occasion, the mercantilist policies of the emerging princely states.[33]

But this story could not be complete without an account of how the collective spirit of yore had given way to the individuation of interest which characterized later stages of evolution, and which ushered in new paradigms for the transaction of rules. One approach, championed by Courcelle-Seneuil, was to seek the individualist ethic – and the system of economic liberty ultimately born from it as jus gentium and the law merchant – in the irresistible attractions of commerce with the world at large.[34] A different view was that individualism tended to grow from within a successful collectivity. Roesler formulated this process as one of the iron "laws of evolution" to which property rights were subject: aided by novel ideas of natural law, the new mind-set attempts "to extricate, as it were, the person from the citizen, and to make his existence independent of the polity [*Civität*]." In the end, property is successful in divorcing itself from its former duties, so that those duties either fall into disuse or, faute de mieux, are assumed by a new bureaucracy.[35]

31. Sombart 1902: 1:184–6. See also Roscher [1854] 1906: §190; Weber [1923] 1924: 234–5.
32. The goal of market regulations, according to Bücher, was always "the ample and cheap provision of the native consumers, and the full satisfaction of the outside customers of local industry" ([1893] 1910: 122). A key function of guilds, on the other hand, was to assure that no single craftsman's acquisitive designs would run riot and destroy the social equilibrium [Bücher 1914: 13]. Sombart's model of guild restrictions posited a good deal more egoism, though not quite of the pecuniary sort. Each individual craftsman's ideal regime was one of "freedom for himself, coercion and constraint for others." But given the incompatibility of these goals in the aggregate, individuals tended to compromise on a regime of constraint for all (1902: 2:29–30). Note that this equilibrium revealed a collective preference not for maximum income, but for maximum personal and social security. See also Sombart, *Die Ordnung des Wirtschaftslebens* ([1924] 1927): 53–4.
33. Bücher 1914: 14–15; Sombart [1924] 1927: 55–6; 1928: 1:363, 809. Bücher considered "collective provisioning" [*Gesamtversorgung*] to be the immediate goal of mercantilist policy.
34. Courcelle-Seneuil [1858] 1891: vol. 2, book 1, ch. 1, §6. Later, he criticized Maine for having neglected this important dynamic in the transition from status to contract (1874: xvi).
35. Roesler 1878: 81–7. "Every system of property ends in revolution," he added,

Naturally, this dynamic model could be applied to the career of the Roman state. In Italy a rude and martial people had developed a system of property geared to nourish the public sphere, but the opulence and stability of the Pax Romana led citizens to refocus their ethical attention on individual rights, and their daily energies on material acquisition: the result was a polished, liberal jurisprudence based on the concept of private property.[36]

The ramifications of these Roman innovations were experienced directly by the Germanic tribes of the north. Inama-Sternegg explained how, along the Roman frontier, the Germans' long-cultivated martial "tribe consciousness" [*Stammesbewußtsein*] was eroded by contact with Roman society. With the Roman presence came new institutions, a new sense of stability, and new possibilities of creature comfort. Under the spell of these new possibilities the tribesmen began to narrow the circle of their personal associations, and to pursue treasure and civic power through private property. Under these circumstances military preparedness could be maintained only "artificially," by executive fiat. Enforced transhumance and repartition of the arable, such as Caesar had noted, was a relative novelty associated with the psychological evolution of the individual German. By the time of Tacitus's report in A.D. 98, individualism had so swept the field that even the magistrate's authority to direct activity toward noneconomic ends had all but expired.[37]

The more backward Saxons preserved their collectivist village institutions well into the Dark Ages, but then in the ninth century Carolingian conquest extinguished their will to resist the new order of sovereignty and individuality (Meitzen 1895: 1:121). Later still, at the dawn of the modern age, these same stirrings of the individualist-capitalist ethic were implicated in the demise of municipal regulation of markets, of the law of guilds, and of the rule of collective inheritance.[38] The extended peasant household, too, fell victim to "the individuality characteristic of modern times" and "the desire for change and improvement in everything" (Laveleye [1874] 1878: 208–9). "With the end of the middle ages," concluded Roesler, "there began an evolutionary process analogous to that of antiquity. Property sought to transform itself into autonomous private power in the pursuit of income and enjoyment" (1878: 110).

"when the spirit of selfish passion, of intellectual and moral corruption, spreads from the possessing and ruling class to the *Volk* as a whole" (111). See also Wagner [1876] 1892–4: 2:§178.
36. Knies [1853] 1883: 189–90; Roesler 1878: 91–6; Schmoller 1901–4: §131.
37. Inama-Sternegg, *Deutsche Wirtschaftsgeschichte* (1879–99): 1:8–12.
38. Brentano [1888] 1923: 29; Laveleye [1874] 1878: 175; Roesler 1878: 115–16; Loria [1893] 1910: 95; Bücher [1893] 1910: 131.

Alongside the process of moral individuation had to be placed that of rationalization. Weber, with whom the concept is most closely associated, traced the roots of institutional rationalization to the aftermath of the Peace of God, pointing as evidence to the emerging gentry's first enclosures ([1923] 1924: 29). Then at the close of the feudal age, according to Knapp, as the mounted knight obsolesced into utter disuse, the manorial lords of East Elbian Germany underwent a wholesale transfiguration from chivalry to modernity. Faced with the dearth of glory to be won on the field of battle, these lords had concluded that their valor would be confirmed by victory in the war of capitalist accumulation; *Gutsherrschaft* and the modern Junker class was born (Knapp 1891: 346–7). Finally, the historical present was understood to be witnessing the extinction of the last remains of those agrarian arrangements which had been geared to suit communal ideals.[39] Soon, if not already, the stick figure *homo oeconomicus* would be adequate to the task of institutional analysis.

## 2    *After* homo oeconomicus

On the other hand, history could be read to the effect that man's evolution had been away from a primeval egoism, toward altruism. After all, did not the institutions of very primitive peoples reveal also the grossest selfishness, lassitude, cruelty, and all-round amorality?[40] And had not the progress of civil society replaced these practices with ones more in keeping with a communitarian ideal? As Leslie stylized this alternative historiosophic reading,

> Both an intellectual and a moral evolution is visible in the successive modes of satisfying human wants – by hunting and cannibalism; by the domestication of animals, with slavery instead of the slaughter of captured enemies; by agriculture, with serfdom gradually superseding slavery; and by free industry and commerce, instead of conquest and piracy. ([1876] 1879: 228)

Schmoller's approach was similar, though more complex in that the evolution's trajectory was not monotonic:

> The psychological transformation of the old communitarian peasant, who first managed his affairs without greed, and who then was subjected to a serfdom which in many ways oppressed him and through which he grew impassive, into the sly egoist and calculating petty entrepreneur, into the freeholder of the

39. Weber [1923] 1924: 34–6; Knies [1853] 1883: 197. Specifically, according to Laveleye, the individuation of property was furthered by "the passion for clearness and precision in juridical matters, which the [modern] jurist imbibed from the study of the Roman law" ([1874] 1878: 208).
40. For examples, see Bücher 1908: 19–22, 41, 81; 1914: 3; Schmoller 1901–4: §29.

modern age, and now most recently into a hearty small- and middle-holder, who once again feels for the community and who seeks out honorary posts in village and bureau: all this is one of the most engaging chapters in the cultural and economic history of Central European history. (1901–4: §103)

The transcendance of crude egoism appears to be also what Seligman had in mind when he wrote that the economic interpretation of history "is substantially true of the past; it will tend to become less and less true of the future" ([1902] 1907: 157–8). Here we can only outline the dynamic by which man's higher nature was supposed to supersede his more elemental, selfish tendencies.

In the Judeo-Christian tradition, which touched all our economists for better or worse, revelation was recognized as the royal road to morality. While some practitioners of the new science stayed close to this paradigm,[41] others saw value in explanations that were secular, systematic, and evolutionary. Friedrich List, to name one early example, believed that it was the development of commerce which had done most to broaden humanity's ethical horizon.[42] Some six decades later, John Commons's "Sociological View of Sovereignty" (1899–1900) made the same point, now in more fashionably scientistic terms. Noting recent experimental findings on childhood psychic development, Commons found a parallel emergence of "reflective self-consciousness" at a specific historical moment in the development of societies. This state of mind "came suddenly upon the breakdown of narrow tribal and local control, and the rise of commerce and money in the place of agriculture and barter." Its institutional significance was bound up in the capacity for comity and cooperation in the public sphere. "Such capacity is based, in the last analysis, on a belief in the moral perfection of the unseen powers that rule the world. Such a conviction alone can sustain that optimism by which hopeful, united action persists." The effects of this development could be seen in Greece, Rome, and in all later constitutional states; its capstone was the more recent creation of an impartial judiciary to make and interpret the society's "working rules" for it.[43]

41. Roscher is a prominent example: see, e.g., his *Grundlegung,* where he calls religion "the highest goal, and at the same time the deepest cause, of the life of the mind" ([1854] 1906: §16 n).
42. List [1837] 1930: 341; similarly Courcelle-Seneuil 1874: xvi. This optimistic interpretation of modernity fits what Albert Hirschman (1977, 1982) has termed the *"doux commerce"* tradition in economic thought.
43. Commons [1899–1900] 1965: 33–6, 53–8; 1924: 142. He noted further that morality presupposed a certain cushion on the margin of existence.

The ethical motive is, indeed, a human and not an animal attribute. But it cannot assert dominion during the period of struggle for sur-

A rather more nebulous scheme of institutional evolution was offered by Gustav Cohn in his *Foundations of Economics* (1885). For Cohn, the tendency of cultural progress was "the elevation of natural disharmony into harmony." Specifically, the long view suggested to Cohn that "the dictatorship of the ego" [*die Willkür des Ich*] would ameliorate in the fullness of time; the more that unenlightened self-interest [*das thörichte Ich*] receded, the more dispensable would become the array of rules – private property foremost among them – which had formerly been a necessary spur to individual effort and temperance (1885: 415–19). Gustav Schmoller's *Outline of General Economic Theory* (1901–4) made essentially the same point in greater detail, with an evolutionary model wherein law first supplants custom, and then moral conviction supplants law (§25–33). Schmoller's concept of emerging morality owed something to Smith's *Theory of Moral Sentiments* and Spencer's *Principles of Ethics,* both of which he cited approvingly. The end toward which civilization was moving was clearly the rule of individual conscience: the perfected conscience would not cease to seek the individual's well-being, but it would accept freely the constraint, previously enforced by custom and law, of not interfering with the well-being of others.[44] The sources of this dynamic were complex but rooted primarily in material existence. The evolutionary perspective on rules, wrote Schmoller, revealed that

> all the economy's natural powers help determine whatever reorganization this social framework undergoes. For instance, a new technique will certainly effect a new social and ethical ordering of the economy; and just as certainly, the generally established ethical concepts and ideals of moral behavior [*Sittlichkeit*] will work their effect on the way the new technique is reflected in customs and institutions.

Finally we may point to Werner Sombart's *Order of Economic Life* (1924) as yet another instance of how modernity could be interpreted as other than the triumph of hedonism. For Sombart, the liberal age did not spell the death of ideology, but merely its relocation from a traditional social grounding to what he called a "materialist-nominalist metaphysic."

> vival. This is the period of subterfuge, diplomacy, strategy, brute force, keen intelligence. Only in the lulls of competition, or in the final victory of perfected and centralized organization, is it possible to introduce the ethical purpose. ([1899–1900] 1965: 109)

44. The rules of ethical behavior were simplicity itself: "Assert and perfect yourself; give to each his own; feel yourself a member of the whole to which you belong; be humble before God, confident yet modest before man. This sort of thing is taught today in all corners of the world, by all religions" (Schmoller 1901–4: §23).

Goaded by the successes of natural science, liberal reformers had conceived an atomic moral universe and concluded that the individual must, on principle, be granted the broadest range of discretion. Moreover, liberalism was fast giving way to another organizing principle, one which in important ways bore comparison with the older collectivism:

> What we are witnessing here is a process of transformation of an economic existence that was at first principally naturalistic in form – i.e. formed in accordance with the principles of liberalism – into a normatively regulated one. It is a process which has been underway for several generations, and which in recent years has been accelerated somewhat. (Sombart [1924] 1927: 59–63)

Reversing the republican foreboding of the previous section, which viewed progress as the enemy of solidarity, the perspectives we have rehearsed here saw the contemporary historical forces turning, in Schmoller's words, "urges into virtues, persons into characters, societies into ordered and harmonic collective powers" (1901–4: §30).

Broad generalizations aside, the idea of evolution from egoism toward idealism found its way also into the analysis of specific rules. The origin of quiritary property law, for example, Marshall traced to "the breadth and nobility of the Stoic character," which had taught the Roman jurists to distill the universal from the accidental elements of justice ([1890] 1895: app. A, §4). And the example of Roman property rights, in turn, was found partly responsible for the gradual establishment of permanent tenure among the German tribes in the 150 years between Caesar's and Tacitus's reports (Miaskowski 1890: 8). Later the improved standing of (upper-class) women resulted in the institution of "legitimate" inheritance, which afforded to the children of one's legal wife the entirety of his bequest (Weber [1922] 1978: II, ch. 4, §1). Above all, ideology was linked to the prevalence of bondage in the classical world. For Roscher, the ancients' penchant for slavery was obviously attributable to their "religious inferiority"; consequently, the triumph of Christianity won a large share of the credit for slavery's abolition.[45]

The institutional innovations of the High Middle Ages were also viewed as at least partly pursuant to the evolution of values. The emancipation of Western Europe's serfs, in particular, was understood to owe at least something to the teachings of Christianity and – increasingly in the early

---

45. Roscher [1854] 1906: §§70, 75; Roesler 1878: 102; Madrazo 1874–6: 1:263–4; Wieser [1901] 1929: 367–8.

modern age – the resurgence of natural law.[46] The privatization of crown, municipal, and village properties also reflected the new spirit of individual enterprise (Schmoller 1901–4: §131).

The high tide of liberalism in the nineteenth century was credited with furthering enclosure of village commons into private holdings (Weber [1923] 1924: 29–30) and especially with besieging the last remnants of unfree labor in Russia, the new world, and elsewhere.[47] "In the end," wrote Sax, "collectivist altruism put paid to slavery, and lately it has grown so strong that even its toleration by any state is not accepted" (1887: 164). Having achieved these basic goals, modern bourgeois morality opened new frontiers by eliminating concubinage, contractual enslavement, and other obnoxious derivatives of the liberal principle (Weber [1922] 1978: II, ch. 8, §ii).

## IV    Beyond rationalism

Perhaps the most radical step of all in this long march away from the "normal science" of chapter 2 was taken when economists relaxed the assumption of boundless instrumental rationalism. The nomothetic proclivities of the new science continued to find expression in this brave post-Cartesian venture, however, most commonly in appeals to general propositions which could be empirically confirmed, falsified, or at least impugned. An obvious line of recourse was to the naturalist's concept of instinct. For example, Weber believed that it was a reflex reaction against "original ethnic difference" that best explained the genesis and entrenchment of strict caste rules in the Indian subcontinent ([1923] 1924: 116–17); much as, for Sombart, the converse development of guilds and civic associations *within* homogeneous groups was rooted in causes that lay "beyond all considerations of expedience. They are the instinctive expressions of a need for solidarity with one's peers" (1902: 1:125).

Reports of "primitive" institutions offered economists a rich vein to be mined for evidence of systematically ingrained irrationality; and the

46. Leslie [1876] 1879: 228; Brentano 1893: 84; Knapp, "Die Bauernbefreiung in Österreich und Preußen" (1894): 419–21; Fuchs 1898a: 299–300; Simkovich 1909: 603–5; Ely 1914: 812; Weber [1923] 1924: 99. De las Casas's crusade for the rights of indigenous Americans was similar in its motivation and its efficacy (Knapp 1889: 144).

47. Sedgwick 1836: 251; Colmeiro, *Historia de la economía política en España* (1863): 282; Wagner [1876] 1892–4: 2:§§37, 40; Cunningham 1896: 5; Weber [1923] 1924: 415. Leroy-Beaulieu too accorded to philanthropic impulses a role in the demise of American slavery, albeit a role subordinate to economic causes ([1895] 1900: 529).

evolutionary tendencies they identified paralleled the findings of developmental psychology. When Veblen looked at primitive property relations, for example, he found the savage, like an infant, profoundly indisposed to distinguish self from surroundings. According to what he termed "folk-psychology," "such meager belongings of the savage as would under the nomenclature of a later day be classed as personal property are not thought of by him as his property at all; they pertain organically to his person" (1898a: 357).

Many primitive institutions were similarly predicated upon a time horizon so vanishingly short that it could only indicate cognitive myopia, not a legitimate application of time preference or of discount for risk. Economists developed the impression that the savage "disregards the future" (Roscher [1859] 1903: §8) and that he was, in general, "a child of the moment" (Bücher 1908: 19–22, 41, 81). Natural man lacked "the idea of saving," opined Inama-Sternegg (1885: 20), because "not dead, but only living possessions appear to be important." The result was a "great juxtaposition of surfeit and dearth: juxtapositions of the sort that arise when one does not know enough to lard away the surplus of one period for a later one." All this helped to account for the relative absence of property rights over productive resources, and the widespread practice of funerary destruction of a decedent's worldly possessions.[48]

If the institutions of precivilized society reflected an undervaluation of the future, then later agrarian institutions tended to the opposite error of *overvaluing* the past. Habit, in other words, was identified as a key inertial element in the evolution of law. Institutional inertia in this sense must be distinguished from "path-dependent development": the latter indicates that the constraints to which the rational actor must adjust are, in part at least, the result of past choices; the former, to which we call attention here, indicates that the actor is simply conservative and may pay a price for it in terms of forgone utility. This seems to be what Marshall had in mind when he wrote that "it is probable that while the influence of custom over

---

48. Roscher [1859] 1903: §8; Bücher 1908: 23. For a rationalist explanation of same, see Posner 1980: 23. This tendency to infantilize the hunter-gatherer mind extended well beyond institutional analysis. Inama-Sternegg went so far as to deny that primitives shared in the "principle of economy," which he defined as "the striving to achieve the highest utility with the least expenditure" (1885: 19). Bücher agreed: "The *Naturmensch* cannot, as it were, weigh two ideas against each other" (1910: 22–7; see also Kulischer 1899: 835–7). Bücher deployed this psychological model to great effect in his influential *Arbeit und Rhythmus* (1896), wherein he argued that the crucial transition from the hand-to-mouth hunter-gatherer economy to a more industrious lifestyle was a case not of rational adaptation, but merely of one pre-reflective instinct (playfulness, "rhythm") winning out over another (indolence).

prices, wages and rent has been overrated, its influence over the forms of production and the general economic arrangements of society has been underrated."[49] Similarly Commons's finding that

> customs cannot be changed radically or suddenly, since they arise from the most elementary fact of living creatures, Instinct and Habit, which are the mere repetition of acts found by experience to be preservative of life, of enjoyment, and of survival in the struggles of competition. This repetition goes from one generation to another in such a way that custom is analogous to heredity.[50]

Institutional inertia was identified especially with the patriarchal and hieratic culture of peasant societies. "The peace of society," wrote Bagehot,

> then reposed on a confused sentiment, in which respect for law, as such – at least law in our usual modern sense – was an inconsiderable element, and of which the main components were a coercive sense of ingrained usage, which kept men from thinking what they had not thought before, and from doing what they had not before done; a vague horror that something, they did not know well what, might happen if they did so; a close religion which filled the air with deities who were known by inherited tradition, and who hated uninherited ways.[51]

This hypothesis was brought to bear on the puzzling longevity of communal property rights over land in the Old World: a common argument was that the original conquest or clearing of land was typically a collective effort, so that it was in some sense natural that the communal ideal be unreflectively transposed and preserved when that land was put under the plow.[52] Extending this line of reasoning, it was argued that the first lordly

49. Marshall [1890] 1895: app. A, §2. See also part VI, ch. 10, §3; Colson 1907: 3:53.
50. Commons, *Institutional Economics* (1935): 45, 73–4. See also Commons 1924: 147; Cohn 1885: 414. For a modern application of this approach to the theory of the firm, see Nelson and Winter's *An Evolutionary Theory of Economic Change* (1982).
51. Bagehot [1876] 1978: 244–52. According to Commons, in the patriarchal era "each despot is sovereign in his own family, but he submits to accepted customs, not because they have coercive sanctions against him, but by mere habit" ([1899–1900] 1965: 40).
52. Hanssen [1835–7] 1880: 2, 29–30; Roscher [1859] 1903: 317; Keussler 1876: 1–3; Stein 1881: 15–20; Meitzen 1895: 1:129–30, 234; 2:682–4; Inama-Sternegg 1896; Knapp 1896; Schmoller 1901–4: 371; Weber [1922] 1978: 370–1. As Knapp (1896: 5) put it, to posit an original social contract for property rights was no less fanciful than the old Norse myths wherein land was distributed by the gods. See also Laveleye [1874] 1878: 73; Engels [1884] 1972: 226.

estates had arisen, in Germany at least, on precisely those waste tracts which had been cleared by individual initiative. The folk law (known as *Bifäng*) which validated this sort of freehold surely "intended" it as a buttress to the village community, not as the open challenge that it ultimately became: but the point was that the rule, once entrenched, had gradually taken on a momentum of its own and could be used to subvert its original purpose (Meitzen 1895: 1:137; R. Hildebrand [1896] 1907: 125–37). In time, feudal institutions themselves struck root, survived beyond their useful lives, and even were transplanted to novel milieus (especially in the Levant and the Americas) where they lacked even a genetic connection.[53] Similarly the European law merchant was found to have been waging, since the High Middle Ages, an uphill struggle against the prejudices of rulers, legislatures, and public opinion at large in favor of the archaic and cumbersome civil law.[54]

In general, institutional inertia seemed less relevant the closer one came to the present day;[55] but at least one economist, observing the sorry progress made in rationalizing the land tenure regime of French Algeria, pointed to the hard lesson being learned, that ancient practices would stand their ground even in the face of enlightened economic reasoning and policy (Colson 1907: 3:50).

## V    Conclusions

Relaxations of the *homo oeconomicus* model held great attraction for economists who lived in a positivist age, and who genuinely believed in instrumental rationalism as an explanatory device, but who nevertheless could not stomach the procrustean simplifications that underpinned our Apollonian chapter 2. In their loftier moments we have seen clearly the economist's pleasure at an empirical challenge well met, at the amorphous circle once again squared.

Those same moments of synthesis, however, have been in large part responsible for the reputation of nineteenth-century institutional econom-

---

53. Wagner [1876] 1892–4: 2:50–1; Page 1900; Sombart 1902: 1:337; Weber [1923] 1924: 90.
54. Courcelle-Seneuil [1858] 1891: vol. 1, book 2, ch. 1, §2. Courcelle-Seneuil considered the cognitive "inadequacy" of lawmakers to be "a necessary and permanent fact, like the weakness of an infant."
55. Schmoller codified this phenomenon as follows: "In the more distant past a static system of custom [*Sitte*], which is not distinct from law and religion, rules all life's domains. This cannot perdure, because free individual morality, which itself seeks, finds and chooses that which is right, exists at a higher level and must be striven for. . . . Thus does the whole domain of ethics come into flux; that is necessary and healthy" ([1874–5] 1898: 59).

ics as something less than science. Against this criticism we should weigh the virtue that most economists were intellectually honest enough to recognize the irreducible idiosyncrasies introduced by the plurality of human values, and by the bounded rationality with which human ends are pursued, elements that sabotage all mechanistic models. Even Schmoller, whom we have seen joining the search for the grail of institutional determination, accepted that the history of property has traversed different paths in different situations, and that those differences are largely unpredictable without very specific knowledge of circumstance. For example, in the final analysis the modernization of agrarian relations was underdetermined:

> Where a strong monarchy protected the peasantry, small- and middle-holdings by and large survived; where feudal and manorial circumstances led to political dominance of the nobility in parliament, in state administration, and in the administration of their own affairs, there large landholdings spread rampant. In all this, the personal character of peasants and nobles naturally played a role: a strong, capable peasantry sustained itself longer and more easily; an intelligent and advanced nobility, one qualified for political and military service, extended its properties more easily and atrophied less readily than one that was apolitical, hedonically absorbed and alienated from life on the land.[56]

To some extent, surely, this and the many other instances of their kind stand as admissions of failure: failure to capture the uniformity underlying the apparent randomness. But a likelier reason is that the economists saw the flies in their ointment and, being unable to fish them out, dutifully called the reader's attention to them.

By this same generous criterion should we judge the larger project reprised in this chapter and the last. It is true, at the end of the day much ambiguity remained. Economists were alive to the potential for a theory of rules that rested on the same basis as the general theory of exchange, that is, on the rational pursuit of wealth; but with only a few exceptions, each of them recognized too that verisimilitude required a more complex understanding of utility than Classical economics had on offer. And even this broader conception left more than a few empirical data beyond the

---

56. Schmoller 1901–4: §126. What made explaining history difficult, of course, made predicting the future virtually impossible:

> Only under certain conditions shall the property relations of the present day become untenable: when greater and middling property quite forgets its public duties, when the majority of the larger landowners sink to the state of epicurean rentiers, when and where unsound practices of subdivided tenure [*Zwergpachtverhältnisse*] or general overindebtedness prevail. These dangers can be worked against, and indeed have been for some time. (§131)

ken of science. It is only in comparison with willful ignorance of the social basis of rules, of the sort that characterized economics before the new science, that this takes on the appearance of progress. Upon reflection on the distance traveled, it is no mean achievement.

This chapter has filled some sizable lacunae in our understanding of the "old" institutionalism. But does it require us to revise anything that we thought we already knew? In two respects, it does. First, the received view of the "German Historical School" of economists, and of *mitteleuropäisch* historicism in general, suggests that the Germans should have been over-represented in the subset of economists who adduced the analytical category of culture and nation, who construed modernity as the triumph of individualist values over the communal ones, and who pointed out the limits of rationality and their significance for the new science; on the other hand, Germans should have been all but absent from the group that celebrated a brave new world of humanist conscience. In fact, Germans predominated in all these groups, much as they predominated in the new science as a whole. Nationality per se, that is, is a surprisingly poor predictor of an institutional economist's position on the importance of values vis-a-vis environment, and on the best way to make sense of the heterogeneity of values. The conclusion suggests itself that nineteenth-century economics was more ecumenical than the conventional nation-centered approach reveals.

Second, the conventional history of social evolutionism leads us to expect that the first decades of our period, lying closer to the heyday of civic humanism, when the tension between the modern celebration of comfort and individuality was set against the ascetic virtues of rude society, would feature the mode of interpretation that discovered altruism "before *homo oeconomicus.*" Conversely, the latter decades should present an evolutionism increasingly at ease with modernity and optimistic regarding its potential for nonpecuniary motivation, and hence more likely to view it with the equanimity that characterized our section "after *homo oeconomicus.*" In fact, though, both approaches were prominent throughout the period. Perhaps this should not surprise us overmuch: after all, one century is not a very long time in the history of human thought, even if it was a century of wrenching social change. Our deep-seated capacities for both nostalgia and modernism thrive on dislocation, and by 1835, let us not forget, the West had been experiencing profound social change for quite some time.

Economic historians will also profit from reflection on the findings of their more distant predecessors. Consider, for example, Stefano Fenoaltea's 1988 essay on the open-field system. In his methodological introduction, Fenoaltea casts a net broad enough to cover all the hypotheses we have reviewed in this chapter. Economists should take care, he warns, not to assume that institutions can be explained only by chrematistical argument: "widespread misconceptions to the contrary, economic rationality means only that individuals make choices on the basis of preferences over alternative outcomes; it does not imply any particular structure of preferences" (1988: 171–2). Alas, this commendably broad-church approach to the problem is vitiated by Fenoaltea's subsequent claim that the economic literature "has yet to discover a meta-agricultural benefit that would indeed be worth a perceptible loss of productivity."[57] There the possibility of ideological motivation is left, or rather abandoned; but we have shown in this chapter that the premise is not true. Economists participating in the new science were quite uninhibited in their inquiries into human motives. We can only speculate that a closer familiarity with the ideas aired in this chapter would bring projects like Fenoaltea's into closer congruity with his principled ecumenism. At the end of the day, his materialist explanation of the open-field system may very well turn out to be the right one; but it will be more robust once it has given the communitarian devil its due.

57. Fenoaltea 1988: 174. Fenoaltea's only references to the literature of nonpecuniary motivation are from noneconomists (Vinogradoff and Maitland), and these he dismisses – unfairly – as ahistorical (178).

# 4

## A new normative science:
## Institutional success and failure

Early in chapter 1 we adduced, as one cause of the tardiness of the explanatory science of rules, the highly judgmental timbre of political economy's early contributions to jurisprudence. *Explanation,* in other words, had been slighted by *evaluation.* But this did not mean, conversely, that the new explanatory agenda, once entrenched, necessarily eschewed the normative applications of its insights. In practice, few of our economists attempted to sublimate the traditional categories of "good" and "bad" in favor of anything so bloodless as "probable" and "improbable." And this is not to be wondered at. The "positivist turn" that we have identified ought, perhaps, to blunt the activist spirit that causes other students to dwell on what might be; but the urge to take sides is so strong that it insinuates itself inexorably into social science, suffusing even very deterministic approaches with defeatist or triumphal tones. In this chapter we shall answer two broad questions that were corollary to the new science: (1) What were the ends to which good laws were supposed to serve as means? In other words, what were the *criteria* of institutional success? And (2) What were thought to be the *political determinants* of institutional success and failure? The first question is as old as political economy; it will be developed here primarily as an adjunct to the second problem, which assumed a prominence unheard of before, and outside of, the new science. The "constitutional" problem was the essence of this new normative science of law.

What sort of political constitution "should" economists advocate, in keeping with the axioms of their discipline? To venture an answer is to invite controversy. Nevertheless, as a point of departure let us assert that the optimal constitution would be a *contractarian* one. In the baseline two-agent case, this means that party and counterparty should decide rules through bilateral negotiation, just as in the marketplace. In the more realistic case of many parties interested directly, and many more interested indirectly through "spillover" effects, it implies legislation by consensus. Now, the economists in question here were of far too practical a bent to tarry long at so ideal an ideal type. This was, after all, the age of the Social Question in Europe and America, and of the fear that modern society might come apart at its seams without some workmanlike effort to reconcile the classes. But if the constitution prescribed by economic principles was deemed unworkable, did research converge upon a single second-best option? The answer is that it did not.

If there is a theme in this chapter, it is one of dissonance and dissension within the college of economists. Only a few practitioners of the new science (primarily Schmoller and Wagner) are remembered at all today for their political opinions, and these as uncritical "social monarchists." There is something to be said for this characterization of the political philosophy of *Kathedersozialismus;*[1] but as a generalization to cover all the economists we have met so far, it is far from adequate. Their ranks numbered also democrats, meritocrats, anarchists (in the sense of opposing the state, though approving of law), and more than a few who argued several and contending sides, as the occasion suited. The only unifying theme we dare postulate is a gradually increasing fatigue with politics per se, which resulted, in the fin de siècle and after, in a growing belief that good law was best served by mandarin rule, or – and here a cautious resurrection of the contractarian ideal – by spontaneous transaction within civil society.

There is little doubt that economists of the new science, whatever their political affiliation, believed their analytical insights to hold profound practical implications as well. We see this in Graziani's admonition to the law faculty at Siena that "legal philosophy must regenerate itself at the running font of the social sciences; only from them can it truly learn the laws of life, from which juridical norms are to be derived" ([1893] 1894: 44). It is also in Laveleye's assertion that "since the decline of states has always been led by the imperfection of institutions and laws, which produce economic disorder, one may well believe that the progress of the social sciences will permit escape from this vicious circle, and will assure to humanity indefinite progress" ([1882] 1902: 15). Or in Franz Oppenheimer's claim that social science "was developed, attacking and destroying superstition, and thereby assisting in preparation of the path of [the state's] evolution" ([1907] 1914: 273).

Admittedly, these are just the sort of claims that had been made on

---

1. On the influence of the social monarchists, see Ascher, "Professors as Propagandists" (1963); and Pyle, "Advantages of Followership" (1974).

behalf of political economy since its infancy. What made this new-model normative institutional economics truly novel was its greater concern with politics, and particularly with the constitutional matrix whence working rules issued. This new concern was probably driven in part by a heightened sense, derived from the sort of reasoning reviewed in the last two chapters, that given a society's physical, political, and psychic environment, its laws were in some sense "determinate." It was driven, too, by the greater empiricism of the new positive science, which pointed up the relativity of good law vis-à-vis evolutionary circumstance. Thus the motivating problem was not merely Which rules are best?, or even Which political system will enact the rules which we know are best?, but also Which political system will enact the rules that are most appropriate to a society's peculiar requirements? In this respect it was genuinely new.

## I      Defining the public interest

First of all let us consider the normative criteria against which institutions were measured, and according to which they were judged adequate or wanting. By way of introduction and foil, we offer a brief, reasoned history of the concept of "welfare" up to the present juncture in applied economics (as opposed to "welfare economics" proper, which is naturally subtler and more disputatious on these points). Through the long centuries predating the emergence of political economy, philosophers and moralists were not bashful in their imaginations of a good society. The Aristotelian (or consequentialist) tradition, where social results mattered and law was set instrumentally subordinate to them, was in some sense antipodal to the Stoic (or formalist) tradition wherein the integrity of justice mattered more than the social state that followed from it. But neither tradition evinced the least inhibition about claiming to know, in detail, what was best for other people.

Modern economic thought, on the other hand, has been profoundly influenced by the utilitarian strand of ethics, which began uncoiling from the tangled skein of moral philosophy at about the same time. Today we are struck by the great hubris and the spurious precision of the utilitarian calculus of pleasures and pains; but in its own day it must have been far more shocking for its modesty and its ethical agnosticism, verging on amorality. For the utilitarian forswore on principle all claims to knowledge of what the good society should look like to the naked eye, insisting only that it should bear a formal relation to the preferences of its members. This claim of value-freedom, as reassuring to nascent social science as it was scandalous to hoary social philosophy, found a home in economic thought. Among other things, it is reflected in the centrality of "wealth" as a summary statistic of exchange values: values which might be meaningless or even repugnant to the scientist, but which, by definition, mean something to the parties concerned.

But there were problems with this happy utilitarian formulation. Its claim to impartiality was dogged by the fact that utility could be aggregated only if the sensations of distinct persons could be measured and reduced to a common denominator. To doubt the possibility of such extraordinary insight was to vitiate the whole utilitarian project; but to insist on it was to invite the conclusion that one was merely reading one's own preferences into one's subject matter. Worse, perhaps, the economist who sought to avoid controversy by espousing the commonsense principle that all human psyches were essentially identical could, in practice, achieve just the opposite effect. For this assumption, in conjunction with the principle of diminishing marginal utility, led ineluctably to the conclusion that each farthing was "worth" more to the pauper than to the prince, and more to the sot than to the sturdy burgher. The redistributive implications of such a stance could chill one's sense of right, not to say one's academic career.

The Paretian "revolution" in normative economics is best viewed as a response to these problems, most especially as a further measure of modesty in the service of professional detachment. Pareto's principle – that one social state is to be judged better than another if, and only if, all parties prefer it (a subset may be indifferent) – is advantaged in modern discourse not principally because of the insights it affords, but rather because of the sticky problems it evades. Alternatives involving winners and losers, which of course means nearly the whole set of alternatives met with in the empirical world, lie conveniently beyond its ken. When the theorist refers to "allocative efficiency," she usually has in mind the locus of Pareto optima described by society's utility possibilities frontier. The applied economist, on the other hand, will typically broaden the concept's coverage with some sort of compensation principle, one that allows a redistributive, Pareto-noncomparable alternative to be judged superior *if* the injured party *could be* compensated in such a way as to produce a Pareto-dominant compromise, regardless of whether the transfer actually takes place. More so even than under the classical utilitarian dispensation, "success" in this case comes to be identical with the maximization of exchange value in the aggregate, that is, with the wealth of nations.

Our purpose in this sketch has not been to unmask a pattern of craven backpedaling in the development of economics. Indeed, the pursuit of professional detachment and consensual assumptions has much to recommend it: not by luck alone is the unified program of economic inquiry the envy of other social sciences. Moreover, we have suggested that the primacy of exchange values in assessing the public interest stems not so much from a misplaced fixation on commodities, as from a worthy disavowal of moral tutelage. Our principal purpose has been, rather, to set out the trade-offs facing researchers in the field, the better to understand how and why the economists of this study differed from their successors. Simply stated: if contemporary normative economics has sacrificed a large measure of common moral sense in the pursuit of consensus and analytical rigor, the practitioners of our "new science" were likelier to make the converse trade. They kept present in their gaze a wider range of the traditional ethical concerns, even at substantial cost in terms of clarity and intersubjective reach. Where contemporary economists have converged over the formal "impossibility" of a social choice mechanism meeting certain reasonable standards,[2] economists of an earlier era worried more over the practical merits and demerits of specific constitutions. Where a narrowly Paretian moral compass has led latter-day economists to trace the taproot of institutional failure to mutually beneficial deals left unstruck (and thus ultimately to information, transaction, and enforcement costs),[3] the earlier group was prone (1) to define success and failure more broadly and (2) to countenance a wider range of causes. The remainder of this section will inspect the first of these distinguishing traits; the sections to follow will consider the second.

In chapter 1 we noted that the transition from formal to consequentialist ethics was not, of itself, sufficient to turn the old science of law into the new. But we can state with some conviction that even if not all consequentialists were participants in the new science, the converse was very nearly exact. Economists of our group, that is, were predisposed to judge laws more by their social ramifications than by their intrinsic qualities. We may best locate this juncture in ethical thought by reference to the ancient dictum, "Let there be justice, though the world perish." For centuries on end, scions of the Judeo-Christian tradition held the truth of that statement to be self-evident; today it strikes us as absurd. Nineteenth-century economists rested uneasily on the cusp of the modern view, as is evident from their frequent objections that the choice was a false one: that, as Laveleye once put it, "The Just and the Useful pronounce the same commandments" ([1882] 1902: 10). But though Laveleye's sentiment was representative of the profession on the whole, among economists associated

2. Here we refer especially to Kenneth Arrow's *Social Choice and Individual Values* (1951), Amartya Sen's "The Impossibility of a Paretian Liberal" (1970), and the large literature their work has spawned.
3. We refer here especially to the large literature around the concepts of "rent seeking," "directly unproductive profit-seeking" (DUP) activities, and "institutional failure." The best-known applications of this research program to economic history are probably Douglass North and Robert Thomas's *Rise of the Western World* (1973) and Mancur Olson's *Rise and Decline of Nations* (1982).

with institutional analysis it sounded cautious and a little retrograde.[4]
These economists believed that private property was justified not by higher
law, but rather by what Roscher called "reasons of general utility."[5] Thus
when one sees affirmed by the likes of Wagner that "right and expediency,
properly understood, are identical" ([1876] 1892–4: 2:§5), or by Schmoller
that "all moral action is expedient action" (1901–4: §23), one should not
mistake it for a vindication of natural law, or even as an artful compromise
after the manner of Laveleye: for these, as for the bulk of the analysts we
will consider here, a law was just *because* it was expedient.

But what was the common good that was to be expedited? To some
extent, it was simply a broader and more diffuse brand of the reasoned
eudaemonism with which economics has always been associated. All we
need add here is that the maximal output of commodities was not generally deemed an adequate criterion for the evaluation of institutions; in
today's language we might say that these economists espoused something
closer to a "maximin" approach to the problem of production, in that
special importance attached to making the worst-case outcome as toler-
able as possible. This is evident in their greater concern for the defense of
social stability against threats domestic and foreign, and especially in the
significance they placed on the well-being of the humblest laborers.

Where these generations of economists really stand apart, however, is
in the extent to which they invoked desiderata which were independent
of – indeed, often opposed to – the elemental human drive to control
resources. This was a proclivity evident especially among Germans, heirs
to long traditions of conservatism, which treasured the idea of community
[*Gemeinschaft*], and liberalism, which celebrated humanistic cultivation
[*Bildung*]: neither one found much joy in the spectacle of rampant consum-
erism. "Acquisitive interest," according to Schäffle, "is always subordinate
to the collective *moral* purpose, to which end the things acquired are but
means" ([1858] 1873: §279). Or more specifically Wieser:

4. It is true that the socialists, single-taxers and agrarian reformers among them—
   including Laveleye—did invoke the labor theories of value and property in
   their indictments of the status quo. But it is no accident that they chose the
   branch of natural law most obviously fitted to the social outcomes they
   hoped for.
5. Roscher ca. 1851: 134. Schäffle, too, criticized all attempts to legitimate private
   property on the basis of matter having been infused with labor, capital, or talent. Like all institutions, property was legitimated by, and only by, its implications for the common good ([1858] 1873: §321). And Marshall agreed that "the
   tendency of careful economic study is to base the rights of private property not
   on any abstract principle, but on the observation that in the past they have
   been inseparable from solid progress" ([1890] 1895: book 1, ch. 4, §6).

To make persons once again equal, as they were before they abandoned their primal states to pursue victory and conquest, before the course of world history rent them asunder into strong and weak, rich and needy, educated and ignorant, deprived and oversated, workers and consumers; to lead them back to the unity in which they had lived in the beginning: that is the great task. [*Über die gesellschaftlichen Gewalten* ([1901] 1929): 376]

"Civilization culminates not in personal well-being," wrote Richard Hildebrand, standing utilitarian hedonism on its head, "but rather in productive collective labor; . . . civilization never comes down to a simple arithmetic problem, or a simple question of majorities and minorities."[6]

Whatever the yardstick chosen to represent the public "good," it goes without saying that not all laws will measure up equally. For a given society, that is, some rules will encourage the employment of extant resources to maximum benefit, and furthermore to augment the stock of physical, technical, and ideological resources; at the other end of the spectrum, some laws will prove worse than anarchy. Ranged between these extremes, all potential rules are characterized by the degree of social success or failure which they bring in tow.[7] Our principal concern in this chapter is the problem of why certain societies manage to "get the rules right," while others – or even the same societies at other moments in their evolution – succumb to institutional failure.

## II     The primacy of institutional success

Before addressing this problem directly, however, we should in fairness investigate a tendency in the literature of the new science which militated against its consideration: by comparison with both their prede-

---

6. R. Hildebrand 1894: 8–9. Similarly, as he took aim at the radical Republican synthesis: "*Fraternité* and *égalité* never go hand in hand with *liberté*. *Fraternité* and *égalité* are a consequence of coercion or servitude, not of freedom; a fact that will surprise no connoisseur of human nature" ([1896] 1907: 121–2).

7. Note that this spectrum evinced a stronger central tendency than does its counterpart of the present day: in other words the verdict on any given institution was likelier to be mixed. At base, the problem was that these economists valued not just allocative efficiency, not just distributive justice, not just social stability, not just public virtue, and not just national development; rather, they valued all these things in comparable measure, and rare was the legal principle which could earn unqualified approval *or* condemnation on the basis of them. Thus, ironically, if not too surprisingly upon reflection, the very great range of the economists' ethical concerns often led them into a state of deep ambivalence regarding the various means to those ends.

cessors and their successors, economists of this era were likelier to see law as an intrinsically irenic, meliorative force in society. From the foregoing chapters it should be clear that the new science was predisposed to view institutions as serving *someone's* interest, a predisposition that has survived down to the present: where it stood apart was in its greater tendency to see the law furthering, as if guided by an invisible hand, the *public* interest as well. In short, institutional success was sometimes privileged over failure.

We shall dispense with a detailed documentation of this assertion: one need not have read too deeply between the lines of chapters 2 and 3 to have gleaned as much already. Suffice it here to illustrate the point by reference to the example of human bondage, which stands out in earlier and later literature as one of the most salient instances of an institution injurious to the commonweal. In this middle period, by contrast, treatments of patriarchy, chattel slavery, and serfdom were tinged with more than a hint of apology. For the primitive economies in which it was typically found, unfree labor was viewed as an invaluable aid in the promoting the division of labor, economies of scale, the accumulation of capital, and the transformation of sloth into industry;[8] it was even enlisted in the cause of moral improvement.[9] Indeed, it was common to suggest that servitude or clientage was often a boon even to those whose freedoms were extinguished, at least if one considered the sorry alternatives confronting these souls in a brutal and clannish world.[10] And if even slavery could be relieved of its moral stigma, how much easier was it to exculpate the many lesser oddities of property, contract, and tort law known to man!

Several reasons may be adduced for this striking leniency in the evaluation of economic rules. Pride of place must be given to the organic conception of society, which suggested a structural-functional – in other words, a sympathetic – interpretation of law, of the sort that nowadays tends to

8. Roscher [1854] 1906: §68; Mangoldt [1863] 1871: 20–1; Schäffle 1875–8: 2:142–3; Wagner [1876] 1892–4: 2:§§26, 33; Loria [1893] 1910: 6–7; Bücher [1893] 1910: 98; Meitzen 1895: 1:165–6; Hadley 1896: 28–33; Wittich 1897: 49; Schmoller 1901–4: §§88–90, 124; Ely 1903: 48; Oppenheimer [1907] 1914: 66. For dissenting views, see Roscher [1854] 1906: 189–90; Walras 1896: 143; Schäffle 1875–8: 2:307–8.

9. Schmoller, e.g., found that the stabilization and intensification of production with which patriarchy was associated had lengthened the life span of parents and, ultimately, facilitated affective bonding and "higher cultural endeavor" (1901–4: §§88–90).

10. Molinari 1853b: 611; Minghetti [1859] 1863: 481; Schäffle 1875–8: 3:93; Wagner [1876] 1892–4: 2:§§29–31; Miaskowski 1890: 10–11; R. Hildebrand [1896] 1907: 143; Brodnitz 1912: 148–9.

be limited to treatments of cultural exotica. One might debate whether this proclivity, in turn, owed more to the legacy of Romanticism, to the fashionable principles of evolutionary selection, or to the object lessons of failed colonial experiments in social engineering: most likely, these all worked hand-in-glove. The significance of Romanticism for moral philosophy has been summarized by Georg Iggers, in his assessment of the historian Ranke:

> For him all products of history and everything that operates within the context of a historical society are concrete, objective values. Such a position involves an extreme optimism regarding history and nature which Ranke shared with other adherents of the Historical School and with many thinkers in the Romantic tradition. It assumes that there is no real evil in nature. ([1968] 1983: 72)

This sensibility affected the German economists most deeply, and not just the hidebound conservatives among them like Adam Müller (who went so far as to insist that "the existing political system is the nation's true capital-stock"; [ca. 1808] 1931: 3), but also latter-day progressives like Schmoller, who likened the emergence of law out of national custom to the development of bone out of cartilage in the human infant (1901–4: §26), and Bücher. Bücher, who described the economy as a complex of institutions, viewed the result as an accretion of popular genius:

> Humanity has fashioned [the economy] through a development of many millenia, and generations without number have inscribed it with the results of their reflection upon the suitable organization of their existence. Only very gradually have we made our way to the present state of affairs, and forces are constantly at work to reshape and improve it. (1914: 82–3)

The insight of natural selection worked to similar effect, by means of a rhetoric that was more mechanistic than teleological. That basic mechanism, of nature's "positive check" against extremes of social parasitism, was posited most clearly by Schäffle:

> The given organization of this world allows scope to capriciousness and abuse of power – who would care to dispute this in the face of thousand-fold experience! But such abuse is not without limits, not unaccountable. The guarantee of material justice lies in punishment by enervation and self-annihilation through injustice, as imposed by social selection.[11]

11. Schäffle 1875–8: 2:81. Compare Wieser's observation: "Just as personal egoism, through the conflict of competition, is exalted into social egoism, and enlisted in the service of public interest, thus the egoism of the ruling political parties is, by the conflicts constantly waged between states, exalted into public

More commonsensically, Marshall argued that

> a body of custom which did nothing but grind down the weak could not long survive. For the strong rest on the support of the weak, their own strength cannot sustain them without that support; and if they organize social arrangements which burden the weak wantonly and beyond measure, they thereby destroy themselves. ([1890] 1895: app. A, §1)

These were both modest propositions, offering pretty cold comfort to the champions of the meek. But the metaphor of biological evolution lent itself also to argument by broad gesture, which came much closer to the goal of acquitting institutions on grounds of their very existence. Schäffle himself played no small part in this. His arguments ranged from the merely tendentious – for instance, that society's hegemonic elements "are of all parties the ones most interested in collective subsistence" – to the downright naive: "Experience teaches that it is simply the interests of individual and collective self-preservation which calls law and custom into being, protects and fortifies it, and governs its transformation according to the historical circumstances of each period" (1875–8: 2:62–6).

Unlike the Romantic moment, the Darwinian one had wide geographic appeal in institutional analysis. It is evident in the Briton Cunningham's remark that "when time is reckoned not by years and decades, but by generations and centuries, we see that the greatest revolutions are possible; better forms of social organisation have gradually superseded less satisfactory types, and have survived till some other type proved itself fitter still" (1896: 183). Similarly, the Italian Graziani argued that each one of the successive historical systems of property, whatever its faults, amounted to "an organism more efficient than its predecessor, fitter to satisfy needs which have grown in extent and intensity" (1904: 321). And in North America, where the rhetoric of social Darwinism was perhaps most warmly received, its message of axiomatic optimism tinged institutional evaluation across the political spectrum, from the Yale conservative Hadley to the Wisconsin progressive Commons.[12]

---

spirited egoism, and made to serve the general interest of the people" ([1914, 1923] 1928: §77).

12. According to Hadley, "The fact that the present organization of capital is a result of historical development, and that present forms have survived where others failed, is the strongest proof of their vitality" (1896: 149–50). This is not far from Commons's assertion that

> as a matter of causal sequence the working rules [his jargon for laws and institutions] are designed primarily to keep the peace and promote collective action. . . . Primarily the rules are necessary and their survival in history is contingent on their fitness to hold together in a continuing concern the overweening and unlimited selfishness of individuals pressed on by scarcity of resources. (1924: 137–8)

Still another reason behind the relatively sympathetic interpretation of the institutional record was, quite simply, that the standards of "success" were lower in those days. That is to say, latter-day critics have tended to measure actual rules against the best rules imaginable, whereas a century ago the more common counterfactual was a Hobbesian one of no rules at all. Thus Max Weber, whose approach to law was hardly Panglossian, nevertheless defined the economic order as "the division of real powers of disposal over goods and economic services, arising *consensually* [*einverständnismäßig*] through a process of compromise of interests" ([1922] 1978: II, ch. 1, §1). By this Weber did not mean that these were ipso facto the best of all possible rules for all interested parties; but it was significant to him that they arose by virtue of being mutually preferable to the likely alternatives. Likewise, Walter Bagehot was inclined to excuse the rigid caste systems that ruled many ancient societies, not because they were particularly felicitous but because, in the absence of a true police power, they minimized friction and at least kept civilization from dissolving in conflict.[13]

Finally, the presumption in favor of institutional success may have to be traced also to the incomplete exorcism from the new science of what we have called the "old science" of law. Recall that a hallmark of that older approach to the law was the practice of isolating one kind of rule as "true" right, and dismissing all others as unworthy of explication. Now the advent of the new science always meant an explanatory treatment of one's favored institutions, if for no other reason than because it added a certain ballast, a determinacy to what was otherwise merely desirable; but undesirable institutions were often denied that same consideration. Liberal French economists, in particular, betrayed a penchant for portraying liberty and property as ineluctable social data, turning a resolutely blind eye to the fact that they were by no means universal. Thus when Paul Leroy-Beaulieu wrote that "all [rights] have their origin in the nature of things, in human instinct, and in the necessities of man's adaptation to the conditions of his environment," he was clearly drawing conviction from

13. Bagehot [1876] 1978: 244. This was consonant with J. S. Mill's more general finding that

> tribunals (which always precede laws) were originally established, not to determine rights, but to repress violence and terminate quarrels. With this object chiefly in view, they naturally enough gave legal effect to first occupancy, by treating as the aggressor the person who first commenced violence, by turning, or attempting to turn, another out of possession. The preservation of peace, which was the original object of civil government, was thus attained; while by confirming, to those who already possessed it, even what was not the fruit of personal exertion, a guarantee was incidentally given to them and others that they would be protected in what was so. (1848: book 2, ch. 1, §2)

the fact that entitlements counted as "rights" only insofar as he approved of them in the first place. The rest, which would have been evidence of institutional failure, escaped consideration.[14]

If this sort of principled aversion to criticism had been absolutely hegemonic within the economics profession, then we could profitably close the discussion here. But in fact this was not the case. To all but the truest of true believers, experience left no doubt but that much human potential was stymied by bad laws, that the invisible hand of institutional selection could all too easily turn against society, its putative master. Now given the poignant contingency of good law, it is not surprising that opinions were aired, explicitly or implicitly, as to sources of difference. In other words, the degree of institutional success or failure was most often perceived to be a dependent variable, so that attention naturally focused on the independent variables driving it. In taking up this problem, economists of the new science were engaging an ancient discourse on the political constitution.

The basic elements of the economists' contribution to this discourse may be descried already from the preceding chapters. The model of *homo oeconomicus* underpinning chapter 2, entailing as it does a determinate human behavioral algorithm, suggests as its constitutional corollary that only the distribution and redistribution of powers can afford real purchase over institutional outcomes. The optimal distribution of public power has always been the central problematic of constitutional thought – the political philosopher's philosopher's stone, so to speak – but few were those who imagined that political *power* could be treated without some allowance for the lability of political *ideology,* or what the humanists called "virtue." As chapter 3 suggested, even economists, whose profession was predicated on man's acquisitive nature, were inclined to recognize the possibility of diverse behavioral patterns. This acknowledgment carried huge implications for the optimal constitution, and for the degree of institutional success to be hoped for from even the best-considered of legislative mechanisms. Its rhetorical import was also great, as witness in the distance between the following quote from Schmoller on the one hand, and the positivistic formulae of present-day "constitutional economics," on the other:

> Passions and stupidity can occasionally gain the upper hand,
> can impose class rule, can permit the organization of economic
> life to fall into such deformity that new, healthier life can arise
> only on the grave of an entire civilization. But such occasions,
> such degenerations, in no way abolish the general law of prog-

---

14. Leroy-Beaulieu [1895] 1900: 545. See also Cherbuliez 1848: 26–7; 1862: 214–16; Leroy-Beaulieu [1888] 1910: 114; Colson 1901–7: 3:i.

ress: they do not relieve true and good persons of the duty always to work towards the end that, for any given level of technology, of capital accumulation and of population density, the most perfect form of economic organization will be discovered and implemented. (1901–4: §28)

In raising these questions were practitioners of the new science following boldly where their powers of observation led, or chasing a will-o'-the-wisp into a morass from which social science later had to be extricated? As is so often the case, one's finding on this question depends on what one is looking for in scholarship.

## III    Society and state

As a rule, political philosophers have had little trouble arriving at the desirability of legislation through a state apparatus. For our purposes we may define a state very generally as a person (or group of persons) who issues directives, and who backs those directives with threats of coercion that are so credible that they only exceptionally need demonstration; laws are the most general of such directives. Economists, despite their association with the possibility of spontaneous order and the allied dictum of laissez-faire, have typically accepted the idea that each economy – in effect, each society – must be coextensive with a state if it is to function properly. In general, our group of economists was no exception. The alternative to a rational state was seen not as some happy anarchy, but as the rule of the mighty: at best, a sinister oligarchy; at worst, nature red in tooth and claw. The result would hardly meet the goals of allocative efficiency or distributive equity, or even that of quashing civil violence.

For similar reasons, most new-science economists were skeptical also of the "night watchman" state, the one strictly limited to the protection of negative liberties and the enforcement of all contracts freely entered into. As noted above, this constitution made of legislation a spontaneous, ad hoc affair, the result of a market for promises very much like the nexus in which commodities are exchanged. To be sure, economists were as alive as anyone to the presumption of welfare enhancement attaching to such metarules which, by enforcing what were sometimes called "spheres of freedom" around each citizen, maximized the scope for social – or even, in the extreme, bilateral – transaction of specific rules. But the problems were manifest as well. In the first place, this constitution presupposed an initial distribution of rights: if this distribution were iniquitous, or merely incomplete, then the results of exchange would surely be tainted as well. Accordingly, only state intervention, wrote Schäffle, "can prevent that that which autonomous parties find to be 'just' does not become injustice with respect to third parties and to the collectivity. In civil and criminal, indeed in all fields of legislation, basic norms must be upheld with a view to the whole, to the 'public interest'" (1875–8: 1:657–9). Moreover, even if the initial distribution of rights were ideal, subsequent negotiations would be subject to significant transaction costs. We have already shown in chapter 2 that the success of bilateral legislation – especially the commutation of relatively inefficient corvée labor dues – was understood to hinge, among other things, on a society's greater or lesser monetization. And when, as was usually the case, rules had to be multilateral in order to function properly, the obstacles to transaction were multiplied. Wieser, for example, explained how network externalities could easily feed into political paralysis:

> In order to gauge correctly the power of mass habit, one must consider how greatly the power of individual habit is heightened by the fact that each individual is reinforced in his personal inertia by the general state of inertia. Even if he himself were inclined to yield [to institutional innovation], he would nevertheless still feel constrained so long as he knows that the rest have not yet yielded themselves; and the rest also feel constrained, because each one ever believes himself overwhelmed by the great mass of the others. (1905: 11)

Whatever the precise etiology, decentralized lawmaking was blamed for various institutional dysfunctions, including the inefficiency of open-field agriculture (Weber 1904: 454) and the self-defeating results of unilateral moves toward free trade.[15] Even the humblest village community could not have sprung from a social contract, reasoned Hildebrand, inasmuch as this would have presupposed improbable reserves of "public spirit or inborn self-abnegation" ([1896] 1907: 108).

The upshot of these considerations was that the public interest was best served by a single *mind,* one enjoying the prerogative of legislation for society as a whole. This metaphor was no more than implicit in most economic literature of the period – except, characteristically, in Schäffle's artless prose: "In its external function, the state represents the same thing for the social body which the central part of the motor nervous system, together with the muscular organs subordinate to it, represents for animal (i.e. unitary, centralized) motion" (1875–8: 1:671). More concretely, he explained that "formation of law through the state's legislation, ordinance and disposal offers great advantages, in that law is unified and directly supported by the authority and power of the whole social body. It rules out conflict, indecision, and doubts over the law's compulsory nature, [and

---

15. List [1841] 1930: 179. It may surprise those who know List's work only by reputation to learn that he considered a future world government to be therefore a precondition to human perfection.

so] can encourage self-help."[16] But how then should society's mind work? Economists who engaged this problem ended up treading a well-worn path between the two great, flawed monoliths of political philosophy, *representation* of interests and *authority* of leadership. Their common grounding in economic theory therefore did not issue in a bold reformulation of the problem of good government; but it did affect subtly the conclusions reached.

## IV     Representation

According to the representative ideal, the problem of public choice is best solved by weighing the opinions of all enfranchised citizens. The interests which strive at large in civil society are not to be feared, that is, but brought together to deliberate, to contest and compromise, and ultimately to be put to an electoral trial. Roscher, heir to the liberal Göttingen tradition of resistance to authoritarianism, put it thus:

> With democracy, where even the lowliest citizens feel themselves part of the sovereign power, we find naturally the greatest *interest of all in the state* as well: i.e., in the case of a competent people, political insight and capacity for sacrifice are most widespread. . . . The citizenry looks on the state as its own work, its own property.[17]

History seemed to many to demonstrate the superior institutional results obtainable through representative government. For German economists in particular, the rude participatory democracies of the ancient Teutons seemed a paragon of legislation in the public interest.[18] Among primitive tribes of their own day, Baumstark (1865: 101–13) and Schmoller (1901–4: §§124–5) found much to admire also in the democratic traditions of the American Plains Indians who, very much like the Germans of Caesar's day, understood the need to retain the polity's eminent domain over land; by invidious contrast, less highly politicized tribes (especially in Africa and Oceania) gave full rein to private appropriation and gradually slipped into the clutches of monopoly, aristocracy, and clientage.

16. Schäffle 1875–8: 1:658–9. See also Schüz [1836] 1976: 154; Schäffle [1858] 1873: 2:§279; Wieser [1914, 1923] 1928: §75.
17. Roscher, *Politik* (1892): 313. On the liberal politics of the German Historical School, which has often been overlooked in the English-language literature, see Eisermann 1956: 31, 87; Bruch 1985; and W. Smith 1991: 14. On an early contribution to constitutional economics in England, see Milgate and Stimson, *Ricardian Politics* (1991).
18. E.g., Inama-Sternegg 1879–99: 1:81; Stein 1881: 17–18; Meitzen 1895: 1:138–40.

The village communes of agrarian society were also lauded as worthy vessels of the commonweal. Laveleye was especially forthright in his defense of these "small, independent rural democracies," a typical example of which was the popular assemblies convened to arbitrate irrigation rights in Moorish Spain – the so-called *acequieras*.

> The wisdom of the decisions of this tribunal, composed solely of peasants, was celebrated throughout Spain. . . . The associates were self-governing and self-adjudicating; they administered freely their own interests, they elected their own officers, they deliberated upon and passed laws. This was at one and the same time republican government and the parliamentary system.
>
> ([1874] 1878: 130, 239)

According to Meitzen and Bücher, the Germanic village councils too had managed their communal assets effectively; according to Hanssen, they were able to carry through the piecemeal privatization of their open fields as required to stimulate cultivation.[19] And thereafter, according to Lewinski, popular legislation generally succeeded in devising land reforms that worked the desired redistribution while maintaining incentive efficiencies. "The village community," he wrote, "tries to divide the land in such a manner as to injure as little as possible the interest of every man in an intensive cultivation." To the cynic this seems an impossibly sanguine view of majority government; but for Lewinski it was the rule rather than the exception: "Where the economic disadvantages of a [re-]distribution of [private] land were so great that they outweighed the advantages, the community recoiled from these measures."[20] Similarly, in concluding his paean to the Alpine village cooperative, Bücher declared that

> what has always appeared most admirable in these *Allmenden* is the very fact that we are dealing with a piece of popular legislation, with absolutely popular institutions which, like the folksong, was made by the *Volk* itself, which has drawn it forth from the depths of its legal conscience and moral sensibility. [The *Volk*] has tailored them to fit its needs; therefore they fit a good deal better than any laws which are composed on the [bureaucrat's] drawing-table. (1902: 22)

Laveleye deeply regretted that oligarchic usurpation had done down

19. Meitzen 1895: 1:138–40; Bücher 1902: 13–14, 22; Hanssen [1870] 1880: 491–2.
20. Lewinski 1913: 48–59. This democratic self-restraint was noteworthy especially in Finland and northwest Russia, where the soil was so stony that many fields – specifically, the ones that required large infusions of individual effort before they could be put under the plow – were perpetually exempted from redistribution (64).

these little republics everywhere but a few zones of exception like Frisia, Switzerland, Andorra, Serbia, and the American frontier.[21] But this did not mean that representative government belonged to a world now irretrievably lost. Parliamentary democracy in the Western nation-state was given a large measure of credit for the recent eradication of slavery and serfdom, by the special strength of what Commons called the "partnership of the capitalist and wage-earning classes" against the rapacity of aristocratic minorities.[22] Laveleye himself placed his socialist hopes in a vaguely articulated democratic renaissance, something akin to Oppenheimer's future utopia of "freeman's citizenship," which could be counted on to smooth away the burrs of social and economic strife ([1907] 1914: 287–8).

Thus were mustered the best arguments for legislation by representation: but the economists' reservations were more fulsome still. It is one of the sharpest indications of how much times have changed, for better and worse, that a century ago one could question in explicit terms the desirability of popular sovereignty without endangering one's place in polite company. Unlike some conservative theorists, economists were not prepared to reject democracy out of hand. The problem, rather, was that it required some very elusive moral preconditions in order to succeed. Discussion of these preconditions typically culminated in broad gestures toward the classic distinctions of self-discipline versus passion, virtue versus corruption, solidarity versus individuation, and good faith versus opportunism. Of these pairs, healthy democracies always cultivated the former; but the intrusion of the latter would invariably poison the well from which good laws were drawn. Even Roscher, whom we quoted above in support of representative government, insisted that it was a blessing only to nations that excelled at

> that knowledge and attention to law, that self-discipline, which are the cause of true freedom. . . . Thus do so many intellectually and morally competent nations reach their apex in the period when they have approached most nearly a true, sound de-

21. Laveleye [1874] 1878: 239. Of these, the first three were saved because their pastoral orientation "required no hands for the cultivation of the soil, and therefore did not necessitate the introduction of corvée as in agricultural districts"; Serbia was advantaged, ironically, in that the Turkish yoke bore down especially hard on the native nobility; the reason for American exceptionalism was not given.
22. Commons [1899–1900] 1965: 77–8; Leslie, "The Wealth of Nations and the Slave Power" ([1863] 1879): 61.

mocracy; while incompetent peoples begin their decline at that selfsame moment.[23]

The drawbacks of representative government were understood to be manifold. To begin with, the great multifariousness of interests made rational deliberation complicated in the extreme. As Wieser put it, metaphorically, "When a thousand persons are assembled for the purpose of agreeing on a common decision, they will never achieve their purpose if they all do what is done in order to reach agreement at the "retail" level [*im Einzelverkehre*]: that is, if they all begin talking" ([1901] 1929: 350). Moreover, practical reason suggested that a unanimity rule, while desirable on a priori grounds, would in practice become a recipe for impasse. But conversely, to the extent that the democratic constitution increased the chance for decision by allowing minority (or, conceivably, majority) preferences to be overridden by vote, it became ever likelier that the governing faction or coalition would prosecute an interest that was not the public's own. "Since each party represents only a part of the citizenry," wrote Wilhelm Hasbach in his treatise *Modern Democracy* (1912), "it must assert its interests at the expense of the minority. . . . It is one of the most striking characteristics of democracy, that it denies open influence to persons and groups who stand outside the party machinery, while it bestows influence most richly upon secret, dark powers" [*Die moderne Demokratie* (1912): 586–7]. Specifically, there was reason to fear the political franchise's falling in the hands of a majority which might imagine that it stood to gain more than it lost from a redistribution of wealth. As Cunningham put it,

> In any community where a great deal of power is in the hands of the poor, and the balance of wealth does not coincide with the balance of power, there is a danger lest great schemes for redistributing property should be undertaken, not because it is right, but because the mass of the voters hope that by such redistribution they themselves will make some personal gain. (1896: 214)

Schmoller agreed, arguing in even stronger terms that

> the theory of popular sovereignty is an absurdity, in the sense that it has been conceived up to now: by it every prevailing majority of the people or of the parliament may redistribute property after its whim, and it can and should exclude the upper classes from national leadership. As such it would become none other than class rule by the laborers. Affairs would reach a state

---

23. Roscher 1892: 311–14. See also Knies, "Niccolò Machiavelli als volkswirthschaftlicher Schriftsteller" (1852); Roscher [1854] 1906: §§16, 74, 78, 84; Schäffle 1875–8: 1:674–5; 2:72–3; Schmoller 1901–4: §97.

compared to which our old German bureaucracy [*Beamten-staat*], despite all its failings, would be a model of justice and reason.[24]

Ancient history appeared to give ample testimony to democracy's pitfalls: confident rationalism brought about first manhood suffrage, then political cynicism; and these latter, in time, ushered in the spectacles of bread, circuses, and intractable social polarization.[25] Regarding the later Teutonic tribal assemblies and Slavic village councils, Weber observed that their political response to looming shortages of free land was a typically counterproductive one of enforcing equality through curbs on private initiative.[26] Contemporary democracy harbored specters of its own, from communist agitation (which Roscher defined as "the exaggeration of the democratic principle of equality") to ill-considered consumerist trade regimes, which Sombart disparaged as "the philistine policy of shopkeepers" and which he set in sorry contrast to the golden age of mercantilism and etatism.[27] Admittedly, Swiss democracy did not seem to bear out these forebodings; but in Hasbach's view this was the exception that proved the rule; for the Swiss stood out also in terms of "spirit and character," as well as in the relatively equal division of wealth to which their economy had given rise spontaneously (1912: 606–7).

Even if democracy did not fail the public interest directly, it might well do so indirectly, by permitting a drift toward the tyranny of self-interested minorities. Once again, classical antiquity was thought a rich source of cautionary tales. Bruno Hildebrand, for instance, saw in the histories of Sparta, Athens, and the Roman Republic alike the tragedy of democracy's failure to sustain itself in the face of social differentiation, each epic end-

24. Schmoller, "Demokratie und soziale Zukunft" ([1912] 1920): 111. See also Roscher [1854] 1906: §78; Schäffle 1875–8: 2:72.
25. According to Roscher, the entire Hellenic world suffered when "all that we may term tradition, political folkways and national legal sensibility [*Rechts-gefühl*] turned to rationalism; and rationalism in turn flung itself, with frightful exclusivity, into the conflict of rich and poor" (ca. 1851: 116–17). "Therefore it is not a fairy-tale of anxious philologists," he concluded, "that Athens fell as a result of degenerate democracy" ([1854] 1906: §16). See also Schmoller [1912] 1920: 111.
26. Weber 1904: 464–7; [1923] 1924: 33–4. So wrong-headed were these measures, in fact, that Weber counted the resulting open-field hodgepodge as prima facie proof that they predated the emergence of strong executive government.
27. Roscher ca. 1851: 115–17; Sombart [1924] 1927: 58–9. On the Tocquevillean reservations of the Austrian economists in particular, see Fuchs, *Geistige Strömungen in Österreich, 1867–1918* (1949): ch. 1; and especially Nyiri, "The Intellectual Foundations of Austrian Liberalism" (1986).

ing in oligarchy and enervation of the body politic.[28] Various economists quoted Pliny's verdict that *Latifundia perdidere Italiam* ["The great estates were Italy's perdition"] and noted that a functional democracy would never have permitted the balance of economic power to become so skewed that the polity faced its own liquidation.[29] And yet the pattern had been repeated again and again, right up to the present. Modern British politics, Laveleye noted ominously, constituted "an exact repetition of the history of property at Rome" ([1874] 1878: 242). Similarly, Weber's early studies of contemporary Germany's great East Elbian estates led him to conclude that neither the Junkers nor the "petty-bourgeois" [*Spießbürgerlich*] social-democratic or liberal parties could be trusted to put the national interest (i.e., in this case, "depolonization" and recolonization with Germans) ahead of their short-term material gain: a conclusion not at all far from the analysis of his dissertation on the history of Roman agriculture, which also pinned much blame on an unholy legislative alliance between the patriciate and urban commercial interests, which succeeded in commodifying landed property.[30]

Successful democracy, in short, demanded national qualities that were quite beyond the reach of most societies; and those few that were able to square the circle for a time were forever challenged to preserve the delicate

28. B. Hildebrand, "Die sociale Frage der Vertheilung des Grundeigenthums im klassischen Althertum" (1869): 13–25, 139–52.

29. The political problem of antiquity (roughly, the Polybian cycle) was explored by Knies [1853] 1883: 182–90; Schäffle [1858] 1873: §21; Laveleye [1874] 1878: 160–74; Roesler 1878: 91–6; George 1879: 372–4; Schmoller 1901–4, §§125–6, 131; Oppenheimer [1907] 1914: 121–73, 285–7. Roesler, e.g., noted that as a result of Stoic and plebeian influences, "The collectivity of the [Roman] nation lost possession of the political power which they had held according to the republican constitution; that power passed into the hands of the politically powerful minority, the oligarchy, which was also dominant in terms of wealth. This was the road to the Republic's collapse" (1878: 96).

Similar results were gleaned from the ethnological literature by Bücher (1879: 281, 311–13; 1914: 88–9); and Baumstark (1865: 93–113).

30. Weber, *Die römische Agrargeschichte in ihrer Bedeutung für das Staats- und Privatrecht* (1891). Weber's documents on the East Elbian question (composed 1892–97 for the Verein für Sozialpolitik) are neatly summarized in Keith Tribe's "Prussian Agriculture – German Politics: Max Weber 1892–97" (1983). Weber also doubted the value of village democracy along the lines of the Russian *obschina,* since these in practice tended to become the suborned creatures of the local *kulak* class ([1923] 1924: 32–3).

Wieser did not see British parliamentarism as a problem in Britain; but he, too, thought that it would be a grave error to import it wholesale to countries – specifically, to Austria – where it was not naturalized [*Über Vergangenheit und Zukunft der österreichischen Verfassung* (1905): 155–7].

synthesis of vigilance and self-denial, since institutional success seemed to carry the seeds of its own reversal. Sooner or later, Schmoller observed,

> the spirit of sacrifice, of dedication to the common good, re-
> treats or disappears. The traditional ideals fade, . . . the acquisi-
> tive drive takes on new, mostly ugly forms, becoming greed and
> social insensitivity. Class struggles begin; softness, luxury and he-
> donism penetrate the younger generations, at the same time that
> industriousness, martial spirit and commitment to duty dimin-
> ish. (1901–4: §276)

The result was political sclerosis – what he called (quoting Bagehot) "a hard-baked cake of customs and laws" – and the end of progress.

Of the economists who remained nonetheless convinced of the representative ideal's ultimate soundness, many were led to tinker at its margins: like Veblen, who suggested that parliamentarism could serve to obviate many of the drawbacks of direct democracy; or Schäffle, who favored a corporative legislature with representation on the basis of economic function, rather than an individual franchise.[31] Other meliorist democrats faced the problem of political culture squarely, like Wagner when he asserted that the roots of better institutional performance lay "in the moral, the intellectual, and especially in the economic edification of the *Volk,* in the moral self-discipline of all economic classes, and in a properly orga-nized, competently operating organ of popular representation, along with good administration" ([1876] 1892–4: 2:§121). Or Bücher (1902: 21), whose study of the Swiss example led him to conclude that truly demo-cratic legislation would create the conditions of its own success, by assur-ing all popular elements a stake in the common enterprise. But more com-mon still was the conclusion that representation was more the stuff of pious hopes than of workable political platforms. For this larger group, the visible hand of government would, in many cases, best be the mailed fist of authority.

## V     Authority

The authoritarian ideal has a long pedigree in the history of eco-nomic thought. Whatever their differences over policy, eighteenth-century theorists like James Steuart in Scotland, the Physiocrats in France, the German cameralists, and even a goodly number of German Smithians, shared an infatuation with the possibility that the awesome power of des-potism could be harnessed by right reason as a force for the social good. This idea went into remission during the age of high liberalism, and conse-

---

31. Veblen, Review of Kautsky, *Der Parlamentarismus, die Volksgesetzgebung und die Socialdemokratie* (1894); Schäffle [1858] 1873: §279.

quently it is seldom met with in literature from the first half of our period of study. But after about 1870 the authoritarian idea resurfaced, most strikingly (and predictably, if only with hindsight) in the writings of German and Austrian economists.

The value of strong executive government was clearest when the alternative was self-interested rule by cabal. As noted above, oligarchy's putative evils were not limited to the redistribution of wealth from poor to rich; it was also thought to behave rather like the sorcerer's apprentice, releasing social and economic demons which threatened its own survival, but before which it was powerless to act constructively. List, for example, favored representative government in principle, but he acknowledged that there were times of such institutional degeneracy – or, more precisely, arrested institutional development – that the republican form was not equal to its tasks. "In such a state of affairs," he wrote in 1841,

> the constitution guarantees not simply the interests of the nation, but also the permanence of the regnant social ills. But it is in the interest and the nature of the absolutist form of government to stamp out those ills; with it is afforded the possibility that a ruler who excels in power and insight may come to power, one who will advance the nation by centuries and who will assure national survival and progress for all time to come.[32]

Sixty years later, Schmoller agreed: in such moments of extremity the "genial dictator" was called for, the "strong monarchical power" that would take matters in hand and restore social peace (1901–4: §132). Bruno Hildebrand saw this ideal type of the messianic lawgiver incarnated in Sparta's Lycurgus, Athens's Solon, and Rome's imperial Caesars.[33] The occasional successes of early modern absolutism lent some substance to this vision as well. It was a hidden blessing, argued Bücher, that so much of the European continent escaped the grasp of expansionist city-states: for while the zones that did fall under urban hegemony (principally in Italy) were visited with aristocratic exploitation of the harshest sort, the more feudal backwaters were saved by the eventual rise of territorial princes, whose holistic "state concept" [*Staatsgedanke*] was more nearly coextensive with the public interest.[34] For German economists in particular, the peasant protection policies of Austria under Maria Theresa and Joseph II, and especially of Prussia under the Hohenzollern, needed only be compared

---

32. List [1841] 1930: 341–4, citing the authority of Machiavelli. List's favorite examples of enlightened absolutism were France under Colbert (120–3), and Russia under the modern Tsars (147).
33. B. Hildebrand 1869: 13–15, 18–25, 139–52. See also Roesler 1878: 97.
34. Bücher [1893] 1910: 134–5. See also Laveleye [1874] 1878: 249; Roesler 1878: 110; Wieser [1914] 1923: §§75, 77.

to the "Junker republics" surrounding them to prove what a difference an enlightened despot makes.[35] Small wonder, then, that so many of them also looked upon the new German Empire with equanimity, to say the least, and that Wieser advocated the adoption of its authoritarian constitution in his native Austria (1905: 17, 155–7; 1910: 95–102).

Rather more daring, but nevertheless common, was the suggestion that authority might be a welcome alternative even to consensual or representative government. According to Loria ([1893] 1910: 117, 123–4) and Pareto (1896–7: §659), excessive political liberty could work to the detriment of a relatively underdeveloped society: a despot (especially, noted Loria, one kept sweet by his tax base's easy exit to adjacent states) would pursue the public interest by enforcing the sort of associations and divisions of labor upon which individuals in a homogeneous bargaining nexus are so seldom able to agree by their own devices. More generally, authority could be a valuable corrective to the failures of democracy outlined above. In contrast to democracy, wrote Hasbach, where "irrational forces" seize the affairs of state, the prince and his counselors could serve as a bulwark of calm reflection (1912: 579); likewise for Wieser, collective action usually demanded "forceful leadership and the subordination of the masses, if effort is to be crowned with success."[36]

Again, history seemed to offer some support to this view. Bücher argued that the iron authoritarianism of the Inca state had produced results far superior to what the Andean people (admittedly, a people of exceptionally slight "intellectual initiative," who were all too happy to submit to coercion) could have achieved on their own (1879: 313); according to Loria, the ancient Asiatic despotisms achieved much the same results – thanks, in this case, largely to sharp competition among rulers for peasant clients ([1893] 1910: 123–4). Regarding Europe, Meitzen found the ancient patriarchal Celtic clan resistant to the sort of public-choice dysfunctions from which the German tribal assemblies suffered, in demonstration of which he proffered an example from Irish history. Around A.D. 600, Meitzen wrote, Ireland's growing population and the availability of improved agricultural practices conjoined in a striking case for privatization of the vast tracts of land which had hitherto been collective property. But while Germany – which was more developed, and therefore had reached this crisis stage some centuries earlier – long labored under the burden of political bargaining in the public sphere, the powerful Irish chieftains cut the Gordian knot by simple fiat. Subordinate households in the clan were al-

---

35. Schmoller, "Der Kampf des preußischen Königthums um die Erhaltung des Bauernstands" (1888a): 254–5; Knapp 1891: 348–9; 1894: 414; Fuchs 1898a: 299; Miaskowski 1890: 17–19.
36. Wieser [1914] 1923: §77; see also Schmoller [1912] 1920: 111.

lotted sufficient land in freehold so that they gained in economic security and independence, while the chieftain compensated his own loss of social leverage by reserving some of the clan land as demesne. Thus was what we today call a "Pareto" improvement achieved straightaway; Germany, by contrast, had to await the articulation of its own lordly class, each lord plenipotentiary in his own bailiwick, before its commons could follow economic logic into the private sphere (1895: 1:167–8, 194–7).

But again, the pitfalls of authoritarian legislation could appear every bit as daunting as those of representative government. The vision of benevolent despotism was recognized as begging the central question: to wit, why a despot should willingly (and despots, by definition, act *only* willingly) keep to the narrow path of benevolence. The facile absolutist syllogism – fathers are patently benevolent, government is but fatherhood writ large, ergo rulers are benefactors writ large – was therefore discounted, for example by Schäffle, who argued that "a patriarch, an individual or a cadre of notables, if it knows and loves its constituency and possess thereby a natural legal authority for it, creates law and brings it into general recognition with the greatest of ease; whereas the distant and cold-tempered state is unable to achieve anything of the sort."[37] Even Wieser, by and large a defender of authority, had to acknowledge the likelihood that it would run beyond the writ of public interest: "The superiority of the leadership, securing success to the masses, results in power to the leaders. This power ultimately becomes autocracy, despotism. The lament that the people are oppressed by the powers whose efficacy is the gift of those who become its victims, is as old as the history of the human race" ([1914, 1923] 1928: §76). Another, more hopeful way of posing the problem was to recognize, like Schmoller, as a necessary condition for institutional success that "the strong, great individuals seek satisfaction not in small-minded egoism, not in greed and hedonism, but in broad political ambition, in dedication to great common goals" (1901–4: §276). But like Wagner's program for vibrant democracy quoted above, this pious credo betrayed more than a little anxiety.

Once again, history was called upon to testify to the misadventures of authoritarian legislation. For Wieser, the vessels of republican Rome's greatness were indeed her dictators, her magistrates, and her jurists; but the true wellspring of that greatness was the virtue of the nation itself, its "self-discipline, its greatness of will, its power to obey and to rule." The Civil Code, Rome's finest gift to posterity, was consequently also "a super-

37. Schäffle 1875–8: 1:658. This jibes with Schäffle's general observation that the absolutist state prefers above all to play social classes off against one another, to its own exclusive benefit ([1858] 1873: §279).

lative achievement of unshakably firm will, . . . a will that successfully shunned the cacophony of passion, in order that the logic of judgement could be heard." Thus did the value of Roman authority depend critically on the mettle of the citizens; and thus also, when conquests led to incorporation of peoples unfit for so demanding a political culture, was the republic doomed to militarization, overcentralization, and ultimately extinction.[38] Other economists stressed the malfeasance – by cupidity, overcaution, or sheer ignorance – of the modern absolutisms. Subjected to criticism were not only such bêtes noires as Turkey, Spain, and Russia[39] but also the monarchs and bureaucrats of England, Germany, Austria, and even Hawaii.[40]

## VI     Advice to the world-weary

So at the end of the day the economists, for all their claimed insights into the mainspring of social action, could not set aright the central conundrum of life within the state. We might well expect that the realization of this hard truth, and the disillusionment that it brings in tow, would be a life-cycle phenomenon, striking economists each in midcareer so that at any moment in time the discipline would harbor both young Promethians and aging skeptics. In fact, though, this does not seem to have been the case. Impatience with traditional political formulas seems to have set in only in the last quarter of the nineteenth century, reaching a crescendo early in the twentieth. Among the many latter-day economists who did not turn for solace to a specious political *Wertfreiheit,* three trends may be identified in the normative science of legislation.

First, there is some evidence that by the twentieth century, institutional economists were finally coming round to the belief – long maintained by their colleagues in the law faculties – that fraught points of institutional

38. Wieser [1901] 1929: 366. Rome's latter-day weakness, Wieser believed, was the inheritance of all modern states. It was therefore as a check against this danger of military centralism, rather than out of any special affection for representative government, that Wieser advocated on principle "the development of healthy, powerful parties," which would wield some veto power over executive decisions. He held up as a model the excellence of the Viennese "republic of music" [*Musikstaat*], where creative activity was the preserve of the composers, and yet final power of fame and obscurity rested with an engaged and vigilant audience ([1901] 1929: 350–1; 1905: 5–6, 170).
39. List [1841] 1930: 106–17; Roscher ca. 1851: 124; [1854] 1906: §87; Wieser [1901] 1929: 366–7; Simkovich 1909: 603–5.
40. Bücher 1879: 281; Knapp 1894: 419–27; Hadley 1896: 133; Brentano [1901] 1923: 64; Bücher 1902: 7–8; Wieser [1914] 1923: §76.

selection might best be left to a judicial mandarinate. Through most of the period under consideration, this was not a creditable idea within the new science. As noted in chapter 1, in fact, denunciation of traditional jurisprudence was something of a ritual ablution concomitant to an economist's declaration of the sociological outlook. At best, jurists had been seen as blinkered by their rarified training; at worst, they were the servants of raw power, what Loria called "the most implacable enemies of the laboring classes and the most zealous defenders of feudal and capitalistic usurpation."[41]

Slowly, the animus toward lawyers began to ebb. In large part this must have been due to another phenomenon noted in chapter 1, namely, the rise of "legal realism" or "sociological jurisprudence," which led to conclusions very much in keeping with the new science in economics. Additionally, the growing intervention of American economists in this discourse may have militated toward this same end, since in the United States the apparent successes of the case law method suggested that it might really be possible to establish a mandarinate, that is, a technocracy of the law which would offer the decisiveness of executive rule, plus the benefits of specialized training, minus the susceptibility to corruption. Such, at least, was the message of Homer Hoyt's 1918 article "The Economic Functions of the Common Law." Hoyt did not deny a role for legislation, but he insisted that judge-made law, duly constrained by precedent, also played a vital – and dangerously underappreciated – part in maximizing joint economic values. On the one hand, by throwing sand in the wheels of legal change, precedent helped individual agents calculate the consequences of their decisions, helped all agents in the mutual adaptation of expectations and behavior, and ultimately lowered the costs of compliance and enforcement.[42] On the other hand, and more significantly in the long view, Hoyt lauded common-law procedures for facilitating incremental change in the legal order, in accordance with "the spirit of the times":

> Judges are instructed by the theory of the common law to construe liberally statutes in favor of common usage, and to construe strictly statutes in derogation of that common usage. Thus

41. Loria [1893] 1910: 107. See also List [1841] 1930: 103, 127–8; Roscher ca. 1851: 113; Knies [1853] 1883: 181; Scheel, "Die wirtschaftlichen Grundbegriffe im Corpus juris Civilis" (1866): 343–4; Schmoller [1874–5] 1898: 72; Schäffle 1875–8: 3:384–5; Wagner [1876] 1892–4: §20; Scheel 1877: 10–11; Menger [1883] 1985: 232.

42. Hoyt 1918: 187. To quote him: "Common law decisions leave tracks in the legal wilderness. If these tracks establish a beaten trail by the constant travelling over the same route, the public has no difficulty in following, just as by constant repetition an old principle wears a pathway in our mental processes, so that obedience to it becomes instinctive."

a change in the face of the average standards of the community
is resisted to the uttermost, while the statute designed to bring
the common law in line with the development of community
standards is aided in every possible way.[43]

In short, although judge-made law was undeniably authoritarian in some
sense, its evolutionary path "is neither made by nor for the benefit of any
autocracy, but is made by the masses for their own benefit" (196).

Hoyt's position on the common law was quite close to the one later
enunciated, far more famously, by John Commons in *The Legal Foundations of Capitalism* (1924). "The common law," according to Commons,
"did not signify *any* kind of custom or habit whatsoever, but only those
customs and habits which had been followed as guides in the decision of
disputes and were therefore the approved, good and workable customs to
the exclusion of bad and disruptive practices."[44] At the highest level of
abstraction, Commons held that the judicial mandarinate served something approaching the normative function of the hypothetical auctioneer
in neoclassical economics: "The courts, in their decisions, endeavor, by
means of common rules, to make the nominal value or prices, represent,
as nearly as practicable, the psychological value, or anticipation, and the
real value, or quantity, of commodities and services. Their goal is a scheme
of 'reasonable value'" (1924: 9). Shorn of social-scientific jargon, Commons's point was that under the judicial mandarinate "every transaction
is weighed at every point according to what is deemed to be a public purpose."[45] This sentiment has found resonance throughout the "law and economics" movement of the later twentieth century, albeit with more conviction among jurists than economists.

43. Hoyt 1918: 194. This position was presaged in Courcelle-Seneuil's introduction to the first French edition of Maine's *Ancient Society*. Courcelle-Seneuil
acknowledged the theory of natural law as "the noblest and most important
of the conceptions within which civilization has developed." He insisted, however, that natural jurisprudence at its best was not founded on a speculative
reconstruction of the primal state, but on the critical study of historical experience in order to distill universal truths: law "from the ground up," as it were,
along the lines of the jus gentium (1874: xix).
44. Commons 1924: 136–7. In support of this proposition Commons adduced the
1602 Case of Monopolies, as well as various decisions on legal tender and
female and child labor (227, 242–3, 329). This aspect of Commons's thought
was applauded by Karl Diehl in *Die rechtlichen Grundlagen des Kapitalismus*
(1929): esp. 21–2. It is surely significant, in this connection, that the title of
Diehl's book was an exact German rendition of Commons's *Legal Foundations
of Capitalism.*
45. Commons 1924: 326. Commons did, however, acknowledge that judges could
make mistakes and (especially) fall behind the times (55–6).

If recourse to technocracy was one way of vaulting the horns of the political dilemma, then the second answer was more daring still: it questioned openly whether the social and economic "body" really needed to be governed by an overarching "mind" in the first place. Recall that earlier in this chapter we raised this possibility of spontaneous legal order, only to dismiss it as a nonstarter in the opinion of most of our economists. But spontaneous law held a certain appeal for some economists throughout these decades, and its appeal broadened with the passing years.

As we portrayed (or caricatured) it above, society without a single sovereign state was generally recognized as a political free-for-all. Lacking all constitutional sanction against cabalism and coercion, it seemed to abandon the field of legislation to precisely those human impulses which the law was meant to tether. But it was also possible, with only a modicum of imagination, to divine loftier principles at work in spontaneous institutional selection. The conceptual leap was to accept that valuable rules might emerge quite independently of conscious design, as social equilibria arrived at and adjusted through processes of discovery, rivalry, and ad hoc negotiation. To say that a law was "irrational," in other words, was not tantamount to calling it bad.

Skeptical as it was of the more extreme rationalist claims, it is not surprising that this jurisprudential philosophy drew more on the lessons of history than on first principles and thought experiments. Carl Menger captured the spirit of this endeavor in an appendix to his *Investigations on Method* (1883) titled "The 'Organic' Origin of Law and the Exact Understanding Thereof." At the dawn of civilization, Menger emphasized, law was not "the expression of the organized *total will* of the nation."

> Still much less was it realized as the result of the reflection of an individual, or even of a national council, aimed at the welfare of all. It arose, rather, *in the minds of the individual members of the population* with the increasing awareness of *their interest, the individuals' interest.* What benefits all, or at least the far greater majority, gradually is realized by all.

In effect, laws developed to maximize joint value through the offices of what we today might term a "Rawlsian veil," which enforced civil peace not by Leviathan but by enlightened self-interest in a fluid environment. But its value was not limited to primitive, undifferentiated societies. To the contrary, spontaneously generated law "broadens and deepens gradually with increasing intercourse and the growing insight of individuals into their interests. It is affirmed by custom and is shaken and finally altered by the change of those conditions to which it owes its origin."[46] An organized state would be hard pressed to do so well.

46. Menger [1883] 1985: app. VIII; Schmoller [1874–5] 1898: 47–8 may be read to

As early as the 1860s and 1870s, Hans von Scheel had argued vaguely that "multifarious, organically growing" economic institutions of this sort were peculiar to the ancient Germans, in contradistinction to the Roman tradition of statutory law and the "doctrinaire legislation" of modern rationalists, neither of which were embedded in the needs of livelihood like the Ur-German alternative (1866: 343–4; 1877: 10–11). Around the turn of this century the heterodox antilegislative interpretation of tribal politics came to be stated more forcefully and in greater detail. Meitzen's empiricist survey of 1895 laid some groundwork for these claims, for instance by arguing that the sparsely settled Finnish nation had managed to establish functional property rights without first erecting a sovereign state – indeed, without regular social intercourse of any kind (1895: 2:193–4). Meitzen reaffirmed, however, the conventional wisdom that Teutonic politics had stood out as a precocious instance of constitutional democracy. Not so Richard Hildebrand, who argued that the individuals wielding authority within the German tribes (the people Julius Caesar had called their *magistratus ac principes*) did so not on the basis of any constitutional enablement, but merely because they could:

> In peacetime . . . there were no authorities outfitted with executive powers stipulated for specific ends, but *only de facto power brokers* [Machthaber] *or chieftains . . .* whose *influence* was *purely personal* and which therefore did not extend *beyond kinship. . . .* The prince was characterized by "heft and status," not "office and dignity."

Hildebrand's point was that jurists (including Maurer, Gierke, Brunner, and Schröder), historians (Sybel, Below, and Lamprecht), and economists (Hanssen, Laveleye, and Bücher) had alike mistaken for political cooperation [*Genossenschaft*] something quite different: political dominance [*Herrschaft*].

> Among the ancient Germans at the time of Caesar, at least, there was as yet no "state" (not even the so-called "gentile state" [*Geschlechterstaat*]), no municipality [*Gemeinde*], no "officeholders," no "citizens." . . . We are dealing here with a personal exercise of influence . . . which mocks every juristic construct.

"It is curious that the modern citizen cannot imagine life at primitive stages of development without a 'constitution,'" Hildebrand concluded, "and never even raises the question of why one would be required" ([1896]

---

broadly similar effect. Menger did not believe that his analysis was a mere reformulation of historicist orthodoxy. At another point in his study, he criticized the "historical" (and Classical) economists, as well as the historical jurists, for having neglected this mechanism of institutional selection ([1883] 1985: book 4, ch. 2).

1907: 66–76, 107, 121–2). This was an analysis that Werner Wittich (1897: 59), reviewing Hildebrand's book for the *Historische Zeitschrift,* called "fully accurate."

Classical antiquity too could be cited in support of the spontaneist position; for notwithstanding the florescence of sovereignty in that era, the state was hard pressed to keep up with the growth of commerce beneath and beyond its purview. According to Courcelle-Seneuil, the competition between purely Roman law, which often became hostage to legislative dysfunction, and the jus gentium, which developed gradually within the geopolitical interstices of the age, was illustrative of a basic principle of modernization: valuable property rights tended to develop, largely, "thanks to the diversity of states and régimes" (1878: 174–6). In the classical age and ever since, he argued, doctors of natural law have not reasoned axiomatically so much as they have "taken inspiration from this grand and continuous phenomenon of commerce, and have introduced its principles bit by bit into the City" (1874: xvi–xix).

But the locus classicus of spontaneous law was bound to be the Middle Ages, not classical antiquity. In the process, oligarchy came as close to legitimacy as it ever would, as when Pareto argued that aristocracy was often the most formidable enemy of despotism, such that "one can say, in a certain sense, that the peoples owed their liberty to their aristocracies."[47] Likewise decentralization – even disorganization – was duly rehabilitated. As Weber explained it, under medieval conditions

> [the] very elements of "backwardness" in the logical and governmental aspects of legal development enabled business to produce a far greater wealth of practically useful legal devices than had been available under the more logical and technically more highly rationalized Roman law. Quite generally one may observe that those special institutions which, like those of medieval commercial law, were particularly well suited for the emerging modern capitalism, could arise more easily in the context of a society which, for political reasons, produced a variety of bodies of law corresponding to the needs of different interest groups. ([1922] 1978: II, ch. 8, §ii.4)

Similarly, Pareto lauded the institutional flexibility and progressivity of the ancient and medieval "associations" that had mediated between the individual and the state.[48] In step as state sovereignty revived – indeed,

---

47. Pareto 1896–7: §659. See also Bücher [1893] 1910: 107.
48. Pareto 1896–7: §660. Therefore, Pareto noted, elimination of these "intermediary organisms" was a top priority of effective despotisms.

according to Meitzen, as early as the consolidation of Carolingian hegemony – these advantages dissipated.[49]

Although modernity was no golden age for spontaneous law, to the extent that such law survived it was appreciated as a continuing force for good, even in the more advanced territorial states. On the one hand, much good law had survived from earlier centuries. As Wieser explained, "The essential part of the prevailing, private economic system is unwritten law, and survives by its inherent power."

> That this salient component of the social constitution should
> have remained unwritten law, can be explained only from the
> fact that it possesses the incisive power of sound historical evolution. The private economic constitution has attained unchallenged authority, which was its own even before the beginning
> of the capitalistic era, because of its historical success. ([1914,
> 1923] 1928: §75)

Here Wieser was following the lead of his teacher Menger, who had also argued that the "organic" component of the legal corpus "advances the welfare of society . . . perhaps to a greater degree than any social institution which is the work of human intention and calculation." ([1883] 1985: app. VIII). Even the diplomatic system of nation-states was not proof against the felicitous evolution of rules to meet social needs: as Schäffle noted, the articulation of international law on the basis of ad hoc diplomacy had yielded far better results than could be expected from any supranational, plenipotentiary "World Areopagus," which would inevitably become the cat's-paw of the great powers.[50]

What lesson did this history hold for contemporary society? Above all else, it was that the modern state's legislative competencies had somehow to be circumscribed. According to Marshall, for instance, the evolutionary perspective taught that "it is the part of responsible men to proceed cau-

---

49. Meitzen 1895: 1:121. In this Meitzen was following Justus Möser's well-known (and oft-applauded) indictment of high feudalism in his *Osnabrückische Geschichte* (1768): "Lost was even the name and the true conception of property, and the entire imperial realm was transformed everywhere into feudal estates, leaseholds, copyholds, and peasant farms, as it pleased the head of the Empire and his vassals" (translated in Knudsen 1986: 104–5). On the anti-imperial, antipapal, corporatist [*ständisch*] legacy of the German Enlightenment in general, see Reill 1975: ch. 1.

50. Schäffle 1875–8: 1:652–3. Courcelle-Seneuil had praised the international law of commerce in similar terms: "This law, uniform for all nations, is destined to replace gradually the diverse civil laws and to become the ordinary common law of all civilized peoples, the human law *par excellence*" ([1858] 1891: vol. 2, book 1, ch. 1, §6).

tiously and tentatively in abrogating or modifying even such rights as may seem to be inappropriate to the ideal conditions of social life" ([1890] 1895: book 1, ch. 4, §6). Arguing more forcefully, Pareto put this point in terms any economist could understand. He derided both popular socialists and *Kathedersozialisten* for apotheosizing a state believed, wrongly, to possess "all power, all science, all virtue"; in truth, "it is to free competition that one must leave the task of eliminating imperfect [institutions], and to propagate the best ones" (1896–7: §§655, 659). Even some of these *Kathedersozialisten* themselves recognized the value of customary and unmediated rules and believed that the virtuous state would afford them due latitude (Schäffle 1875–8: 1:654–9; Schmoller 1901–4: §29).

The third development, and the most radical departure by far, was the suggestion that the very problem of optimal jurisprudence was gradually being obviated by the inexorable march of progress. To a large extent, this proposition was part and parcel of the model outlined in chapter 3 as "After *homo oeconomicus*," whereby man's intellectual and ideological evolution had begun to purge civilization – and would purge it further in the future – of those rules which reflected the iron logic of crass egoism. To be sure, in that context the implication was one of law *becoming better,* not of it *withering away;* and the earlier contributors to the discussion stuck to that vision. Theirs especially was to consider the tonic influences of Christianity and Natural Jurisprudence, but they did not seriously consider the possibility of human perfection paving the way for harmonic anarchy. Not so some of the later generation. Loria, for one, implied as much in his evocation of primitive harmony, a harmony which, like Marx, he believed would be regained once society had been prised from the grip of capital. In a society of true equals, Loria asserted, "the law simply amounts to a technical classification of the acts and abstentions which are to the advantage of the citizens of the state." Individuals would submit to these "laws" without prompting or sanction, because such would be their interest ([1893] 1910: 78–9).

   This vision was possible even without presupposing, as did Loria and Marx, enforced social equality. Writers like Schmoller (1901–4: §29) and Emil Sax (1887: 162), who saw the emergence of mutualism, altruism, and conscience as essential aspects of higher social evolution, tended accordingly to predict the gradual superannuation of that fetter on man's predatory nature, law. As Schmoller put it, liberalism had misread the course of social evolution as prescribing greater individual freedom from collective constraint; socialism, conversely, erred in predicting a future where collective purpose would override personal whim. In fact, the coming millennium was one where people's ethical sense would be so highly developed that they no longer sought to trespass on the rights of others. With this the age of law would yield to the age of morality.

Technocracy; spontaneous order; the power of progress to resolve contradiction: these themes of "advice to the world-weary" will be immediately recognized as the economist's stock-in-trade. Thus we may cautiously conclude that the new normative science, even having renounced the strict contractarianism most in keeping with economic axioms, nevertheless remained within their gravitational field. On the other hand, by venturing into constitutional philosophy in the first place, these economists – or at least some subset of them – may well and truly have gone beyond their sociological brief, to indulge in the sort of speculative, tendentious argument that has branded institutional economics, rightly or wrongly, to this day. It is therefore an opportune moment to turn to the final questions motivating this study: What influence did the economists' new science exert beyond its own circle? Why was its standing so truncated within economics in the decades after 1930? Can we expect its star to rise again over the academic horizon?

# 5

## The way to oblivion

It is difficult to measure the true impact of the economists' new science on other disciplines, or on succeeding generations of economists. Much of the problem is that the movement's leitmotifs – institutional evolution, rationalism, materialism, civic virtue – were generally "in the air" at that time. Thus there exists, on the one hand, the danger of neglecting lines of real influence which ran not directly and acknowledged, but rather were mediated through a common, largely anonymous fund of intellectual capital. On the other hand, there stands the converse danger of specious credit, of assigning the new science influence by the mere fact of its correlation with developments elsewhere, when in fact those developments might have proceeded apace even in the hypothetical absence of the economists' contribution.

Our accounting in this chapter will be less ambitious than the "atmospheric" approach, and I hope less prone to error. Insofar as is possible, we shall reason on the basis of things explicitly said of the new science and its practitioners, and to a lesser extent on the basis of conspicuous silences. The new science was not without its admirers; but the weight of evidence in this chapter will point to indifference, verging into open hostility. We will document this fact by examining in sequence several disciplines which were potentially amenable to the new science's approach: history (section I), the "younger" social sciences (sociology, anthropology, etc., in section II), jurisprudence (section III), and economics itself (section IV). Conclusions follow in section V.

The new science approached oblivion via a number of paths. Enumeration of those paths will be a task for the pages to follow. For now suffice it to emphasize two overarching themes, one external to the new science per se, the other internal to it. The external factor is the professionalization of social inquiry. The economists under study gloried in a heroic phase of social science, when old disciplinary boundaries were freely breached and a grand, unified theory of man seemed to be taking shape. Over the past century, however, beauty has increasingly been found in specialism. Consequently scholarly boundaries have been more jealously guarded, and interdisciplinary boldness has come to be viewed as crass dilettantism. The internal factor, which will be explored in section IV below, was the rhetorical excesses and the analytical imprecision which grew increasingly prominent in the work of later practitioners of the new science. Either one of these forces alone would have posed a grave threat to the integrity and status of the new science; together, they were a sure recipe for its demise.

## I    History

The clearest avenue for the new science's penetration into the historical profession was through the budding specialty of economic history. In historians like Georg von Below, Karl Lamprecht, Henri Pirenne, and Eberhard Gothein, the economists' approach to law found an attentive, if not uncritical, audience. Lamprecht, for example, studied economics under Hanssen, wrote his dissertation under Roscher's direction, and was in his turn instrumental in recruiting Bücher to Leipzig University's growing circle of interdisciplinary scholars.[1] Lamprecht's quest for a grand unified social history was shared also by Ludwig Felix, who hoped that his multivolume comparative study of property would be "welcomed by the friends of not only economic, but also historical studies,"[2] and by the legal historian Paul Vinogradoff. In his history *Villainage in England* (1892), indeed, Vinogradoff announced that the evolution of legal historiography toward social science was well-nigh complete:

> Historians are in quest of laws of development and of generalisations that shall unravel the complexity of human culture, as phys-

1. This "Leipzig Circle" included also Friedrich Ratzel, Wilhelm Wundt, and Wilhelm Ostwald. See Roger Chickering's *Karl Lamprecht* (1993): 294; and W. Smith 1991: 204–18. Chickering argues further that, despite the disciplinary boundary separating them, Roscher remained the great formative influence on Lamprecht's thought (50–1).
2. Felix, *Entwicklungsgeschichte des Eigenthums unter kulturgeschichtlichem und wirtschaftlichem Gesichtspunkte* (1883): 1:vi. Among economists, Felix drew most heavily on the works of Hanssen, Roscher, Laveleye, and Meitzen.

ical and biological generalisations have put into order our knowledge of the phenomenon of nature.

There is no subject more promising from this point of view than the history of social arrangements. It borders on political economy, which has already attained a scientific standing; part of its material has been fashioned by juridical doctrine and practical law, and thereby moulded into a clear, well-defined shape; it deals with facts recurring again and again with much uniformity, and presenting great facilities for comparison; the objects of its observation are less complex than the phenomena of human thought, morality, or even political organisation. (vi–viii)

This spirit of interdisciplinary endeavor found its way into histories of classical antiquity,[3] of the Middle Ages,[4] and of early modern Europe.[5]

Across the Atlantic, the same process was helping to shape the thought of two American historians, Frederick Jackson Turner and Charles A. Beard. Turner's biographers have identified his intellectual debt to Francis A. Walker, to his Wisconsin colleague Ely, and especially to Loria, who had anticipated his "frontier thesis" and with whom Turner maintained

3. Ettore Ciccotti's *Il tramonto della schiavitù nel mondo antico* (1899), e.g., referred readers to Cairnes, Rogers, and Marx. More strikingly still, Karl Johannes Neumann's *Die Grundherrschaft der römischen Republik* (1900) averred that G. F. Knapp's work on Prussian manorialism and its dissolution would serve well as a template for antiquity: his revision of the Roman experience was founded "not on new source materials, but rather on rigorous consideration of the view of agrarian history that I owe to my honored colleague Knapp, who has become my teacher" (36–8).

4. E.g., references to the work of Hanssen, Nasse, Inama-Sternegg, Bücher, Rogers, Wittich, Meitzen, and others may be found in the following historical works: Frederic Seebohm, *The English Village Community Examined in Its Relations to the Manorial and Tribal Systems and to the Common or Open Field System of Husbandry* (1883); Georg von Below, "Der Osten und der Westen Deutschlands: Der Ursprung der Gutsherrschaft" (1900); Felix Rachfahl, "Zur Geschichte des Grundeigentums" (1900); Maksim Kovalevskii, *Die ökonomische Entwicklung Europas bis zum Beginn der kapitalistischen Wirtschaftsform* (1901–14); Gaillard T. Lapsley, "The Origin of Property in Land" (1903); Hermann Wopfner, "Beiträge zur Geschichte der älteren Markgenossenschaft" (1912–13); and Howard L. Gray, *English Field Systems* (1915). We may note also that Ernst Bernheim's *Lehrbuch der historischen Methode* (1903: 633) alerted students to Schmoller's work in the economics of medieval law and politics.

5. See, e.g., Georg Grupp, "Die Anfänge der Geldwirtschaft" (1897); Below, "Unfreiheit" (1898); Lamprecht, "Geschichte des Grundbesitzes" (1910); and Jerome Blum, "The Rise of Serfdom in Eastern Europe" (1957).

an occasional correspondence.[6] Beard, whose *Economic Interpretation of the Constitution* (1913) fit even more snugly into the research program of the new science of law, wrote glowingly of Turner's approach, acknowledged the influence of Marx and Seligman, and was almost certainly familiar with the writings of Loria.[7]

But this ecumenical spirit was never to carry the day within the guild of historical scholarship. Predictably, the faults most often found were overgeneralization and evidentiary insouciance. In France the reaction against the economists' incursions into institutional history appears to have been rather mild, if we are to judge from Fustel de Coulanges's measured critique of Laveleye in the *Revue des Questions Historiques*. Fustel allowed that the comparative method was "infinitely fruitful; but only on condition that the facts which are compared have a real resemblance to one another, and that things which are widely different are not confused."[8] Alas, Laveleye's use of sources did not meet even this low standard:

> A story or sentence from some traveller is quoted about each of these nations. As to this I have one remark to make: there is nothing rarer or more difficult than an accurate observation. This truth, which is recognized in all other sciences, ought also to be recognised by every one who is dealing with history; for history is precisely that one of all the sciences in which observation is most difficult and demands the greatest attention. (Fustel de Coulanges [1889] 1891: 114)

Consequently, he advised social scientists to play to their strengths and leave history to the experts. When hypothesizing a law of social behavior or development, he warned,

> do not invoke history in its favor. Present your theory as an abstract idea which may be valuable, but with which history has nothing to do. Let us not have sham learning. In saying this I have at heart the interests of historical science. There is danger

6. See *The Early Writings of Frederick Jackson Turner* (1938): 71–2, 198; Fulmer Mood, "The Development of Frederick Jackson Turner as an Historical Thinker" (1943): 306–7; Lee Benson, "Achille Loria's Influence" (1950): 190–6. As Benson has put it, Loria "was the direct source of two of Turner's most important ideas, i.e. American evolution recapitulates all the stages of man's social and economic development, and the corollary that this recapitulation offers an invaluable scientific laboratory for the study of the past."

7. Beard [1913] 1935: xiii, 5, 15. Strong circumstantial evidence linking Beard to Loria is marshalled in Benson, *Turner and Beard* (1960): 106.

8. Fustel de Coulanges, "Le problème des origines de la propriété foncière" [1889] 1891: 129.

lest, from love of a theory, a whole series of errors should be forcibly thrust into history.[9]

In Germany the new science's confrontation with history was harder fought. In some measure this fact must be ascribed to the personality of Karl Lamprecht, the champion of nomothetic historiography and no stranger to bombast. Lamprecht's career was seen by many as a standing challenge to the "Prussian" school of history, that is, to the heirs of Ranke's textual method and his idea of the state as historical protagonist. In turn, Lamprecht's professional discredit in an acrimonious *Methodenstreit* bade ill for structuralist history (Chickering 1993: 149–61, 262–4). From the 1890s onward, German economic history was subordinated to the primacy of political events. Below, the dean of this new orthodoxy, was not coy about the shortcomings he perceived in the economists' approach to institutions. In 1897 he faulted Meitzen's competence in constitutional and administrative history (1897: 475); in 1901 he warned against "the errors of evolutionist fanaticism" evident in the works of Bruno Hildebrand, Bücher, Schmoller, and Sombart;[10] in 1903, he concluded that what Lamprecht and his allies were doing was not really history at all:

> When one sets oneself the goal of investigating the corresponding legal and economic institutions of the nations, and of collecting these correspondences methodically, the process of textual analysis and stipulation of individual facts – a process which Lamprecht views with contempt – cannot be dispensed with.[11]

At the Conference of German Historians held in Nuremberg in 1898, the ascendancy of Below's view was made patent. The occasion was Eberhard Gothein's paper "How Did the Manorial System [*Grundherrschaft*] Arise in Germany?" Although the immediate target of Gothein's criticism was the economist Wittich, he used the occasion to voice his more general objection to "the tendency of Moderns, and particularly of economists, to 'construct' historical development according to a biased principle." The

9.  Fustel de Coulanges [1889] 1891: 152. This sort of objection may be found also in Rioult de Neuville's review of Laveleye (for the same journal), and in Henri Sée's treatise *The Economic Interpretation of History* (1929): 114–15.
10. Below, "Über Theorien der wirtschaftlichen Entwicklung der Völker" (1901): 30. Against the economists' universalizing stage theories of development, Below maintained that "it is in fact the exceptions that are interesting, or at least not less important than the rules" (33).
11. Below, "Das kurze Leben einer vielgenannten Theorie" ([1903] 1926): 23. Below criticized Richard Hildebrand on the same grounds: "He values comparison too highly, and the direct interpretation of sources too little. . . . The broad view must be complemented with meticulous work in elucidation of concepts, and with reliable interpretation" (21).

ensuing discussion from the floor confirmed that Gothein's was the majority view.[12] As a rule, German historians kept to the high ground of scholarly rigor in their strictures against the economists' contributions.[13] But reading between the lines, one can only wonder what role ethnic pride may have played in reinforcing the historians' distaste for universalizing models. That this may have been operative is suggested by G. Liebe's comment, in reviewing Hildebrand's *Law and Custom,* that "the historian will protest against a conception of humanity so indiscriminate that it leave unexplained why the Germans have made history, whereas the Bashkirs have not" (1900: 286).

## II    The younger social sciences

Where traditional historians took exception to the new science, the other branches of social science – sociology, anthropology, social psychology, and the like – might likely have proved more receptive. For these disciplines, in their infancies at least, celebrated the same nomological approach to social knowledge that the economists practiced, and the historians regretted. Moreover, political economy, as the oldest and best established of the social sciences, enjoyed an institutional prestige which could not be ignored, if for no other reason than that it held sway over so much social-scientific talent. In the pantheon of modern sociology, for example, stand many men who held degrees or chairs in political economy (Weber, Pareto, Sombart, Schäffle, Loria, Oppenheimer, Stein, Wieser); and most of these men, in turn, we have encountered in previous chapters of this study.[14] Practitioners of the new science of law proved to be avid consumers of ethnological research, and there is at least some evidence that the favor was returned. H. J. Nieboer's *Slavery as an Industrial System: Ethnological Researches* (1900), for instance, maintained a plainly economistic explanatory model and referred freely to the contributions of Cairnes, Loria, Bagehot, Ashley, Cunningham, and Inama-Sternegg.

12.  Gothein, "Wie ist die Grundherrschaft in Deutschland Entstanden?" The paper and ensuing discussion were summarized in the *Zeitschrift für Kulturgeschichte* 5 (1898): 451–3. Only Lamprecht, apparently, defended the economists.

13.  See Eduard Meyer, "Die wirtschaftliche Entwicklung des Altertums" ([1895] 1910); Meyer, *Die Sklaverei im Altertum* ([1899] 1910): 210; Robert von Pöhlmann, *Geschichte des antiken Kommunismus und Sozialismus* (1893–1901): 1:4–6; J. F. Normano, "Karl Bücher: An Isolated Economist" (1931).

14.  On the link between economics and sociology, see Oppenheimer, "Nationalökonomie, Sociologie, Anthropologie" (1900); and Volker Kruse, "Von der historischen Nationalökonomie zur historischen Soziologie" (1990).

Similarly, in 1911 Max Moszkowski delivered a lecture to the Kiel Institute for World Economy entitled "On the Economic Life of the Primitive Peoples": though Moszkowski's talk was ostensibly an ethnological report of his observations in Southeast Asia, its model of the evolution of property rights bore the unmistakable imprint of the new science.[15]

But by and large, the economists' new science was not much more welcome in this milieu than among the historians. Occasionally the resistance was due to plain ignorance of the endeavors of the new science;[16] usually, the problem was more subtle. In the first place, the younger social sciences were imbued with the same synoptic vision of their subject that had led Comte to inveigh against partial approaches to knowledge.[17] Although

15. Moszkowski, *Vom Wirtschaftsleben der primitiven Völker* (1911). Moszkowski argued that at the lowest state of the "appropriatory economy" [*Raubwirtschaft*], man could survive simply by plunder of nature's abundant "capital," so that there was nothing to be gained from specifying title to the output. But there existed another class of objects, those made by human hands, over which property had *always* extended. Rights of this latter sort were functional, and "psychologically quite understandable," because in their absence natural acquisitiveness would lead individuals to try and ride free on the efforts of others. As society progressed to higher stages, each characterized by production more intensive in both labor and man-made capital, a widening role for private ownership of consumption goods and (especially) capital goods was assured. As Moszkowski put it, "The more effort one expends in an [agricultural] task, and the less certain is success, the more jealously will one stand guard over it, the less will one grant others a share in the fruits of this labor. At this point agrarian communism ceases" (5–36).

   See also the ethnological treatments of property in Edward Westermarck's *The Origin and Development of the Moral Ideas* (1906–8), which referred to Bagehot, R. Hildebrand, and J. S. Mill, and in Wilhelm Schmidt's *Das Eigentum auf den ältesten Stufen der Menschheit* (1937–42): 1:5–10, which referred to Laveleye, Bücher, Hanssen, Roscher, Lewinski, Wagner, and others.

   In the literature of the sociology of law, repeated references to Laveleye and Loria may be found in C. Nardi-Greco's *La sociologia giuridica* (1907), and in Gabriel de Tarde's *Les transformations du droit* ([1893] 1909).

16. This seems to have been an especial problem among "scientific" socialists. Paul Lafargue wrote in his *Evolution of Property from Savagery to Civilization* (1890: 1) that "political economists have laid it down as an axiom that Capital, the form of property at present predominant, is eternal; they have tasked their brains to show that capital is coeval with the world, and that as it has had no beginning, so it can have no end." Engels's *Origin of the Family, Private Property and the State* (1884), too, appears to have been innocent of developments within academic economics.

17. E.g., M. A. Vaccaro's *Le basi del diritto e dello stato* ([1893] 1898) quoted from

this attitude did not conduce inexorably to derogation of the elder science, in practice it often did. C. Nardi-Greco, for example, in his *Juristic Sociology* (1907), objected to the "unilaterality" of historical materialism; and anthropologists like Heinrich Schurtz charged economists with "the overhasty construction of schematic theoretical edifices" in approaching the origins of property.[18] Statements such as these evinced an almost oedipal desire to stand alone, to establish the place of twentieth-century social science against a superannuated progenitor. And practitioners of the new science, for their part, occasionally threw down the gauntlet by doubting the need for a new discipline in the first place (e.g., Loria [1893] 1910: 380–5; R. Hildebrand 1894: 32).

Moreover, latter-day social science has increasingly come under the sway of other, competing nomothetic paradigms. Already around the turn of this century, the gravitational pull of these new paradigms was eroding further the prestige of economics, not least its tradition in the analysis of law. For an example, we may turn to Raphael Petrucci's *Natural Origins of Property* (1905). Recall that practitioners of the new science had typically approached the problem of explaining primitive property regimes by showing how highly rational – "modern" – minds would have converged on the same solution given the same tastes, endowments, and techniques. Petrucci's approach, by contrast, was to document meticulously the phenomena among lower forms of life that could sensibly be classed as property as well: what emerged salient from his account was the continuity between the behavior of "lower" human and "higher" animal societies. This was a subtle shift of emphasis, to be sure, a mode of argumentation that was not entirely unknown to economists, either. But by substituting

---

Comte's *Cours de philosophie positive,* "Social phenomena are so profoundly interconnected that genuine study of them could never rationally be separated. Any isolated study of the diverse social elements is therefore, by the nature of the science, profoundly irrational" (lviii).

This spirit is reflected with apparent benignity in René Worms, "La sociologie et le droit" (1885: 41): "What we ask is that the social sciences, instead of shutting themselves up in jealous isolation, as they sometimes tend to do, should unite, reach comity and penetrate one another." Significantly, however, it is *sociology* that is expected to be the vehicle of this happy result.

18. Nardi-Greco 1907: 314–15; Schurtz, "Anfänge des Landbesitzes" (1900): 246–7. With seemingly false generosity, Schurtz announced that "I do not have in mind a polemic against the older assays of Laveleye, or the more recent ones by Hildebrandt [*sic*], Oppenheimer etc.; let the facts . . . speak for themselves." Cf. also Alfred Vierkandt, "Die wirtschaftlichen Verhältnisse der Naturvölker" (1899): 183–4; Eduard Hahn, *Das Alter der wirtschaftlichen Kultur der Menschheit* (1905): 30.

the biological discourse of instinct for the economic discourse of choice, Petrucci was able to portray himself as opening a new field of inquiry.[19] This evolutionist gambit was played also by Ernest Beaglehole in his *Property: A Study in Social Psychology* (1931). Beaglehole pronounced social psychoethnologists like himself better equipped to explain basic human institutions than economists. "The economist's psychology of human motive in the past," he wrote, "has rarely been noteworthy either for its acuteness or its truth" (13–14). The linguistic model of evolution also won adherents, notably Gabriel de Tarde [*The Transformations of Law* ([1893] 1909)]. In general, as the twentieth century progressed the ideal of behaviorist social science won ground from the introspectionism of nineteenth-century economic inquiry, culminating in the ascendancy of regression analysis among modes of explanation. For latter-day positivists of this genre, the new science of law holds few attractions: I have found only one recent contribution to this genre that even acknowledges its existence, and then simply to dismiss it as "unsystematic, often ideologically biased, non-quantitative."[20]

If the new science found itself pressed on the one flank by advancing positivist pretensions, it was no less challenged on its opposite flank, by the articulation of a self-consciously relativist and hermeneutical tradition of social thought. This opposite tendency doubted frankly the value of all science that purported to reduce social phenomena to universal characteristics of the human individual. To the contrary, it argued that individual motives and heuristics were to be understood in the light of specific cultural environments. This movement had roots in high theory, as in Durkheim's appeal to "social facts" as data irreducible to individual intention, and roots also in the exoticism of the burgeoning ethnological literature.[21] By midcentury its partisans – notably Karl Polanyi among economic anthropologists, Talcott Parsons among economic sociologists – had all but abolished law as an object of inquiry, preferring to posit instead norms, institutions, and shared values, all of which enjoyed more the status of *explanans* than *explanandum*. In sum, the new science had become irrele-

---

19. Petrucci, *Les origines naturelles de la propriété* (1905); similarly Eduard Hahn, *Die Entstehung der wirtschaftlichen Arbeit* (1908): 24, 75, 102. Petrucci's pretensions to novelty are evident in his brief introduction to the relevant literature: "The natural origins of property never having been observed from the point of view that I broach here, this bibliography could fit into a half-page" (viii). Not surprisingly, that brief review included no references to the new science.
20. F. W. Rudmin, "Cross-Cultural Correlates of the Ownership of Private Property" (1992): 58.
21. See especially W. Smith 1991 for a reasoned account of this development.

vant to most mainstream sociologists and anthropologists: economics held little attraction as a vehicle, nor law as a destination.

## III    Jurisprudence

Did the economists' new science fare better among the specialists in society's rules, the jurists? Economists were understandably desirous of influence, and they were increasingly afforded the institutional opportunity. In articles published in 1863 and 1877, Courcelle-Seneuil posed the necessity of teaching political economy to France's future lawyers, largely as a means of inoculation against socialist error. "Above all," he argued, "students must be given a plain and durable idea of the causes of individual property, of interest, and of the place that contract has assumed in modern society."[22] In 1878 Courcelle-Seneuil's campaign was crowned with success, as political economy was officially recognized as a subject in all French law faculties. Thus it was not with forlorn hope that economists wished, as did Heinrich Dietzel,

> that the stuff which nowadays is mostly studied only from the perspective "What is the *nature* of law?" [wie *ist das Gesetz*], will in future also be studied from the perspective "Why is it law?" [weshalb *ist es Gesetz*] – i.e. that the juristic approach will be supplemented with the *staatswissenschaftlich,* and especially with the economic one. (1897: 706)

As we noted in chapter 1, Germany's more inchoate academic scene had long mingled law and economics in the curriculum of *Staatswissenschaft;* indeed, at any given German university the audience of economics lectures was primarily composed of future civil servants whose primary field of study was the law. Traditionally the *Staatswissenschaft* curriculum had been assigned to the faculties of philosophy, not law, but as the nineteenth century wore on this convention was increasingly breached. In universities that were newly founded (Zürich, Bern, Strassburg) or recently reorganized (Vienna, Prague, Freiburg i.B., Graz, Innsbruck, Czernowitz, Würzburg), economics and law were formally united in a single faculty.[23] Moreover, casual empiricism suggests that it had become rather fashionable for jurists to yoke the terms "law" and "economics" together in the titles of

22. Courcelle-Seneuil, "L'enseignement de l'économie politique dans les facultés de droit" (1877): 185; Courcelle-Seneuil, "De la nécessité d'enseigner l'économie politique dans les écoles de droit" (1863).
23. On the evolving relation of law and economics in the German universities, see Gustav Cohn, "Ueber die Vereinigung der Staatswissenschaften mit den Juristenfakultäten" (1900), and Klaus Hennings, "Aspekte der Institutionalisierung der Ökonomie an deutschen Universitäten" (1988).

books, articles, and journals.[24] Was this to be the new science's path to immortality?

We noted in chapter 1 too that the field of law was going through changes akin to the economists' revolt against formalism in general, and natural law in particular. These changes brought the novelties of *Interessenjurisprudenz* to the German scene, for example, and "sociological jurisprudence" and "legal realism" to America. Although it would be too much to claim that political economy was instrumental in the founding of these movements, the new science was occasionally adduced in support of them. Already in 1857, the first volume of H. Dankwardt's *Economics and Jurisprudence* quoted approvingly Roscher's dictum that "jurisprudence gives us but the superficial How; only economics adds the deeper Why." The new science, according to Dankwardt, "by exposing an institution's economic impetus, shows us the way to discover its often obscure origin." Thus political economy

> puts the jurist in a position to create a clear, complete and ordered image of life's actual relations. Everything around us, apparently an endless chaos, loses its random character and is united, right down to the smallest details, into one great organized mechanism [*Getrieb*], powered by the elemental force of human egoism. [*Nationalökonomie und Jurisprudenz* (1857–9): 1:3–11]

Dankwardt, admittedly, was only an obscure Rostock barrister. But even academic jurists evinced some interest in political economy's ferment. In the 1860s Wilhelm Arnold (1826–83), professor in Basel and Marburg, himself wrote of the "link between jurisprudence and political economy, which is lately so much commented upon." "We owe a debt of gratitude to the younger science," Arnold opined of economics, "for having greatly advanced our understanding of the law." Civilists, for example, stood to benefit greatly from this literature: "Would not the Roman law be far more completely revealed to our understanding, if it were explained also in reference to the economic life of that people? For it is exactly the latter that can point up to us better than all else the prime movers of evolution." Arnold believed this interdisciplinary method to bear fruit in the investigation of Greek, Germanic, and modern law as well.[25]

24. This phenomenon was especially prevalent in German-speaking regions, as witness the periodicals *Jahrbuch der Internationalen Vereinigung für vergleichende Rechtswissenschaft und Volkswirtschaftslehre zu Berlin* (1905–1914); *Blätter für vergleichende Rechtswissenschaft und Volkswirtschaftslehre* (Berlin, 1905–26); *Archiv für Rechts- und Volkswirtschaftslehre* (Berlin, 1907–33); *Recht und Wirtschaft* (Berlin, 1911–22); *Wirtschaft und Recht* (Bayreuth, 1934–44); *Wirtschaft und Recht* (Zürich, 1949 to present).
25. Arnold, *Cultur und Rechtsleben* (1865): xii–xiii, 42, 98–9, 105–12. Be it noted,

Arnold's call was perhaps the strongest and most explicit manifesto of allegiance to emerge from jurisprudence; but its echo reverberated from time to time throughout the succeeding half-century. We may point also to Otto von Gierke (1841–1921), professor of law at Berlin, admirer of Arnold and friend of Schmoller, who himself noted the importance of economic theory to the understanding of law.[26] Other European proponents of the cross-fertilization of economic and legal thought included Georg Jellinek,[27] Semen V. Pakhman,[28] Paul Oertmann,[29] Ernst Lands-

in passing, that we are glossing over one important difference between Dank-wardt and Arnold: Arnold insisted that economics, at least up to the time of Knies and Roscher, had been as prone to the errors of materialism and determinism as was jurisprudence to the error of voluntarism. Above all, Arnold called for the mutual fructification of these disciplines. See Arnold's *Zur Geschichte des Eigentums in den deutschen Städten* (1861): 202–3; *Recht und Wirtschaft nach geschichtlicher Ansicht* (1863); *Cultur und Rechtsleben* (1865): 13, 90–8, 103, 120–1.

26. "Since jurisprudence belongs to the sciences of the social existence of man, and since the social being is an organism [*Lebenseinheit*], therefore all other social sciences are, to a greater or lesser extent, auxiliaries in the deeper knowledge of law. Here suffice it to indicate the significance of economic theory for the understanding of German private law and its transformations" [Gierke, *Deutsches Privatrecht* (1895–1917): 1:§12]. For background, see Albert Janssen, *Otto von Gierkes Methode der geschichtlichen Rechtswissenschaft* (1974): 172–7.

27. Jellinek's *Allgemeine Staatslehre* ([1900] 1905) devoted forty-three pages to "the relations of the theory of the state to the other social sciences," including six pages (103–8) to economics, where he cited Marx, Schmoller, and Wieser. Jellinek (1851–1911) was professor of law at Heidelberg.

28. Pakhman envisioned a new jurisprudence that would be "realist" as well as historicist: "Since law itself belongs essentially among the elements of social life, the new science should, while holding its historical ground, enter into closest association with all other disciplines which are dedicated to the exploration of social phenomena. Among these disciplines, excepting sociology in general, it is political economy which should assume pride of place, since economic life represents the most important real foundation of legal development" [*Über die gegenwärtige Bewegung in der Rechtswissenschaft* ([1882] 1986): 13]. Pakhman (1825–1910) was professor of law at St. Petersburg.

29. According to Oertmann, "More and more we gain the following insight: the most advanced outpost of both sister-sciences are reaching out to one another. The great names – men like the Romanist Jhering and the Germanist Gierke on the one side, and the economist Wagner on the other – are already achieving common goals in their fields of research. And it is our task, the task of the younger generation, to follow the example of our worthy teachers!" [*Die Volkswirtschaftslehre des Corpus juris civilis* (1891): 2–3]. Oertmann (1865–1938) was professor of law at Berlin, Erlangen, and Göttingen.

berg,[30] and Paul Vinogradoff.[31] In America, Mark Lichtman's 1927 article "Economics, the Basis of Law" referred to the contributions of Commons, Oppenheimer, Seligman, and Loria; and a collegiate reader entitled *Evolution of Law* (Kocourek and Wigmore 1915–18) included a chapter translated from Loria's *Economic Foundations of Society.*

It is not our intention to belittle the aforementioned acknowledgments of the new science among jurists. But it would be a greater mistake to overestimate the influence of the economic literature. Emblematic of the new science's liminal position is Courcelle-Seneuil's declaration of pleasure, on reading the leading lights of legal history, to see his hypotheses "demonstrated, completed and clarified by *savants* who are unaware of one's works or one's name!"[32] The selflessness is commendable, the pathos yet unmistakable. Despite the economists' best efforts, the process of professional differentiation – and perhaps also some pique at the rising prestige of the social sciences relative to jurisprudence – made neglect, irritation, and rejection the likelier outcomes (see Maier 1990: 228).

The most eloquent testimony to this fact is the very silence of many new-model jurists whose work ran closely parallel to the new science: for example, Rudolf Jhering, whose many books on the social basis of the civil law reveal virtually no cognizance of economic contributions.[33] But

30. Landsberg noted pointedly the debt historical economics owed to historical jurisprudence, but he went on to explain how that debt had been largely repaid. Political economy, "looking backwards historically and around itself statistically, in order to ascertain economic phenomena as exactly as possible, offers a very novel wealth of materials and stimuli to legal history as well. Indeed, this state of affairs places in especial relief the fact that jurisprudence and political economy, though they are by no means inseparably paired, nevertheless exert a strong influence on one another, and have done so historically" [*Geschichte der deutschen Rechtswissenschaft* (1910): 3:761–2]. Landsberg (1860–1927) was professor of law at Bonn.

31. Vinogradoff's advice to historical jurists was that "the position of political economy requires special attention in many ways. The study has reached a high scientific level and, in spite of many controversies and doubtful points, presents the best proof of the possibility of bringing social phenomena within the scope of exact analysis and of generalizing reflection" [*Outlines of Historical Jurisprudence*" (1920–2): 1:75–7]. As examples worthy of emulation he adduced Roscher, Knies, and Schmoller. Vinogradoff (1854–1925) was professor of history at Moscow, then professor of law at Oxford.

32. Courcelle-Seneuil 1874: x–xi, referring particularly to Maine and Fustel de Coulanges.

33. I have come across only one reference to an economist: viz., to Wagner, in *Der Zweck im Recht* (1877–83): ch. 8, §13. The supportive tone of the reference

explicit digs were not wanting, either. Several of the jurists' objections seconded those of the historians. Richard Hildebrand's work, in particular, was faulted for its comparativism, its penchant for generalization, and its slapdash use of sources. Ernst Neukamp, in his *Introduction to an Evolutionary History of Law* (1895), declared Hildebrand's lecture *On the Problem of a General Evolutionary History of Law and Custom* an "absolutely inappropriate" approach to the subject.[34] In particular, he took exception to Hildebrand's claim that the history of law was a task "which mocked disciplinary boundaries": "In contrast I hope to have shown that the depiction of 'the evolutionary history of law' is a task which lies entirely *within* the framework of jurisprudence, and which must be solved by [jurisprudence]" (1895: 188). Rudolf Stammler too found Hildebrand's lecture methodologically unsound: "Philosophy is for him 'a scientific stopgap,' one for which he personally has no use. And he is right about that. . . . The learned mass of material which the lecture assembles does not aid in the slightest the *methodical* clarification of the problem expressed in the title. It is a colorful picture-book."[35] Hildebrand's subsequent book *Law and Custom* (1896) fared little better, as Josef Kohler pronounced its approach "off-target" and warned that "only a methodical historical study of individual populations – to the extent that they still offer a historical dimension – can lead to usable results."[36] In general, wrote Kohler on another occasion, "the layman should leave the themes of legal history to the jurist; for the whole idiosyncrasy of law and of legal evolution is revealed only to him who sees its development daily, before his own eyes."[37]

was more than a little blunted by Jhering's contention that Wagner's insights had long been anticipated in his own work.

34. "Clear results are not obtainable by means of the 'ethnological' method, for the very reason that it is not capable of discovering the 'historical' context of the facts it relates" [Neukamp, *Einleitung in einer Entwicklungsgeschichte des Rechts* (1895): 83–4]. Neukamp (1852–1919) was a judge in the German Imperial Court.
35. Stammler, 1901: 414–15. Stammler (1856–1938) was professor of law at Marburg, Giessen, Halle, and Berlin.
36. Kohler 1908. Kohler (1849–1919) was professor of law at Würzburg and Berlin.
37. Kohler, "Soziologie und Rechtsphilosophie" (1910–11): 560. Cf. similar comments in Berolzheimer's treatment of Schäffle (1904–7: 2:368–70); and in Kohler's 1902 review of Nieboer's *Slavery as an Industrial System*.
    The young legal historian Max Weber was of a similar mind when, in his *Habilitationsschrift* on the agrarian history of Rome (1891: 3), he praised Rodbertus's work on the colonate but went on to note that the "aprioristic

To boundary-conscious jurists like these, economists of the new science were unwelcome visitors, clumsy interlopers who, as Gumersindo de Azcárate put it, "invade alien territory" when treating the history of institutions.[38] When Azcárate and others did cite the economic literature, it was typically as a source of empirical data, not as a novel mode of analysis.[39]

One of the central points of the present study has been that the economists' new science of law cannot be reduced to a simple story of "materialism" or "economic determinism." Analysts, we have seen, were quite free to discount the explanatory power of the *homo oeconomicus* model and yet retain their good standing within the profession of political economy. The "hard cores" of this science were methodological individualism and instrumental rationalism, not historical materialism. Alas, this fact was all too often lost on contemporaries in the legal profession; the result was heightened skepticism. As Giorgio Del Vecchio put it in his 1935 article "Law and Economy," economics was the science of egoistic behavior. Law, on the other hand,

> expresses and somehow reflects a conception – a more or less perfect conception, but one that is nonetheless integral – of the purpose of life and of all the tendencies and aspirations of the human soul, not, certainly, the economic ones alone. . . . Hence the impossibility of a simple economic foundation of law; or in other words, the necessity that the economic factor be subordinated to the juridical one.[40]

The complexity Del Vecchio called for was far from unknown in the literature of the new science, of course. The problem is that so many jurists appear to have remained ignorant of this fact.[41]

economic hypotheses" of the great man's epigones had provided "almost too much of a good thing."

38. Azcárate, *Ensayo sobre la historia del derecho de propiedad y su estado actual en Europa* (1879–83): x–xi, xviii. Azcárate (1840–1917) was professor of law at Madrid.

39. Besides Azcárate 1879-83, see Burkard Wilhelm Leist, *Über die Natur des Eigentums* (1859); Lothar Dargun, "Ursprung und Entwicklungsgeschichte des Eigentums" (1884); Heinrich Brunner, *Deutsche Rechtsgeschichte* (1887–92): §11.

40. Del Vecchio, "Droit et économie" (1935): 1477–9. Del Vecchio (b. 1878) was professor of law at Rome.

41. Economists were tarred with the brush of reductive materialism also in H. Schreuer's 1898 review of Hildebrand 1896; Roscoe Pound, "The Scope and Purpose of Sociological Jurisprudence" (1911–12): 162, 168, 492–5; Dionisio Anzilotti, *La filosofia del diritto e la sociologia* ([1892] 1963): 638; Vinogradoff 1920–2: 79–83; Luigi Miraglia, *Filosofia del diritto* ([1885] 1903): 145–6; Icilio

To be sure, the ranks of jurists engaged in the longitudinal and cross-sectional explication of law were growing over the course of these decades; and among these, more and more were adopting an interdisciplinary perspective. But not only did these newfound interests fail to raise substantially the profile of the economists' contribution, in many cases they actually detracted from it. On the one hand, most jurists interested in social science opted directly for the newest and ostensibly the most synthetic of them all, sociology, and absorbed from it much of the sociologists' indifference (or outright hostility) to economics. "After the creation of sociology," as Michele Angelo Vaccaro put it in *The Foundations of Law and the State* (1893), "it was natural that all the individual social sciences should be overthrown, and that they should be reconstituted upon the *new foundations* with which sociology has furnished each of them."[42] Or to quote Dionisio Anzilotti,

> Precisely because the problem is of such a nature that it must be resolved through sociology – through a sociology that has been stripped of all unilateral and exclusive baggage – it follows that the philosophy of law must make use of its conclusions, and that the connections between [law] and economic science must be established through the offices of the general science of society: the latter, as has been adumbrated above, already guaranties against the dangers of a partial or exaggerated interpretation.[43]

In short, the work of mere economists had little resonance for Vaccaro, for Anzilotti, or for sociological jurists in general.

In a very different vein, legal history and legal ethnology were touched also by the neoidealist movement in philosophy. Neoidealist jurisprudence, and most specifically the neo-Hegelianism of Kohler and his followers, posited an evolutionary process powered not by cause but by telos, by "culture." Culture, according to Kohler, "consists in the greatest possible development of human knowledge, and in the greatest development of human mastery over nature"; it was "the purpose of all human activity, of all human history." The only kind of positivism Kohler would brook was the teleological and holistic Positivism of Comte and his followers,

Vanni, *Il problema della filosofia del diritto nella filosofia, nella scienza e nella vita ai tempi nostri* (1890): 42–3.

42. Vaccaro, *Le basi del diritto e dello stato* ([1893] 1898): lvi. Vaccaro (b. 1854) was professor of law at Rome.

43. Anzilotti [1892] 1963: 638. Anzilotti (1867–1950) was professor of law at Palermo, Bologna, and Rome.
   See also Pound 1911–12: 162, 168, 492, 505; D'Aguanno, *La genesi e l'evoluzione del diritto civile* (1890); Berolzheimer, "Grundprobleme der Rechts- und Wirtschaftsphilosophie samt der Soziologie" (1909–10): 30.

which had identified and researched "the organism of humanity as a whole." This Comtean moment had culminated in "the recognition that humanity has its own laws, laws which rule the whole as an organic mass," and had thereby set the terms of neo-Hegelian social inquiry.[44] With this insight Kohler had apparently struck a resonant chord, as attested by the stream of scholarship filling the avowedly neo-Hegelian journal which he founded in 1907. But this approach to the data of law could hardly have been less compatible with that of the new science: in all, its references to the positive theory of institutions were few, oblique, and deprecatory.[45]

Even yet we have not exhausted all the sources of juristic imperviousness to the new science. Heretofore we have explored the various objections that economists were explaining law poorly; it remains now to appreciate the problem posed by the fact that they were undertaking to explain law at all. It must be remembered, in this connection, that explanation was never to gain general acceptance as the primary mission of legal scholarship. It was rather the differentiation of just from unjust, and of expedient from inexpedient – the same tasks which had once retarded the new science in political economy – that remained the legal profession's primary brief, long after the other social sciences had evolved toward positivist detachment.

Hence it was the normative, and specifically the utilitarian, valence of modern economics that was responsible for that discipline's rising status in the eyes of many jurists, and specifically for the nascent fashion of "law and economics" alluded to above.[46] An influential variant on this theme was the neo-Kantian jurisprudence of Rudolf Stammler and his followers. Stammler's *Law and Economy According to the Materialist Conception of History* (1896) advanced the novel, if hopelessly obscure, proposal that the relation between law and economy be approached as the relation between

44. Kohler, "Wesen und Ziele der Rechtsphilosophie" (1907–8): 15; "Vom Positivismus zum Neuhegelianismus" (1909–10): 167–9, 170–1. See also the appreciative glosses in Pound 1911–12: 155–7, and in Kocourek's introduction to Berolzheimer (1912: xv).

45. As Kohler and Berolzheimer put it in their manifesto, "With the merely positivist or materialist approaches human thought cannot be satisfied, nor can the challenges of history and of social life be met" ["Die Begründung einer Internationalen Vereinigung für Rechts- und Wirtschaftsphilosophie" (1908–9): 435]. See also Berolzheimer, *System der Rechts- und Wirtschaftsphilosophie* (1904–7): 2:§7; 3:162.

46. E.g., Julius Baron's 1877 review of Wagner 1876; and Anton Randa, *Das Eigenthumsrecht* ([1884] 1893): 1–7. On the role of economics in what came to be known as the *Sozialrecht* tradition in law, see especially Walter Wilhelm, "Private Freiheit und gesellschaftliche Grenzen des Eigentums in der Theorie der Pandektenwissenschaft" (1979).

"form" and "content." This was expressly *not* to be understood as a materialist conception, whereby economy causes law; indeed, Stammler rejected causal argumentation per se. Instead, the concept of "economy" had to be understood *teleologically* as a new categorical imperative, a social ideal that could and should be employed by the legislator.[47] Or as Stammler's admirer Fritz Berolzheimer put it in his *Systematic Philosophy of Law and Economics* (1904–7: 1:vii–viii, 3:158–9), the core concept of economy was "the idea of substantive justice [*die Idee des Gerechten nach ihrem Inhalte*]."

All this was a far cry from – not to say an outright rejection of – the principles of the new science, and it was not limited to neoidealist circles. By the turn of the century and beyond, it was not uncommon for jurists of all stripes to inaugurate projects that featured both law and economics; but such pretensions very seldom entailed the *recourse* to economic literature to *explain* law.[48] By embracing the potential of economics for social engineering, these lawyers were all but excluding the work of economists who posited the social determinacy of law.

The potential for animus is indicated in Auguste Béchaux's strictures against the relativism of what he called "the German school" of economists, who had lost touch with the traditions of natural law and moral philosophy, and who thereby had ceased to offer any positive services to jurisprudence. "Far from amounting to progress," Béchaux concluded, "this manner of envisaging economic science leads us back into the errors of past centuries."[49] But it is surely of even greater significance that so few of these neo-Kantian or Progressive apostles of "law and economics" betrayed even a passing familiarity with the new science. As such, they were able to preserve a blissful ignorance of the fact that many economists had come not to aid normative jurisprudence, but to bury it.

## IV   Economics

We turn finally to the greatest of all the new science's failures: to wit, its eclipse in twentieth-century economic discourse. By way of expla-

---

47. Stammler, *Wirtschaft und Recht nach der materialistischen Geschichtsauffassung* (1896): esp. 198–202. Cf. also Diehl, "Wirtschaft und Recht" (1897): 847–8; Max Weber's comment in Voigt, "Wirtschaft und Recht" (1911): 269–70; and Kocourek's introduction to Berolzheimer 1912: xiv.

48. In some cases, economics was deemed relevant as a tool for effective legislation; in others, the juxtaposition merely reflected an academic and administrative category of long standing.

49. Béchaux, *Le droit et les faits économiques* (1889): 17–20. Béchaux (1854–1922) was professor of law and economics at Lille.

nation, three general trends deserve mention. First of all, by the early twentieth century the normative, reformist, and possibilist impulses that had dominated early economic thought had won back much of the ground that had been lost to the more contemplative evolutionism of the nineteenth. Notwithstanding the rearguard actions fought by partisans of "social Darwinism" and/or *Wertfreiheit*, economics was once again caught up in the noble dream of recasting society from a better mold. This drive – what the American institutionalist Walton Hamilton called "a general demand for control" – held important ramifications for the economic analysis of law.[50]

The "demand for control" could easily result in an impatience with the data of law altogether. An early exemplar of this tendency was Karl Marx. The alert reader will have noticed that Marx has gone all but unmentioned since chapter 1; this is because his treatment of law was radically stunted, never advancing far beyond the most general considerations in the introduction to his *Contribution to the Critique of Political Economy*. To some extent, Marx's abstention from institutional analysis must be ascribed to his methodological holism, to his penchant for teleological reasoning, and to the simple fact that his historical investigations focused on one single "mode of production" (the "bourgeois" one), wherein the institutional framework was more or less parametric. But of comparable import must have been the fact that Marx remained at heart a radical reformist. Despite his evolutionist gestures, he was never truly reconciled to the idea that social institutions had an existence independent of human plan: that they could be real, even if they were not "rational." Donald Kelley has argued that Marx's hostility to the historical jurists stemmed from his perception that they were "giving positive law priority over philosophy."[51] This rings true. Marx was more than willing to call down the weight of historical necessity as leverage to individual activism; but dwelling *too* closely upon the actual determination of social institutions would have given too much comfort to quietism.

Not surprisingly, this impatience with law remained common coin among radical economists long after Marx's death. But the new science suffered also at the hands of more gradualist reformers. An important, ironic example of this is the "social-law school" [*sozialrechtliche Richtung*] in early twentieth-century German economics. Led by Karl Diehl (Freiburg) and Friedrich von Gottl-Ottlilienfeld (Berlin), these economists

50. Hamilton, "The Institutional Approach to Economic Theory" (1919): 313. See also Coats, "The First Two Decades of the A.E.A." (1960): 563.
51. Kelley 1990: 257. In support of Kelley's position we may cite Marx's early indictment of Gustav Hugo in his "Philosophische Manifest der historischen Rechtsschule" ([1842] 1975): 205.

owed proud allegiance to Stammler's neo-Kantian innovations in jurisprudence; this entailed "total accordance," as Diehl put it, with Stammler's "basic propositions about the relation between law and economy."[52] Its implications for the economic approach to law are indicated in Diehl's indictment of historical materialism:

> According to this theory, certain economic relations – especially the state of productive technology – are decisive for the shaping of law. Thus, [different] economic relations necessarily bring with them a change in the legal constitution. The truth is precisely the opposite: it is the legal order which first imparts to the economy the norms within which it occurs, and in this legal imposition [*Rechtssatzung*] it is particular views of justice and considerations of expediency which are decisive.[53]

Therefore, while the jurist is concerned with law itself, the economist's attention is properly devoted to "the real life which plays out *within these norms*. What interests him is the actual material organization of legally ordered social life."[54] Consequently for Diehl, as for other theorists of *Sozialrecht*, the relevance of economic theory to law is not as a tool for understanding *why* law *is*, but rather as a practical guide to *what* law *should be*.[55]

Stripped of its philosophical overlay, this same basic insight powered many other economists' approach to law in the twentieth century. In

52. Diehl 1897: 821. For a more nuanced account of his position on Stammler, see Diehl 1941: 70–86.

    For Gottl-Ottlilienfeld, even Stammler's formulation did not accord to social norms the conceptual priority they deserved. The plain fact about law, wrote Gottl, was "*that it simply has nothing to do with the economy!* The very idea, that economy and law relate to one another as 'content' and 'form', is untenable" [*Volk, Staat, Wirtschaft und Recht* (1936): 193].

53. Diehl 1941: 17. See also Diehl 1929; Gottl-Ottlilienfeld, *Bedarf und Deckung* (1928): 189–96.

54. Diehl 1923–4: 1:39. Similarly Diehl 1929: 34; 1941: 29, 136.

55. Consider also Andreas Voigt's rather dismissive attitude toward explanation in the following passage from his "Wirtschaft und Recht":

    > To understand law means to grasp its economic or social purpose. This is also the proper guiding principle of the modern legal movement: judicial interpretation of law according to its purposes, tracing the true and actual motives of law, not merely philological-historical interpretation from the text of laws and from the historical accidents motivating the legislator. (1911: 443)

    In styling this claim we are admittedly leaving out of account the few explanatory pages on property rights in volume II of Diehl 1923–4, an omission that seems justified considering that (1) the whole chapter on "Economy and Law" in volume I is devoted to normative issues and (2) the rights he explains are ones he anyway approves of on ethical principle.

America, Progressive economists viewed the law as a key weapon in their arsenal of social reform, and the amenability of common-law judges to economic argumentation only whetted their zeal. As Walton Hamilton, the first economist appointed to the Yale Law School, put it, his interdisciplinary mission was guided by the twin propositions that (1) legal reform should incorporate the economic insight, and (2) economic reform should use the law instrumentally (1929: 56). Reformist economics, sociological jurisprudence, legal realism: the heady result was what Herbert Hovenkamp (1990) has styled "The First Great Law & Economics Movement," and while we might quibble with the breadth of that claim, from a strictly normativist and anglophone perspective it holds more than a grain of truth. But it was a movement that had no use for the positive "law and economics" of the new science.

A similar relation of law and economics was posited in the German *Ordnungspolitik* movement, organized in 1936 by professors at the University of Freiburg (notably the economist Walter Eucken and the jurist Franz Böhm) around a series that later evolved into the journal *ORDO*. In the inaugural preface to the series, titled "Our Task," Eucken and his co-editors indicated just how little their intervention would draw upon the explanatory science of law. The current impasse in jurisprudence, they reasoned, could be traced to the "fatalism" and "relativism" of Savigny and the nineteenth-century historical jurists who followed him. "This confidence in the inner silent forces seemed innocuous but, in reality, as later events demonstrated, it proved extremely dangerous." Marx was held up as one unfortunate product of this historicism, who in his turn added to the determinist momentum. By the fin de siècle,

> the prevailing view was that "the private law in force at any given time, as the system of private interrelationships between citizens, represents at all times the spirit of the prevailing social and economic situation." The politico-legal task of science can only ascertain in each case the most recent social and economic situation and make recommendations as to how the law should adapt itself to this situation. Confronted with such a fatalistic attitude the lawyer can only adjust to the economic conditions. He does not feel that he has the strength to shape them.[56]

"How can the intellect shape events," the editors asked rhetorically, "when it accepts them as inevitable?" German economists, far from combating this trend, had joined the historicist tide and thereby had proved themselves, too, "essentially no longer capable of transcending everyday experience" (Böhm et al. [1937] 1989: 20–21). *ORDO*'s task was thus to rescue

---

56. Böhm et al., "Unsere Aufgabe" ([1937] 1989): 16–17. The quote contained in the passage was from Karl Geiler.

both economics and law, and to place them in a position of mutual fructification; but it left no doubt that explanatory science would not be part of that task.[57]

As the century wore on, mainstream normative economics lost even this connection to jurisprudence. A. C. Pigou, in some respects the founder of modern welfare economics, lacked even a passing interest in law or in public choice,[58] preferring instead to hypothesize the administration of public affairs through an omniscient, unitary bureaucracy. Despite fitful attempts (by Knight and later Coase) to object that the law held possibilities unaccounted for in the Pigovian model, government by legal rules came to look an increasingly blunt and old-fashioned tool for constructing the good society.

The second broad factor to which we call attention is the professionalization of economics itself. From a broad perspective this development was of greater moment than the normativist call for "law and economics"; professional specialization was, so to speak, the grain against which "law and economics" had to cut. In what did this new specialism consist? Its roots stretch back to the last third of the nineteenth century, notably to the discoveries of the marginal principle and of general equilibrium. These new theories opened broad vistas of fruitful research, but their significance for the economic analysis of law was inauspicious. As economists' attention was drawn to the interaction of many agents in a perfectly defined and enforced market order, less attention was paid to the question of why society's rules come into being in the first place, since laws – unlike market prices – often emerge from the context of small-numbers interaction and political or physical coercion. There was nothing inevitable in this phenomenon, of course: Menger, for example, was a leader in both the marginalist revolution and in the new science of law. But the temptation to play exclusively to one's professional strengths was strong. Most market analysts came to view the problem of rules as irrelevant, if not positively threatening.

The "neoclassical" synthesis in positive economics made quick inroads throughout Europe and America, driving the positive science of law before it. In Germany the divorce of law and economic analysis was relatively

---

57. Eucken's *Grundlagen der Nationalökonomie* ([1940] 1950: 315) followed this brief in that he called on the one hand for the renewed cooperation of law and economics, while stipulating on the other hand that their cooperation should be for the express goal of establishing the optimal economic constitution.
58. Pigou, *Wealth and Welfare* (1912) and *The Economics of Welfare* (1920). See Ronald Coase's comment in Kitch 1983: 218; and Alan Peacock, *Public-Choice Analysis in Historical Perspective* (1992).

difficult, owing to the centripetal force of the *Staatswissenschaft* tradition. Still the divorce took place, if only a little later. Already in 1906, Georg von Mayr was arguing in his *Concept and Subdivision of the Staatswissenschaften* that *Staatswissenschaft* in its "literal meaning" comprised political science and law only. These were to be distinguished from economics and the other social sciences, which were *Staatswissenschaften* only in the "figurative sense," and even that due to the historical accident of German scholarship. By rights, to include economics among the sciences of state was "a wholly incongruent description of a field of knowledge which deals with the state only to a relatively slight extent."[59] By the time of the Great War, Schmoller's party had lost control of the German economics establishment, and it would remain in the academic wilderness until very recently: "Right up to our own time," wrote Knut Borchardt in 1977, "the historical-institutional dimension of nineteenth-century authors has been looked upon as a mark of the backwardness of German economic science."[60]

The main stream of mid-twentieth-century economics was not, in sum, an environment hospitable to the explanation of law. The Keynesian revolution disturbed the neoclassical synthesis and created a new field of macroeconomics, but it did little to spur the endogenization of rules into economic reasoning. Developments in the immediate postwar decades were even less auspicious, as the "Formalist Revolution" in economic theory displaced much of what remained of empirical and institutional concerns, replaced verbal argumentation with the language of mathematics, and devalued the history of economic thought.[61] Only this course of events can

59. Mayr, *Begriff und Gliederung der Staatswissenschaften* ([1906] 1921): 25–6, 101, 111.
60. Borchardt 1977: 148; see also Rüdiger vom Bruch, "Gustav Schmoller" (1988): 223–5. Regarding the more general field of Public Choice, Bruno and Rene Frey reported in 1973 that German thought had grown wholly dependent on Anglo-American initiatives: "Links to those German economists of the nineteenth and the first half of the twentieth century who were interested in the integration of economic and political thinking (Friedrich List, Adolf Wagner, Emil Sax, Friedrich von Wieser, Lorenz von Stein, Hans Ritschl, Edgar Salin, etc.) practically do not exist" ["The Economic Theory of Politics: A Survey of German Contributions" (1973): 81].
61. See Benjamin Ward, *What's Wrong with Economics?* (1972): 35–44. As Alan Peacock has formulated the choice facing young economists of his generation, the "mathematical formulation of economic propositions . . . no longer required extensive knowledge of and commentary on the work of others." Henceforth, "the history of economic ideas appeared to have too high an opportunity cost as an input into the basic training of economists. . . . The personal satisfaction derived from discovering new facts about and presenting new insights into the works of dead men would be bought at the risk of losing promotion, remaining a junior lecturer whilst others were pushing out a

account for Paul Samuelson's comment, noted at this study's outset, that institutions were "matters which economists have traditionally chosen not to consider within their province" (1947: 8).

The third and final broad factor we shall explore concerns that rump of the economics profession that continued to engage the problem of explaining rules. Even in its Classical, nineteenth-century formulations, the new science was unpalatable enough to most twentieth-century economists, for all the foregoing reasons; but its fate was sealed by the innovations of its latter-day practitioners, who drifted ever further from the economic approach of methodological individualism and rational choice, toward a "sociological" one of methodological holism and irrationalism.

Prominent among these innovations was the elevation of human irrationality to a central principle of legal history. As an aid to clear thought, neoclassical economists have tended to assume that human agency amounts to rational calculus in the pursuit of stable preferences. Now we have already confirmed in chapter 3 that the new science, even in the midst of the "age of materialism" of which political economy was the paragon, had always entertained doubts about *homo oeconomicus*. But whereas for the founding fathers the irrational aspects of human nature had been consigned primarily to the earliest stages of social evolution, for many latter-day analysts irrationality – whether instinctive or ideological – was essential to understanding modern law as well.

After some precocious stirrings among impatient radical economists in the nineteenth century,[62] the "modernity of the irrational" came into its own in the later brands of institutional analysis associated with such luminaries as Weber, Sombart, and Veblen. Weber, as is well known, maintained that rationalism had history on its side. But in *Economy and Society,* his last and most general theoretical piece, charisma and taboo emerged as major forces in institutional evolution, forces not yet poised on the brink of history's dustbin. The concept of "binding rules," Weber theorized, was founded on the "regularities" of "psycho-physical reality." The logic of adaptation to an evolving environment [*Änderung der äusseren Lebensbedingungen*] was not irrelevant, of course; but the actual institutional profile of a given society was found beholden much more directly

stream of articles in major journals and becoming 'upwardly mobile'" (1992: 5–9).
62. Here we refer especially to Loria's invocation of bourgeois "morality" as a force diverting the exploited ego from its true interests, and of course to Marx's use of the concept of "false consciousness" (Loria [1893] 1910: 13–72). These concepts ran against the grain of their generally materialist-rationalist institutional analysis, but they were necessary stopgaps given the fact that the revolution had not yet occurred.

to the nonrational factors of traditionalism (or more precisely, the human aversion to "innovation"), which obstructs adaptation, and charisma (the capacity of individuals for "abnormal experiences"), which occasionally overcomes tradition.[63]

The development of Sombart's thought also indicates the rise of the irrational. In the first edition of *Modern Capitalism* (1902), irrational impulses helped shape economic institutions right up to the threshold of modernity, at which point capitalist rationality gained the ascendant. In the book's later editions, however, the relevance of the *homo oeconomicus* model to early modern institutions was much diminished: significantly, the chapter titled "The New Legal Order" [*Das neue Recht*], which in the 1902 edition had established the distributional logic underpinning legal evolution in Europe's nascent territorial states, was omitted altogether. The apparent shift in Sombart's thought was confirmed by the more general considerations in his *Ordering of Economic Life* (1924), where the ideological aspect of law was transformed into a general category, free of historical qualification: "In a particular economic order there reigns obviously a particular 'spirit', which emerges pursuant to particular principles, i.e. to a particular legal mentality [*Rechtsgesinnung*]." Modern legislation was thus the creature of an unreflective liberal ideology, just as the old world had conformed to instinct and "collective consciousness."[64]

To this intellectual ferment Veblen – and the American school of "institutional economics" he helped found – contributed a basic revision of the term "institution" itself, from explicit social norm to "settled habits of thought common to the generality of men."[65] The change was an im-

63. Weber [1922] 1978: II, ch. 1, §2. The following passage from his chapter
    "*Rechtssoziologie*" gives some sense of the complex relation between (rational)
    adaptation and (irrational) magic:
    > Charismatically qualified persons can receive the inspiration for new
    > norms without (or at least apparently without) the intervention of con-
    > crete causes, and specifically without any change in external circum-
    > stances. This manner of thing has often occurred. As a rule, however,
    > when shifts in economic or other conditions of life require new norms
    > for problems that have not yet been solved, these norms are produced
    > through magical means of all sorts. ([1922] 1978: II, ch. 8, §ii)

64. Sombart [1924] 1927: 3, 54–9. Compare Oppenheimer's 1921 lecture to the
    Kiel Institut für Weltwirtschaft, in which he proposed to combine two novel
    psychological theories in a general theory of law: (1) the "phenomenological,"
    i.e., the neo-Kantian categorical imperative deriving from a priori reason, and
    (2) the "genetic," based upon the empirical observation of a "*Wir-Interesse*"
    existing alongside the more commonly remarked "*Ich-Interesse*" of self-
    preservation. Like Sombart, Oppenheimer claimed to explain much, when in
    fact he was clarifying very little.

65. Veblen, "The Limits of Marginal Utility" ([1909] 1961): 239. According to
    Hamilton's article "Institutions" for the *Encyclopedia of the Social Sciences*,

portant one, inasmuch as it shifted attention from the *constraints* binding the rational mind, to the *content* of a mind that had few intrinsic qualities at all. Veblen was at pains to distance himself from the utilitarian anthropology:

> For mankind as for the other higher animals, the life of the species is conditioned by the complement of instinctive proclivities and tropismatic aptitudes with which the species is typically endowed. . . . Human activity, in so far as it can be spoken of as conduct, can never exceed the scope of these instinctive dispositions, by initiative of which man takes action.[66]

Ownership, for example, is and always has been "a cultural fact and has to be learned; it is a cultural fact which has grown into an institution in the past through a long course of habituation, and which is transmitted from generation to generation as all cultural factors are" (1898a: 360). This insight was the foundation for Veblen's theory of property in his famously satirical *Theory of the Leisure Class* (1899); from it flowed too his prediction that in future a "mechanistic" mind-set would increasingly supplant its "supernatural" predecessor in the minds of workers, who would in turn recognize the institution of property to be a vestige of natural law, and would rebel against it.[67] In essence, as Richard Langlois has argued, Veblen's behaviorist psychology "wished to rid economics of any sort of human intelligence and purpose."[68] The critique of boundless rationality in Veblen's thought, as in the thought of latter-day institutionalists in general, was qualitatively not so different from the doubts we heard voiced in chapter 3; but it was presented in terms so challenging as to make compromise with the utilitarian insight all but impossible. While this is by no means a self-evidently bad thing, one may readily appreciate how little appeal it held for economists of the mainstream.

An analogous problem was presented by the tendency of twentieth-

"in ordinary speech ['institution'] is another word for procedure, convention of arrangement; in the language of books it is the singular of which the mores or the folkways are the plural" (1937: 8:84). Consequently, for Hamilton, institutional economics amounted to "a study of the conventions, habits of thinking, and modes of doing which make up the scheme of arrangements which we call 'the economic order'" (1919: 311). See also Dorfman 1946–59: 3:439.

66. Veblen, *The Instinct of Workmanship and the State of the Industrial Arts* (1914): 1. Compare Hamilton, who argued that "a theory of motives must be used which is in harmony with the conclusions of modern social psychology," and that therefore institutionalism "must find the roots of activity in instinct, impulse, and other qualities of human nature" (1919: 316–17).

67. Veblen, 1899: ch. 2; Veblen, *An Inquiry into the Nature of Peace and the Terms of Its Perpetuation* (1917): 363–6. See also Walker 1977: 222–35.

68. Langlois, "The New Institutional Economics" (1986): 4. See also David Seckler, *Thorstein Veblen and the Institutionalists* (1975).

century institutional analysis to relax the nomothetic presumptions that had underpinned the new science since its inception. In its place developed a more idiographic mode of explanation, one which (like its contemporary, Freudian psychopathology) told persuasive stories about institutional faits accomplis, but which offered little more than a pretense of predictive power. This is implicit, for example, in Weber's invocation of charisma as an important factor in the origin of lordly property rights at particular times and places ([1923] 1924: 62). Wieser's attempt at a covering law of constitutional history, like the tradition of civic republicanism whence it derived, also begged more questions than it answered:

> Where the masses degenerate, lasting oppression is the outcome of the process. However if the people preserve the vigor of their manhood, they will eventually throw off the yoke of their oppressors under new leadership. They will recover their liberty at the stage of development which they had attained. Then in the process of evolution the same cycle is repeated with new actors.
> ([1914, 1923] 1928: §76)

Or as Commons put it, "Every individual, every judge and every official of government has a different set of habits and emotions from every other individual, and the resulting emotions of value are the very center of individuality" (1924: 325). Again, all this is undoubtedly true, but it must have been a most unwelcome observation in an age when physics was the queen of sciences and most fields of social inquiry were judged by their royal likeness.

Less appealingly, twentieth-century epigones also impaired the new science's standing by experimenting with holistic ontology and methodology, and with the associated concept of teleological causation. This tendency was not unknown to the new science in its classical phase, of course: ever since Weber's long essay on Roscher and Knies, a stock criticism of nineteenth-century historical economics has been around its supposed "emanationism," its postulation of stages of development driven, in quasi-Hegelian fashion, by world-historical necessity. This criticism is not altogether specious; but the preceding chapters of this study have demonstrated that the reification of society and history were in no way intrinsic to the new science of law, and that the economists engaged in it in no way saw themselves as foot soldiers in a Hegelian revolution. It was only around the turn of this century that any real grounds were afforded to this reading of the movement.

The change is evident is the works of Bücher and Loria. It will be recalled that Roscher, Knies, and the older generation in general predicated the stages of institutional development primarily upon deeper seated trends in the economic environment and in individual civic virtue. In Bücher's *Emergence of the Economy* (1893), however, this restrained nominalism had to make way for holistic and teleological reasoning. Innovations in medieval economic organization, for example, were driven by "the necessity of economic progress," and by the fact that "the nascent exchange-economy was seeking to widen its own scope" ([1893] 1910: 103–4, 131). Similarly, regarding the institutional design of the new nation-state,

> the unification of economic forces advanced hand-in-glove with the bending of private interests to the higher purposes of the collectivity. . . . In the deepest foundations of the movement which led to articulation of princely absolutism, there slumbers the world-historical idea that humanity's new, greater cultural tasks required a unified organization of entire peoples – a great, living community of interest – and that this could only spring from the soil of a common economy.[69]

From his own very different ideological perspective, Loria too used the organismic metaphor in describing a legal system that seemed to have a purpose independent of individual interests, and in explaining why the law of his own day had grown "rigid," as if "stricken with a kind of paralysis." The simple reason for this dysfunction was, in his words, that the law "is no longer inspired with economic life, and thus fails to respond with sufficient readiness to modern demands" ([1893] 1910: 74–6, 102).

In later decades this organicism grew more commonplace; gradually it was fused into a sort of functionalism. Andreas Voigt, for example, in his 1911 article "Economy and Law," argued that "all legal prescriptions must be explained by reference to economic or, more generally, social need."[70] Similarly, Eugen Peter Schwiedland's contribution to the volume *Contemporary Law and Economy* (1912) asserted that

> the demands of custom and law are largely a question of *collective security* [*Gesamtheitsschutz*], in the sense in which this is generally understood. Custom and law seek the self-defense of the collectivity, they seek to order social co-existence in the collective interest; the individual, with his personal feelings and desires, is but a cipher in the face of these expressions of selfish collective sensibility [*selbstisches Massenempfinden*].[71]

---

69. Bücher [1893] 1910: 135–6. Not even the high tide of contemporary liberalism, Bücher argued, could deflect the modern state from these *Kulturaufgaben* (140–1).

70. Voigt 1911: 240. Thus "each economic epoch has, by and large, managed to provide itself with the appropriate legal order."
    Similarly Navratil (1905: 291): "Society intends either to enforce the laws that are favorable to a particular course of economic development, or else to use the legal order to obstruct the advance of a different course of economic development."

71. Schwiedland, "Allgemeine Volkswirtschaftslehre" (1912): 29. The work of Oppenheimer (whose first degree was in medicine) is also rife with biological

Holistic functionalism also found an important part in Commons's model of legal evolution. "The state itself," as Commons put it, "is but one of many going concerns, whose sovereign working rules are but a larger collective will, and the behavior of whose officials is a collective behavior."[72] As demonstrated in chapters 2 and 3, there is a good deal more to Commons's theory of law than this opaquely holistic jargon of "going concerns," "working rules," and "collective will"; unfortunately, though, this was to be his major legacy to American institutionalism.[73] For Clarence Ayres, a central figure among the next generation of institutionalists, "social patterns are not the logical consequents of individual acts; individuals, and all their actions, are the logical consequents of social patterns." As such, Ayres concluded, the explanation of institutions "must necessarily be couched in terms of social forces."[74] By the time those thoughts were voiced, in 1951, few economists were any longer listening.

## V    Conclusions

This chapter has documented the ultimate dereliction of the economists' new science and has offered a number of reasons for that fate. From the perspective of the present, the significance of its oblivion is that recent economic approaches to the law have not had the benefit of the insights (and, doubtless, the mistakes) of their long-dead predecessors. It is therefore fitting to close with a brief catalog of the errors and omissions indicative of that neglect.

Inevitably, neglect is the enemy of nuance: Procrustean simplification has focused such attention as there is on the "German Historical School" of economics, despite the very real doubt that what we have been in-

metaphors for the state, and occasional hints of vitalism. E.g., Oppenheimer believed that institutional crisis should be traced to "an external disturbance, which obstructs and distorts the normal course of communal functions, but which is, like all illness, the organism's attempt to expel or neutralize the toxin" (1921: 13).

72.  Commons 1924: 149; see also his article "Law and Economics" (1925).
73.  On Commons's primary commitment to methodological individualism, see also M. Rutherford, "J. R. Commons's Institutional Economics" (1983), and Viktor Vanberg, "Carl Menger's Evolutionary and John R. Commons' Collective Action Approach to Institutions" (1989). On the methodological holism characteristic of American institutionalism, see Geoffrey Hodgson's "Institutional Economics" (1993).
74.  Ayres, "The Co-ordinates of Institutionalism" (1951): 49–50. Ayres offered the interesting observation that technology was prominent among the forces driving institutional evolution, but he apparently did not explore the mechanics of this relation.

specting in this study deserves the simple labels "German" (it was cosmopolitan in practice, and especially in spirit), "historicist" (if it had a methodological conceit, it was more nearly "evolutionist"), or even "school" (practitioners agreed on the basic questions, but not on the answers). We have already doubted the adequacy of the frequent description of the new science as "Hegelian"; and yet this is probably the most forgivable of misreadings, given the fin-de-siècle recovery of idealism, given Weber's undoubted intellectual authority, and given the economists' own weakness for simplified historical models. Less understandable, certainly, is Karl Pribram's charge that "Schmoller's school" was so organismic that it "prepared the soil – for the most part unwittingly – for the subsequent acceptance of the National Socialist creed."[75] On the one hand, the tenacity of such imprecisions in the literature points to the fact that German as a language has grown increasingly foreign to economists over the course of this century; on the other hand, it indicates the more general preoccupation with discovering the intellectual roots of the German catastrophe. Neither phenomenon has been conducive to an appreciation of the new science.

The single greatest misperception on the part of "new" institutional economists is that their nineteenth-century predecessors were hopelessly naive empiricists. At a roundtable discussion of early Chicago "law and economics" convened in the early 1980s, George Stigler was called upon to elucidate the deeper background. His response:

75. Pribram, *A History of Economic Reasoning* (1983): 372. If Pribram's view has an exculpation, it is that National Socialism did not scruple to find ideological precursors among thinkers who were no longer around to rebut the charge. E.g., Justus Remer's *Die geistigen Grundlagen der historischen Schule der Nationalökonomie* (1935), a work which plainly curried Nazi favor, claimed to answer the call "once again to take up valuable traditions which an older generation of German economists created, a generation which was buried decades ago and which now must laboriously be exhumed" (v, 105).

Almost as sinister, given the tendencies of *Sonderweg* historiography, are the overtones of H. W. Spiegel's claim that German historical economics was "a revolt against the Enlightenment" [*The Growth of Economic Thought* (1983): 411]; or H. Stuart Hughes's observation that "the German tradition of economic history represented a curious hybrid of a kind of crypto-Marxism and a romantic notion of the 'spirit' of human communities derived in part from Ranke" [*Consciousness and Society* ([1958] 1961): 303]. The occasion for Hughes's comment is his argument that Weber's thought should be interpreted in part as a wholesome reaction against the historical economists; the error in this view of Weber's agenda is documented in Wilhelm Hennis, "A Science of Man: M. Weber and the Political Economy of the German Historical School" (1987).

> The German Historical School had big names in it like Roscher
> and Schmoller and Vogner [*sic,* presumably an erroneous tran-
> scription of "Wagner"]. All had treatises in which there were
> books devoted to legal institutions – the institutions of property,
> the institution of the family, and so forth. If you look at them –
> I haven't gone through all of them – it is my impression that you
> will be dissatisfied with them on the ground that they were
> largely descriptive rather than analytical.[76]

Ronald Coase argued to similar effect in 1984:

> I know little about the German Historical School but I gather
> from [T. W.] Hutchison that their position was essentially the
> same as that of the American institutionalists. American institu-
> tionalism is a dreary subject and I don't intend to dwell on it
> even though the institutionalists personally were anything but
> dreary people. . . . It certainly led to nothing. . . . Without a the-
> ory they had nothing to pass on except a mass of descriptive ma-
> terial waiting for a theory, or a fire. So if the modern institu-
> tional economists have antecedents, it is not what went
> immediately before. (1984: 229–30)

And likewise Richard Langlois in 1986: "The problem with the Historical
School and many of the early Institutionalists is that they wanted an economics with institutions but without the theory."[77] As characterizations of
the late excesses of institutionalism, these criticisms are not wholly unfair;
moreover, insofar as the earlier historical economists' objections to the
stark generalizations of the Classical school led them into rhetorical excess, they deserve some measure of the blame for their own antitheoretical
repute. But the fact remains that to brand the new science as history from
the magpie's-eye view, as has typically been done, is profoundly mis-
leading.

What is worse, these views are among the better informed ones. Far

76. Stigler, in Kitch 1983: 169. Elsewhere he offered the opinion that while
    nineteenth-century Europeans "talked a lot about the importance of studying
    environmental conditions and the like, they paid no real attention to the insti-
    tutions of the law" (216). Stigler's comment on Commons's *Legal Foundations
    of Capitalism* – "a book that I believe is impossible to read" (170) – does,
    however, ring true!

77. Langlois 1986: 5. In so arguing, Langois was following in the footsteps of
    Veblen himself, who held that "the whole broad range of erudition and re-
    search that engaged the energies of that [i.e., the Historical] school commonly
    falls short of being science, in that, when consistent, they have contented
    themselves with an enumeration of data and a narrative account of industrial
    development, and have not presumed to offer a theory of anything or to elabo-
    rate their results into a consistent body of knowledge" (1898b: 58).

more common among economists is plain ignorance of this historical epi-
sode. This larger group has implicitly seconded the conclusion of Armen
Alchian – one of the earliest and otherwise most insightful of the "new"
institutional economists – that, given the apparent paucity of institutional
analysis in the extant literature of economic thought, "I suspect our main
alternative is to initiate studies of our own."[78] That was in 1965; since then,
"starting from zero" has become something like an article of faith among
"new" institutionalists.

78. Alchian, "Some Economics of Property Rights" ([1965] 1977): 134. Similarly
Evsey Domar in "The Causes of Slavery or Serfdom": "If historians have
always known about the relation between the land/labor ratio and serfdom
(or slavery), they must have tried hard not to scatter too many good, clear
statements in places where I could find them" (1970: 31–2).

This same innocence of the new science led John Umbeck to argue in his
*Theory of Property Rights* (1981: 53) that during the nearly 200 years separating Rousseau's and Alchian's generations, "the relationship between property
rights, contract, and state was forgotten or ignored."

# Epilogue: The "new" new science of law, ca. 1965–1995

Since the mid-1960s or thereabouts, the explanatory approach to law has once again grown fashionable among mainstream economists. Before we take the measure of this "new" institutional economics, let us consider a few of its wellsprings.

First of all, we should mention the reaction against what was perceived as the excessive naïveté of Pigovian welfare economics. It is useful to recall, in this connection, the argument from chapter 1 that the original new science was born in part from skepticism toward the sanguine reformism of many Classical economists. Something similar was brewing in the mid-twentieth century, except that the enemy was now not natural law, but rather Progressive "social engineering." Even at the climax of Progressivism in the interwar years, there remained a subset of economists who thought administrative fiat a poor substitute for the rule of law.

Pigou's proposed solution to the problem of externality was a lightning rod of sorts for this discontent. A disinterested government agency, Pigou argued, should estimate the social cost of spillovers and set corrective taxes and subsidies accordingly. This solution won many adherents (and is articulately defended to this day): considering that it took allocative efficiency as its end, and the price mechanism as its means, this is not surprising. But already in 1924, Frank Knight rebutted that the Pigovian approach neglected the fact that the mere existence of legal rights could, under plausible conditions, solve the problem of externality without recourse to bureaucratic intervention.[1] Knight's objection and his alterna-

1. Knight, "Some Fallacies in the Interpretation of Social Cost" (1924).

162

tive vision were restated more formally, and famously, in Coase's 1960 article "The Problem of Social Cost." The thrust of these contributions was normative, specifically to the effect that (1) law was not merely a redistributive weapon, but a productive tool as well, and consequently that (2) given positive transaction costs, optimal "social engineering" may not be at the level of outcomes, but of rules. They were not, however, without significance for positive analysis. Coase (1960: 19–23) examined, by way of historical illustration, the resolution of nuisance cases at English common law and concluded that judicial decisions did historically serve to minimize transaction costs and to maximize joint economic values. This view of the judicial process implicitly reinforced, and was reinforced by, Coase's findings in his equally seminal article "The Nature of the Firm" (1937), wherein it was argued that the firm can best be understood as a sort of social contract writ small, a set of rules rationally adapted to the economic environment. It was a line of reasoning that offered great encouragement to an explanatory science of law, as attest the number of "new" institutional economists who hold up Knight and Coase as progenitors.[2]

A second source of the "new" new science was the articulation of an economic approach to politics – a research program commonly known by the rubric "Public Choice." This, too, was in some sense the child of welfare economics and the pretensions of the welfare state. On the one hand, its roots stretch to the normative contributions of the Swedish and Italian schools of public finance, and to the social-choice theories of Bergson and Arrow; on the other hand, it was beholden to Schumpeter's more cynical considerations on democratic government.[3] The founding classics of Public Choice – Anthony Downs's *Economic Theory of Democracy* (1957), Duncan Black's *Theory of Committees and Elections* (1958), James Buchanan and Gordon Tullock's *Calculus of Consent* (1962), Mancur Olson's *Logic of Collective Action* (1965) – all investigated the behavior of utility-seeking individuals in their capacities as citizens, representatives, and bureaucrats. The models they postulated were of obvious relevance to an economic theory of law: the more so since law in the twentieth century

2. These include Richard Posner, *The Economic Analysis of Law* (1973); Umbeck 1981: 53–6; North 1981: 21; Thrainn Eggertsson, *Economic Behavior and Institutions* (1990); Gary Libecap, *Contracting for Property Rights* (1989); Yoram Barzel, *Economic Analysis of Property Rights* (1989).
3. See Dennis Mueller's *Public Choice* (1979): 1–3. The more purely intellectual stimulus of the rediscovery of Condorcet and Carroll is not to be discounted either.

has been increasingly a product of legislative fiat, and correspondingly less a creature of spontaneous development.

Third, it seems likely that a sense of crisis in the theory and the pursuit of economic growth helped to push some credentialed neoclassicals in the direction of institutional analysis. To some minds in the middle of this century, the aggregate production function seemed to capture all that was important in the process of economic modernization: capital, labor, natural resources, and a (hopefully) minor residual ("total factor productivity" or "efficiency"). But as the data of experience came increasingly to insist that this residual was (1) a very substantial source of growth and (2) strongly associated with institutional structure, the problem of comparative economic performance came to be seen more and more as a question of why certain societies develop "functional" institutions, why others do not, and why institutionally successful societies tend to lose their edge over the long run. From this perspective, it is no wonder that the explanatory science of law was reborn.

Last, and probably least, we must recognize that the original new science was not utterly forgotten after 1935. Menger, for example, was clearly a great influence on Friedrich Hayek's approach to institutions; and Coase, in turn, has acknowledged Hayek's great impact as his teacher at the London School of Economics in the 1930s.[4] Since then, gestures toward Menger have become virtually de rigueur among institutionalists of the neo-Austrian persuasion.[5] Marx's insights have also been recognized,[6]

---

4. Coase, in Kitch 1983: 217. Hayek's proximity to the new science's interdisciplinary research program is indicated in the following introductory passage from his *Law, Legislation and Liberty:*

> Nowhere is the baneful effect of the division of [social thought] into specialisms more evident than in the two oldest of these disciplines, economics and law. . . . One of the main themes of this book will be that the rules of just conduct which the lawyer studies serve a kind of order of the character of which the lawyer is largely ignorant; and that this order is studied chiefly by the economist who in turn is similarly ignorant of the character of the rules of conduct on which the order that he studies rests. (1973–9: 1:4–5)

5. See, e.g., Andrew Schotter, *The Economic Theory of Social Institutions* (1981): 3–5; Langlois 1986: 5.

6. Frederick Pryor, *The Origins of the Economy* (1977); C. G. Veljanovski, *The New Law-and-Economics* (1982); Pejovich 1982; Jack Knight, *Institutions and Social Conflict* (1992).

as have Wagner's,[7] Loria's,[8] and Commons's.[9] These voices from the past would not have made much difference absent the causes enumerated above; but in conjunction with them, they afforded a measure of legitimacy and gravitas.

The "new" new institutional economics has come increasingly to resemble the original one. Up to the early 1980s, the new practitioners did not stray far from the *homo oeconomicus* model. Works dating from this period consequently have the rigorous, and perhaps reductionist, flavor of the arguments reprised in chapter 2. With regard to property rights over natural resources, for example, Harold Demsetz's classic reference "Toward a Theory of Property Rights" (1967) argues (on the basis of ethnological reports) that the establishment of private property is a function of the resource's value and the costs of enforcement. Evsey Domar's "Causes of Slavery and Serfdom" (1970) makes a very analogous argument, whereby the land/labor ratio and the means of coercion are the key variables. And Richard Posner's *Economic Analysis of Law* (1973) argues that the evolution of torts and contracts at common law has been systematically shaped by judges' concern to maximize joint values.[10] These broad insights have been readily incorporated into new, institutionally oriented economic histories. One such tendency has been called "neo-Malthusian," inasmuch as the balance between population and resources is viewed as a prime mover of institutional evolution: the locus classicus is Douglass North and Robert Thomas's *Rise of the Western World* (1973), which traces European development from A.D. 900 to about 1600. Another tendency might be termed the "rent-seeking" approach, in that it sees institutions in play

---

7. Günter Hesse, "Der Property-Rights-Ansatz" (1980); Hutter 1982; Veljanovski 1982. To quote Borchardt, for the German forerunners

     institutions and rights were . . . in no sense constellations of given parameters of economic action, but rather, to a great extent, variables in a much more extensive system. . . . One needs only peruse the extensive passages on economic organization in the texts of Albert Schäffle or Adolph Wagner in order to get some impression of the diversity – and profundity – of their assays at a theory of organization. (1977: 147–8)

8. Domar 1970: 31–2; Pryor 1977: 228.
9. Veljanovski 1982; Oliver Williamson, *The Economic Institutions of Capitalism* (1985): 3; Vanberg 1989.
10. We will not broach here the problem of whether Posner's view of the judiciary is in fact consonant with the *homo oeconomicus* model in the way that, say, the rent-seeking approach to regulation would be. Suffice it to say that Posner himself appears to consider his work to lie well within the bounds of the economic approach.

in a tug-of-war between allocative efficiency and redistributional politics: prominent here is Mancur Olson's *Rise and Decline of Nations* (1982).

In light of the earlier economists' willingness to diverge from the pecuniary rationality of *homo oeconomicus* (see chapter 3), it is unlikely that "hard" neoclassical institutionalists, were they aware of their predecessors' work, would receive it warmly. It therefore bodes well for a recovery of the new science, that contemporary economists have grown more willing to incorporate the findings of psychologists, sociologists, and evolutionary theorists which cast some doubt on the adequacy of *homo oeconomicus.* Such concepts as "satisficing" and "bounded rationality" have found their way into institutional analysis, as they have into economics at large.[11] An extreme example of this trend is evident in the increasing willingness of economists to employ the principle of "blind," or Darwinian, selection in such a way that even the core assumption of rational choice can be dispensed with. Hayek was among the first to apply this insight to legal evolution, particularly in his works of 1967 and 1973.[12] The origin of *legal* rules, according to Hayek, must be sought in the more primordial *heuristic* rules that guide human society in its earliest development:

> Man is as much a rule-following animal as a purpose-seeking one. And he is successful not because he knows why he ought to observe the rules which he does observe, or is even capable of stating all these rules in words, but because his thinking and acting are governed by rules which have by a process of selection been evolved in the society in which he lives, and which are thus the product of the experience of generations. (1973–9: 1:11)

Eventually, society grows so complex that these heuristics come (again by the process of natural selection) to be explicitly formulated and outfitted with social sanction: law is born (1:43). The great lesson of evolution remains, however, that "*the brain is an organ enabling us to absorb, but not to design culture*" (3:157). Hayek's model has been fairly faulted for imprecision;[13] but its core insight has been bolstered by Nelson and Winter's very

11. Eggertsson (1990: 7–10) has gone so far as to postulate two subschools in contemporary institutional analysis: a "neoinstitutional" tendency, which cleaves to *homo oeconomicus,* and a "new institutional" tendency, which diverges from it. To my knowledge, this distinction has not yet gained general acceptance. Robert C. Ellickson's "Bringing Culture and Frailty to Rational Actors" (1989) provides a helpful guide to trends in the economic analysis of law; on the prospects for economics as a whole, see Hahn 1991.

12. Hayek, "Notes on the Evolution of Systems of Rules of Conduct" (1967), and the first volume of *Law, Legislation and Liberty* (1973–9).

13. Notably by Vanberg's "Spontaneous Market Order and Social Rules" (1986),

influential *Evolutionary Theory of Economic Change* (1982), and through it has spawned a substantial literature of evolutionary institutionalism (see Hodgson 1993: 21–3).

From a very different quarter has come the further objection that a rational-choice approach to law gives short shrift to the motive power of ideology. A leader in this effort has been Douglass North, who himself did so much to entrench the neoclassical model of the state and of law. *Homo oeconomicus* may well be a useful first approximation, North has argued recently,

> but a major point of this study is that institutions, by reducing the price we pay for our convictions, make ideas, dogmas, fads, and ideologies important sources of institutional change. In turn, improved understanding of institutional change requires greater understanding than we now possess of just what makes ideas and ideologies catch hold. Therefore, we are still at something of a loss to define, in very precise terms, the interplay between changes in relative prices, the ideas and ideologies that form people's perceptions, and the roles that the two play in inducing changes in institutions.[14]

This call for greater cultural sensitivity has been voiced also by Alexander Field, Thrainn Eggertsson, Gary Libecap, and Avner Greif.[15] Heterogeneity and indeterminacy have been found to characterize not only ultimate values, but instrumental values (e.g., bona fides versus opportunism, cooperation versus confrontation) as well, all with important implications for politics and institutions. Knowingly or not, these economists have been building bridges back toward the concerns of the new science – not to mention those of Livy, 'ibn Khaldun, and the civic humanists.

Again like the new science (cf. chapter 4), some strands of the more recent institutionalism have taken a "constitutionalist" turn. Having surrendered the dream of engineering not only individual outcomes but even specific rules of action, these analysts proceed to the normative plane by asking what metarules would produce, on balance, the best aggregate set of rules (and hence outcomes). Unlike the practitioners of the new science, how-

---

where it is shown just how close Hayek's postulate of "group selection" comes – no doubt inadvertently – to the methodological holism he had spent his life combating.

14. North, *Institutions, Institutional Change and Economic Performance* (1990): 85–6. See also North 1981: 21, 31–2.

15. Field, "On the Explanation of Rules Using Rational Choice Models" (1979): 62 and passim; Eggertsson 1990: 73–7; Libecap 1992: 223; Greif, "Cultural Beliefs and the Organization of Society" (1994): 914–17 and passim.

ever, latter-day "constitutional economists" have proved to entertain even fewer illusions about the possibilities of majority or minority rule. The leading alternatives have been championed by Buchanan and Hayek.

Buchanan, in *The Calculus of Consent* and especially in *The Limits of Liberty* (1975), pursues a thought experiment of how and to what extent rational individuals will allow themselves to be bound by collective decision rules in a political society. This is social contract theory, and as such it has about it the inevitable whiff of history *als ob.* But given Buchanan's basically individualist and proceduralist ethical values, it is clear that the contractarian principle is more a moral criterion than a realistic simplification. And indeed, he does conclude that government by constitutional consent offers the best prospect of good legislation and a good society.

Hayek, by contrast, is evolutionist in approach and very nearly a constitutional anarchist by conviction. For him, Menger's vision of the "organic" development of institutions goes to the heart of the human race's successes:

> *Man did not adopt new rules of conduct because he was intelligent. He became intelligent by submitting to new rules of conduct.* The most important insight which so many rationalists still resist and are even inclined to brand as a superstition, namely that man has not only never invented his most beneficial institutions, from language to morals and law, and even today does not yet understand why he should preserve them when they satisfy neither his instincts nor his reason, still needs to be emphasized. The basic tools of civilization – language, morals, law and money – are all the result of spontaneous growth and not of design, and of the last two organized power has got hold and thoroughly corrupted them.[16]

Alongside the contractarian and evolutionist tendencies in contemporary "constitutional economics," the Posnerian call for judge-made law also deserves mention. Despite their divergences, these schools of thought share a characteristic impatience with the political processes of the modern nation-state. In this sense, they may well be considered heirs to the later practitioners of the new science.

Will the "new" new science of law escape the original's fate? On the one hand, the outlook for a welcome reception in the cognate disciplines (jurisprudence, history, sociology) is by no means brighter than a century ago. Professional specialization has proceeded apace, and it continues to

---

16. Hayek 1973–9: 3:163 (italics original). See also Robert Sugden's *Economics of Rights, Co-operation and Welfare* (1986), which employs Buchanan's conjectural approach to arrive at basically Hayekian conclusions.

confront the interdisciplinary ideal with mutual jealousy and sheer incomprehension. Moreover, the "new" institutional economics has shown a certain reluctance to translate their research into terms readily assimilable by a lay audience, a habit which rubs rhetorical salt into the real wounds opened by the division of intellectual labor. This, at least, is something of which the new science could never have stood accused.

On the other hand, there are grounds for optimism as well, especially regarding the staying power of institutional analysis within economic discourse. Contemporary economists enjoy greater methodological consensus than ever before and are therefore readier to engage the thoughts, and challenge the excesses, of peers than were their predecessors. Hence it is far less likely that a future generation will be inclined – or if inclined, able – to dismiss the efforts of the new institutionalists as wrongheaded, or even merely as irrelevant to true economic science. Ironically, perhaps, methodological stringency appears to have already forced an incipient rapprochement between the "old" and "new" brands of institutional economics.[17] If the thaw continues, then the original new science of law may yet be rescued from oblivion.

17. See A. W. Coats, "Confrontation in Toronto" (1990), and the symposium of which it is a part.

# Biographical notes

**Ashley**, William J. (1860–1927). Education: history, political economy (Oxford). Vocation: prof. constitutional history and political economy (Toronto); prof. economic history (Harvard); prof. commerce (Birmingham).

**Ayres**, Clarence E. (1891–1972). Education: philosophy (Brown, Chicago). Vocation: prof. philosophy (Chicago, Amherst, Reed); prof. economics (Texas).

**Bagehot**, Walter (1826–77). Education: law and economics (London). Vocation: banker; editor, *The Economist*.

**Baumstark**, Eduard (1807–89). Education: law and *Kameralwissenschaft* (Heidelberg). Vocation: docent in *Kameralwissenschaft* (Heidelberg); prof. *Staatswissenschaft* and *Kameralwissenschaft* (Greifswald).

**Beauregard**, Paul-Victor (1853–1919). Education: law (Paris). Vocation: prof. law (Douai); prof. political economy (École des Hautes Études Commerciales, École des Sciences Politiques).

**Béchaux**, Auguste (1854–1922). Education: classics (Dôle); law and philosophy (Innsbruck, Paris); political science (Louvain). Vocation: prof. law and political economy (Lille).

**Bernard**, François (1859–1920). No further information.

**Block**, Maurice (1816–1901). Vocation: economist; civil servant.

**Braun**, Karl Joseph Wilhelm (1822–93). Education: philology (Marburg); law (Göttingen). Vocation: editor; author; politician.

**Brentano**, Lujo (1844–1931). Education: law (Heidelberg); economics (Göttingen). Vocation: prof. economics, public finance, and economic history (Berlin, Breslau, Strassburg, Vienna, Leipzig, Munich).

**Brodnitz**, Georg (b. 1876). Education: law and *Staatswissenschaft* (Paris, Oxford, Berlin, Leipzig, Halle). Vocation: prof. economics (Halle).

**Bücher**, Karl (1847–1930). Education: history, philology, and economics (Göttingen); *Staatswissenschaft* (Munich). Vocation: prof. *Statistik* (Dorpat, TH Karlsruhe, Leipzig).

**Cairnes**, John Elliott (1823–75). Education: Trinity College, Dublin. Vocation: prof. economics (Dublin); prof. political economy and jurisprudence (Galway); prof. political economy (University College, London).

**Cherbuliez**, Antoine Elisée (1797–1869). Education: law (Geneva). Vocation: Prof. law and political economy (Geneva); prof. political economy (Zürich).

**Cohn**, Gustav (1840–1919). Education: *Staatswissenschaft* and economics (Leipzig, Berlin, Heidelberg). Vocation: prof. *Staatswissenschaft* (Riga, Zürich, Göttingen).

**Colajanni**, Napoleone (1847–1921). Education: medicine (Naples). Vocation: prof. *Statistica* (Naples); writer; politician; sociologist; parliamentarian; journalist.

**Colson**, Léon Clement (1853–1939). Education: engineering and law (Paris). Vocation: lecturer in economics (Paris); engineer; civil servant.

**Commons**, John R. (1862–1945). Education: theology (Oberlin); economics (Johns Hopkins). Vocation: prof. economics (Wesleyan, Oberlin, Indiana, Syracuse, Wisconsin).

**Cossa**, Luigi (1831–96). Education: economics (Göttingen, under Roscher). Vocation: prof. political economy (Pavia).

**Courcelle-Seneuil**, Jean-Gustave (1813–92). Education: law (Paris, no degree). Vocation: prof. political economy (Santiago de Chile); journalist; businessman; civil servant.

**Cunningham**, William (1849–1919). Education: arts (Edinburgh); moral science (Cambridge, Tübingen). Vocation: prof. economics (King's College, Cambridge).

**Diehl**, Karl (1864–1943). Education: (Berlin, Jena, Halle). Vocation: prof. economics (Halle, Rostock, Königsberg, Freiburg i.B.).

**Dietzel**, Heinrich (1857–1935). Education: law and *Staatswissenschaft* (Heidelberg, Berlin). Vocation: prof. economics (Dorpat, Bonn).

**Dupuit**, Arsine-Jules-Etienne-Juvenal (1804–66). Education: polytechnic (Paris). Vocation: engineer; civil servant.

**Ely**, Richard Theodore (1854–1943). Education: general (Columbia); political economy (Heidelberg, Berlin). Vocation: prof. economics (Johns Hopkins, Wisconsin).

**Fuchs**, Carl Johannes (1865–1934). Education: economics (Strassburg). Vocation: prof. economics and public finance (Greifswald, Freiburg i.B., Tübingen).

**George**, Henry (1839–97). Education: informal. Vocation: publicist; businessman.

**Gottl-Ottlilienfeld**, Friedrich von (1868–1958). Education: economics (Vienna, Berlin, Heidelberg). Vocation: prof. economics (Brunn, Munich, Hamburg, Kiel, Berlin).

**Graziani**, Augusto (1865–1938). Education: political economy and public finance (Modena, Pavia). Vocation: prof. political economy and public finance (Siena, Naples).

**Grünberg**, Karl (1861–1940). Education: law, *Staatswissenschaft,* and economics (Vienna). Vocation: prof. political economy (Vienna); prof. *wirtschaftlichen Staatswissenschaften* (Frankfurt a.M.).

**Hadley**, Arthur Twining (1856–1930). Education: general (Yale); economics (Berlin). Vocation: prof. economics; dean; president (Yale).

**Hamilton**, Walton Hale (1881–1958). Education: economics (Texas). Vocation: prof. economics (Chicago, Amherst, Yale Law).

**Hanssen**, Georg (1809–94). Education: law and economics (Heidelberg); *Kameralwissenschaft* (Kiel). Vocation: prof. economics (Leipzig, Göttingen, Berlin); editor, *Archiv der politischen Ökonomie und Polizeiwissenschaft.*

**Hasbach**, Wilhelm (1849–1920). Education: philology and history (Münster, Bonn, Tübingen); *Staatswissenschaft* (Berlin, Greifswald). Vocation: prof. *Staatswissenschaft* (Greifswald, Königsberg, Kiel).

**Helferich**, Johann Alfons Renatus von (1817–92). Education: political economy (Erlangen, Munich). Vocation: prof. political economy (Freiburg i.B., Tübingen, Göttingen, Munich).

**Hildebrand**, Bruno (1812–78). Education: history (Breslau). Vocation: docent in history (Breslau); prof. *Staatswissenschaft* (Marburg, Zürich, Bern, Jena).

**Hildebrand**, Richard (1840–1918). Education: (Leipzig, Bern, Jena). Vocation: prof. political economy and public finance (Graz).

**Hoyt**, Homer (1895–1984). Vocation: prof. economics; real estate consultant.

**Inama-Sternegg**, Karl Theodor von (1843–1908). Education: history and economics (Munich). Vocation: prof. political science (Innsbruck); prof. political economy (Prague, Breslau); prof. *Statistik* and administration (Vienna).

**Kautz**, Gyula (1829–1909). Education: law (Pest); economics (Berlin, Heidelberg). Vocation: prof. economics and law (Grosswardein, Ofen, Pest).

**Keussler**, Johannes von (1843–97). Vocation: economist; historian.

**Knapp**, Georg Friedrich (1842–1926). Education: economics (Göttingen). Vocation: prof. economics (Strassburg).

**Knies**, Karl (1821–98). Education: history and *Staatswissenschaft* (Marburg). Vocation: prof. history, geography, *Kameralwissenschaft,* and *Staatswissenschaft* (Marburg, Freiburg i.B., Heidelberg).

**Lampertico**, Fedele (1833–1906). Education: law (Padua). Vocation: professor (Padua); economist; publicist; parliamentarian.

**Laveleye**, Émile de (1822–92). Education: philosophy (Louvain); law (Ghent). Vocation: prof. political economy (Liège).

**Le Hardy de Beaulieu**, Charles (1816–71). Vocation: prof. economics (Mons [Belgium]).

**Leroy-Beaulieu**, Paul (1843–1916). Education: law. Vocation: prof. political economy and public finance (Paris).

**Leslie**, Thomas Edward Cliffe (1827–82). Education: classics and philosophy (Dublin); law (London). Vocation: prof. jurisprudence and political economy (Belfast).

**Lewinski**, Jan Stanislaw (1885–1930). Vocation: prof. economics and sociology (Warsaw).

**List**, Friedrich (1789–1846). Education: law and cameralism (Tübingen). Vocation: civil servant; publicist; businessman; briefly prof. *Staatswirtschaft* and *Staatspraxis* (Tübingen).

**Loria**, Achille (1857–1943). Education: law (Bologna); economics (Pavia, Rome, Berlin). Vocation: prof. political economy (Siena, Padua, Turin); parliamentarian.

**Madrazo**, Santiago Diego (1816–71). Education: law (Salamanca); logic, history, and political economy (Madrid). Vocation: prof. political economy (Salamanca, Madrid); parliamentarian.

**Mangoldt**, Hans Karl Emil von (1824–68). Education: *Staatswissenschaft* (Tübingen, Göttingen). Vocation: prof. political economy and *Staatswissenschaft* (Göttingen, Freiburg i.B.); civil servant.

**Marshall**, Alfred (1842–1924). Education: mathematics and moral science (Cambridge). Vocation: lecturer in moral science (Cambridge); prof. political economy (Bristol, Cambridge).

**Marx**, Karl (1819–83). Education: philosophy (Bonn, Berlin, Jena). Vocation: publicist.

**Meitzen**, August (1822–1910). Education: law and *Staatswissenschaft.* Vocation: prof. economics and *Staatswissenschaft* (Berlin).

**Menger**, Carl (1840–1921). Education: law and politics (Vienna, Prague, Cracow). Vocation: prof. political economy (Vienna).

**Miaskowski**, August von (1838–99). Education: law (Dorpat, Heidelberg), *Staatswissenschaft* (Berlin, Jena). Vocation: prof. economics and *Staatswissenschaft* (Basel, Breslau, Vienna).

**Mill**, John Stuart (1806–73). Education: principally by James Mill. Vocation: inspector of E.I.C.; parliamentarian.

**Minghetti**, Marco (1818–86). Education: physics, mathematics, and political economy (Bologna). Vocation: editor; author; civil servant; politician.

**Molinari**, Gustave de (1819–1912). Vocation: prof. political economy (Royal Brussels Museum Library); editor, *Journal des Économistes*.

**Navratil**, Akos von (1875–1952). Vocation: prof. economics and public finance (Kolozsvár/Klausenburg/Cluj).

**Neurath**, Otto (1882–1945). Education: political economy (Heidelberg). Vocation: prof. economics (Neue Handelsakademie Wien); philosophy.

**Nicholson**, Joseph Shield (1850–1927). Education: mathematics and moral science (London, Cambridge). Vocation: prof. political economy and mercantile law (Edinburgh).

**Oppenheimer**, Franz (1864–1943). Education: medicine (Berlin); economics (Kiel). Vocation: docent in *Staatswissenschaft* (Berlin); prof. economics and sociology (Frankfurt).

**Page**, Thomas Walker (1867–1937). Vocation: economist.

**Pareto**, Vilfredo (1848–1923). Education: engineering (Polytechnic Institute, Turin). Vocation: prof. political economy (Lausanne); engineer.

**Philippovich von Philippsberg**, Eugen (1858–1917). Education: law and Economics (Graz, Vienna). Vocation: prof. economics and public finance (Freiburg i.B., Vienna).

**Rodbertus-Jagetzow**, Karl (1895–75). Education: law (Göttingen, Berlin). Vocation: barrister; private scholar.

**Roesler**, Hermann (1834–94). Education: law and *Staatswissenschaft* (Erlangen, Tübingen). Vocation: prof. *Staatswissenschaft* (Erlangen, Rostock), adviser to Japanese government.

**Rogers**, James Edwin Thorold (1823–90). Education: lit. hum. (London, Oxford). Vocation: clergyman; prof. economics and statistics (London, Oxford).

**Roscher**, Wilhelm Georg Friedrich (1817–94). Education: *Staatswissenschaft* (Göttingen). Vocation: prof. *Staatswissenschaft* (Göttingen, Leipzig).

**Sax**, Emil (1845–1927). Education: law (Vienna). Vocation: prof. economics and public finance (Vienna, Prague), parliamentarian.

**Schäffle**, Albert Eberhard Friedrich (1831–1904). Education: *Staatswissenschaften* (Tübingen). Vocation: prof. economics (Tübingen, Vienna); minister; editor, *Zeitschrift für die gesamte Staatswissenschaft*.

**Scheel**, Hans von (1839–1901). Education: law (Halle); philosophy (Jena). Vocation: prof. economics (Proskau); prof. *Staatswissenschaft* (Bern).

**Schmoller**, Gustav (1838–1917). Education: *Staatswissenschaft*, philosophy, and history (Tübingen). Vocation: prof. *Staatswissenschaft* (Halle, Strassburg, Berlin).

**Schwiedland**, Eugen Peter (1863–1937). Vocation: prof. political economy (TH Vienna).

**Sedgwick**, Theodore (1780–1839). Education: law (Yale). Vocation: lawyer; businessman; political activist.

**Seligman**, Edwin Robert Anderson (1861–1939). Education: economics (Berlin, Heidelberg, Geneva, Paris, Columbia). Vocation: prof. economics (Columbia).

**Sering**, Max (1857–1939). Education: law and *Staatswissenschaft* (Strassburg, Leipzig, Bonn). Vocation: prof. *Staatswissenschaft* (Bonn, Berlin).

**Simkovich**, Vladimir G. (1874–1959). Vocation: prof. economic history (Columbia).

**Sismondi**, J.-C.-L. Simonde de (1773–1842). Vocation: bank clerk; farmer; politician; economic author.

**Sombart**, Werner (1863–1941). Education: law, economics, history, and philosophy (Pisa, Berlin, Rome). Vocation: prof. political economy (Breslau, Berlin).

**Stein**, Lorenz von (1815–90). Education: law (Kiel, Paris). Vocation: prof. *Staatswissenschaft* (Kiel); prof. political economy (Vienna).

**Veblen**, Thorstein Bunde (1857–1929). Education: philosophy (Carleton, Yale). Vocation: prof. economics (Chicago, Stanford, Missouri, New School for Social Research).

**Voigt**, Andreas (1860–1941). Education: mathematics, natural science, philosophy, and economics (Berlin, Freiburg i.B., Kiel, Heidelberg). Vocation: prof. economics (Frankfurt a.M.).

**Wagner**, Adolph Heinrich Gotthelf (1835–1917). Education: *Staatswissenschaft* (Heidelberg, Göttingen). Vocation: prof. economics (Berlin).

**Walras**, Léon (1834–1910). Education: engineering (Paris), incomplete. Vocation: prof. political economy (Lausanne).

**Weber**, Max (1864–1920). Education: law (Berlin). Vocation: prof. economics and public finance (Freiburg i.B., Heidelberg, Vienna); prof. social science (Munich).

**Wieser**, Friedrich Freiherr von (1851–1926). Education: law and economics (Vienna, Heidelberg, Leipzig, Jena). Vocation: prof. economics (Prague, Vienna); parliamentarian.

**Wirth**, Max (1822–1900). Education: law and *Staatswissenschaft* (Heidelberg). Vocation: editor; publicist; economist.

**Wittich**, Werner (1867–1937). Education: law. Vocation: prof. economics and public finance (Strassburg).

# References

Adams, Henry Carter. 1896. "Economics and Jurisprudence." Presidential address to the American Economic Association. Reprint; New York: Macmillan, 1954.

Aguanno, Giuseppe D'. 1890. *La genesi e l'evoluzione del diritto civile, secondo le risultanze delle science antropologiche e storico-sociale, con applicazioni pratiche al codice vigente.* Turin: Bocca.

Alchian, Armen. 1965. "Some Economics of Property Rights." *Il Politico.* Reprinted in *Economic Forces at Work:* 127–49. Indianapolis: Liberty Press, 1977.

Anzilotti, Dionisio. 1892. *La filosofia del diritto e la sociologia.* Reprinted in *Opere di Dionisio Anzilotti,* 4:495–671. Padua: Cedam, 1963.

Arnold, Wilhelm. 1861. *Zur Geschichte des Eigentums in den deutschen Städten.* Basel: H. Georg.

———. 1863. *Recht und Wirtschaft nach geschichtlicher Ansicht: Drei Vorlesungen.* Basel: H. Georg.

———. 1865. *Cultur und Rechtsleben.* Berlin: F. Dummler.

Arrow, Kenneth J. 1951. *Social Choice and Individual Values.* New York: Wiley.

Ascher, Abraham. 1963. "Professors as Propagandists: The Politics of the *Kathedersozialisten.*" *Journal of Central European Affairs* 23:282–302.

Ashley, William James. 1891. "The English Manor." Introduction to the English translation of Fustel de Coulanges 1889: vii–xlviii.

Ault, David E., and Rutman, Gilbert L. 1979. "The Development of Individual Rights to Property in Tribal Africa." *Journal of Law and Economics* 22:163–82.

Ayres, Clarence R. 1951. "The Co-ordinates of Institutionalism." *American Economic Review* 41:47–55.

Azcárate, Gumersindo de. 1879–83. *Ensayo sobre la historia del derecho de propiedad y su estado actual en Europa.* (Biblioteca jurídica de autores espanoles, 2:8.) Madrid: Imprenta de la Revista de Legislación.

Bagehot, Walter. 1876. "The Postulates of English Political Economy." *Fortnightly*

*Review*. Reprinted in *Collected Works of Walter Bagehot*, ed. N. St John-Stevas, vol. 11. London: The Economist, 1978.

Baron, Julius. 1877. "Jurisprudenz und Nationalökonomie" [review of Wagner 1876]. *Kritische Vierteljahrschrift für Gesetzgebung und Rechtswissenschaft* 19:372–401.

Barzel, Yoram. 1989. *Economic Analysis of Property Rights*. Cambridge: Cambridge University Press.

Bastiat, Frédéric. 1848. "Propriété et loi." *Journal des Économistes*, 15 May. Reprinted in *Oeuvres complètes de Frédéric Bastiat*, 4th ed.: 275–97. Paris: Guillaumin, 1878.

Baudrillart, Henri. 1855. "Du principe de propriété." *Journal des Économistes*, ser. 2, no. 8: 321–42.

———. 1867. *La propriété*. Paris: Guillaumin.

Baumstark, Eduard. 1835. *Kameralistische Encyclopädie*. Heidelberg and Leipzig: K. Groos.

———. 1865. "Die Volkswirthschaft nach Menschenrassen, Volksstämmen und Völkern." *Jahrbücher für Nationalökonomie und Statistik* 5:81–134.

Bazard, Saint-Amand, et al. 1829. *Doctrine de Saint-Simon. Exposition. Première année, 1829*. Translated *The Doctrine of Saint-Simon: An Exposition. First Year, 1828–1829*. Boston: Beacon, 1958.

Beaglehole, Ernest. 1931. *Property: A Study in Social Psychology*. London: Allen and Unwin.

Beard, Charles Austin. 1913. *An Economic Interpretation of the Constitution of the United States*. 2d ed.; New York: Macmillan, 1935.

Beauregard, Paul. 1891. "Droit." In *Nouveau dictionnaire d'économie politique*, ed. Joseph Chailley, 1:741–46. Paris: Guillaumin.

Béchaux, Auguste. 1889. *Le droit et les faits économiques*. Paris: Guillaumin.

Bell, John F. 1953. *A History of Economic Thought*. New York: Ronald.

Below, Georg von. 1897. Review of Meitzen 1895. *Historische Zeitschrift* 78:471–5.

———. 1898. "Unfreiheit." In *Wörterbuch der Volkswirtschaft*, ed. Ludwig Elster, 2:721–77. Jena: G. Fischer.

———. 1900. "Der Osten und der Westen Deutschlands: Der Ursprung der Gutsherrschaft." In *Territorium und Stadt: Aufsätze zur deutschen Verfassungs-, Verwaltungs-und Wirtschaftsgeschichte*, 1–94. Munich and Leipzig: R. Oldenbourg.

———. 1901. "Über Theorien der wirtschaftlichen Entwicklung der Völker, mit besonderer Rücksicht auf die Stadtwirtschaft des deutschen Mittelalters." *Historische Zeitschrift* 86:1–77.

———. 1903. "Das kurze Leben einer vielgenannten Theorie (Über die Lehre vom Ureigentum)." Reprinted in *Probleme der Wirtschaftsgeschichte*, 2d ed., 1–26. Tübingen: J. C. B Mohr, 1926.

———. 1920. "Die Haupttatsachen der älteren deutschen Agrargeschichte." In *Probleme der Wirtschaftsgeschichte*, 2d ed., 27–77. Tübingen: J. C. B Mohr, 1926.

Benson, Lee. 1950. "Achille Loria's Influence on American Economic Thought." *Agricultural History* 24:182–99.

———. 1960. *Turner and Beard: American Historical Writing Reconsidered*. Glencoe, Ill.: Free Press.

Bernard, François. 1886. "L'évolution de la propriété foncière." *Journal des Économistes,* ser. 4, no. 35: 173–99.

Bernheim, Ernst. 1903. *Lehrbuch der historischen Methode und der Geschichtsphilosophie, mit Nachweis der wichtigsten Quellen und Hilfsmittel zum Studium der Geschichte,* 3d and 4th eds. Leipzig: Duncker and Humblot.

Berolzheimer, Fritz. 1904–7. *System der Rechts- und Wirtschaftsphilosophie,* 5 vols. Munich: C. H. Beck.

———. 1909–10. "Grundprobleme der Rechts- und Wirtschaftsphilosophie samt der Soziologie." *Archiv für Rechts- und Wirtschaftsphilosophie* 3:28–35.

———. 1912. *The World's Legal Philosophies.* Boston: Boston Book Co. [Abridged translation of Berolzheimer 1904–7.]

Black, Duncan. 1958. *The Theory of Committees and Elections.* Cambridge: Cambridge University Press.

Block, Maurice. 1890. *Les progrès de la science économique depuis A. Smith.* Paris: Guillaumin.

Blum, Jerome. 1957. "The Rise of Serfdom in Eastern Europe." *American Historical Review* 62:807–36.

Boccardo, Gerolamo. 1853. *Trattato teoretico-pratico di economia politica,* 3 vols. Turin: Roux e Favale.

Böhm, Franz, Walter Eucken, and Hans Grossmann-Doerth. 1937. "Unsere Aufgabe" [preface to Böhm's *Die Ordnung der Wirtschaft als geschichtliche Aufgabe und rechtsschöpferische Leistung*]. Translated "Our Task," in *Germany's Social Market Economy: Origins and Evolution,* ed. Alan Peacock and Hans Willgerodt, 15–26. Basingstoke: Macmillan, 1989.

Böhm-Bawerk, Eugen von. 1881. *Rechte und Verhältnisse vom Standpunkte der volkswirthschaftlichen Güterlehre. Kritische Studie.* Innsbruck: Wagner.

Borchardt, Knut. 1977. "Der Property-Rights-Ansatz in der Wirtschaftsgeschichte: Zeichen für eine systematische Neuorientierung des Faches?" In *Theorien in der Praxis des Historikers,* ed. Jürgen Kocka, 140–56. Göttingen: Vandenhoeck and Ruprecht.

Braun, Karl. 1865. "Zur Fysiologie des Eigenthums und des Erbrechts." *Vierteljahrschrift für Volkswirtschaft und Kulturgeschichte* 3:55–88.

Brentano, Lujo. 1888. "Die klassische Nationalökonomie." Reprinted in *Der wirtschaftende Mensch in der Geschichte: Gesammelte Reden und Aufsätze,* 1–33. Leipzig: F. Meiner, 1923.

———. 1893. "Die Volkswirthschaft und ihre konkreten Grundbedingungen." *Zeitschrift für Social- und Wirthschaftsgeschichte* 1:77–153.

———. 1895. *Ueber Anerbenrecht und Grundeigenthum.* Berlin: O. Haring.

———. 1901. "Ethik und Volkswirtschaft in der Geschichte." Reprinted in *Der wirtschaftende Mensch in der Geschichte: Gesammelte Reden und Aufsätze,* 34–76. Leipzig: F. Meiner, 1923.

———. 1913. "Über Begriff und Wandlungen der Wirtschaftseinheit." Reprinted in *Der wirtschaftende Mensch in der Geschichte: Gesammelte Reden und Aufsätze,* 261–81. Leipzig: F. Meiner, 1923.

Brodnitz, Georg. 1912. "Die Grundherrschaft in England. Ein Beitrag zur vergleichenden Wirtschaftsgeschichte." *Jahrbücher für Nationalökonomie und Statistik* 98:146–78.

Bruch, Rüdiger vom. 1985. "Zur Historisierung der Staatswissenschaften: von der Kameralistik zur historischen Schule der Nationalökonomie." *Berichte zur Wissenschaftsgeschichte* 8:131–46.

———. 1988. "Gustav Schmoller." In *Deutsche Geschichtswissenschaft um 1900,* ed. Notker Hammerstein. Stuttgart: Steiner.

Brückner, Jutta. 1977. *Staatswissenschaften, Kameralismus und Naturrecht. Ein Beitrag zur Geschichte der Politischen Wissenschaft im Deutschland des späten 17. und frühen 18. Jahrhunderts.* Munich: Beck.

Brunner, Heinrich. 1887–92. *Deutsche Rechtsgeschichte,* 2 vols. Leipzig: Duncker and Humblot.

Buchanan, James M. 1975. *The Limits of Liberty: Between Anarchy and Leviathan.* Chicago: University of Chicago Press.

———. 1991. "Economics in the Post-Socialist Century." *Economic Journal* 101:15–21.

Buchanan, James M., and Gordon Tullock. 1962. *The Calculus of Consent.* Ann Arbor: University of Michigan Press.

Bücher, Karl. 1879. *Das Ureigentum.* Leipzig: F. A. Brockhaus. [Translation of and supplementary materials to Laveleye 1874.]

———. 1893. *Die Entstehung der Volkswirtschaft. Vorträge und Versuche.* 7th ed.; Tübingen: H. Laupp, 1910.

———. 1902. *Die Allmende in ihrer wirtschaftlichen und sozialen Bedeutung.* (*Soziale Streitfragen,* 12.) Berlin: J. Harrwitz.

———. 1908. "Der wirtschaftliche Urzustand" and "Die Wirtschaft der Naturvölker." [Addenda to the 6th and subsequent editions of Bücher 1893.]

———. 1914. "Volkswirtschaftliche Entwicklungsstufen." In *Grundriß der Sozialökonomik,* ed. S. Altmann et al., 2:2–18. Tübingen: J. C. B Mohr.

Burrow, J. W. 1966. *Evolution and Society: A Study in Victorian Social Theory.* Cambridge: Cambridge University Press.

Cairnes, John Elliott. 1862. *The Slave Power: Its Character, Career and Probable Designs.* 2d ed.; London: Macmillan, 1863.

Carey, Henry C. 1837–40. *Principles of Political Economy,* 4 vols. Philadelphia: Lea and Blanchard.

Cheinisse, Léon. 1914. *Les idées politiques des Physiocrates.* Paris: A. Rousseau.

Cherbuliez, Antoine. 1848. *Simples notions de l'ordre sociale à l'usage de tout le monde.* Paris: Guillaumin.

———. 1862. *Précis de la science économique.* Paris: Guillaumin.

Chickering, Roger. 1993. *Karl Lamprecht: A German Academic Life (1856–1915).* New Jersey: Humanities Press.

Ciccotti, Ettore. 1899. *Il tramonto della schiavitù nel mondo antico: un saggio.* Rome: Laterza.

Coase, Ronald. 1937. "The Nature of the Firm." *Economica,* n. s., 4:386–405.

———. 1960. "The Problem of Social Cost." *Journal of Law and Economics* 3:1–44.

———. 1984. "The New Institutional Economics." *Zeitschrift für die Gesamte Staatswissenschaft* 140:229–31.

Coats, A. W. 1960. "The First Two Decades of the A.E.A." *American Economic Review* 50:555–74.

Coats, A. W. 1990. "Confrontation in Toronto: Reactions to the 'Old' versus the 'New' Institutionalism Sessions." *Review of Political Economy* 2:88–93.

Cobden Club. 1870. *Systems of Land Tenure in Various Countries.* London: Macmillan.

Cohn, Gustav. 1885. *Grundlegung der Nationalökonomie. Ein Lesebuch für Studierende.* Stuttgart: F. Enke.

———. 1900. "Ueber die Vereinigung der Staatswissenschaften mit den Juristenfakultäten." *Jahrbücher für Nationalökonomie und Statistik* 75:755–69.

Colajanni, Napoleone. 1887. "Di alcuni studî recenti sulla proprietà collettiva." *Giornale degli Economisti* 2:519–32.

Colmeiro [y Penido], Manuel. 1859. *Principios de economía política.* 4th ed.; Madrid: F. Martínez García, 1873.

———. 1863. *Historia de la economía política en España.* Madrid: C. López.

Colson, Léon. 1901–7. *Cours d'économie politique,* 3 vols. Paris: Gauthiers-Villars.

Commons, John R. 1893. *The Distribution of Wealth.* New York: Macmillan.

———. 1899–1900. "A Sociological View of Sovereignty." *American Journal of Sociology.* Reprint; New York: A. M. Kelley, 1965.

———. 1924. *The Legal Foundations of Capitalism.* New York: Macmillan.

———. 1925. "Law and Economics." *Yale Law Review* 34:371–82.

———. 1935. *Institutional Economics: Its Place in Political Economy.* New York: Macmillan.

Comte, Auguste. 1851–4. *Système de politique positive ou Traité de sociologie instituant la religion de l'humanité,* 4 vols. Translated *System of Positive Polity.* London: Longmans, 1875–7.

Cossa, Luigi. 1875. *Primi elementi di economia politica.* 14th ed., translated *Premiers éléments d'économie politique.* Paris: M. Giard, 1922.

Courcelle-Seneuil, Jean-Gustave. 1858. *Traité théorique et pratique d'économie politique.* 3d ed., 2 vols.; Paris: Guillaumin, 1891.

———. 1863. "De la nécessité d'enseigner l'économie politique dans les écoles de droit." *Journal des Économistes,* 2d ser., no. 39: 5–18.

———. 1874. Translator's introduction to Henry Sumner Maine, *L'Ancien droit.* Paris: A. Durand.

———. 1877. "L'enseignement de l'économie politique dans les facultés de droit." *Journal des Économistes,* 3d ser., no. 46: 173–87.

———. 1878. "Conjectures sur l'histoire du droit de propriété." *Journal des Économistes,* 4th ser., no. 1: 161–78.

———. 1892. "Propriété (Droit de)." In *Nouveau dictionnaire d'économie politique,* ed. Léon Say, 2:641–55. Paris: Guillaumin.

Cross, Melvin L., and Robert B. Ekelund. 1981. "A. T. Hadley: The American Invention of the Economics of Property Rights and Public Goods." *Review of Social Economy:* 37–50.

Cunningham, William. 1896. *Modern Civilization in Some of Its Economic Aspects.* London: Methuen.

Dankwardt, H. 1857–9. *Nationalökonomie und Jurisprudenz,* 4 vols. Rostock: G. B. Leopold.

———. 1862. *Nationalökonomisch-civilistische Studien.* Leipzig and Heidelberg: Winter.

Dargun, Lothar. 1884. "Ursprung und Entwicklungsgeschichte des Eigentums." *Zeitschrift für Vergleichende Rechtswissenschaft* 5:1–115.

Del Vecchio, G. 1935. "Droit et économie." *Revue d'Économie Politique* 49:1457–94.

Demsetz, Harold. 1967. "Toward a Theory of Property Rights." *American Economic Review* 57:347–59.

Diehl, Karl. 1897. "Wirtschaft und Recht." *Jahrbücher für Nationalökonomie und Statistik* 69:813–50.

———. 1923–4. *Theoretische Nationalökonomie,* 2 vols. Jena: G. Fischer.

———. 1929. *Die rechtlichen Grundlagen des Kapitalismus.* Jena: G. Fischer.

———. 1941. *Die sozialrechtliche Richtung in der Nationalökonomie.* Jena: G. Fischer.

Dietzel, Heinrich. 1897. "Stud. jur. et cam." *Jahrbücher für Nationalökonomie und Statistik* 69:679–711.

Domar, Evsey. 1970. "The Causes of Slavery and Serfdom: A Hypothesis." *Journal of Economic History* 30:18–32.

Dorfman, Joseph. 1946–59. *The Economic Mind in American Civilization,* 5 vols. New York: Viking.

Downs, Anthony. 1957. *An Economic Theory of Democracy.* New York: Harper.

Dupont de Nemours, Pierre Samuel. 1768. *De l'origine et des progrès d'une science nouvelle.* Reprinted in *Physiocrates,* ed. E. Daire. Paris: Guillaumin, 1846.

Dupuit, Arsine-Jules-Émile-Juvenal. 1861. "Le principe de la propriété". *Journal des Économistes,* 2d ser., no. 29: 321–47; no. 30: 28–55.

Eggertsson, Thrainn. 1990. *Economic Behavior and Institutions.* Cambridge: Cambridge University Press.

Eiselen, Johann Friedrich Gottfried. 1828. *Handbuch des Systems der Staatswissenschaften.* Breslau: J. Max.

Eisermann, Gottfried. 1956. *Die Grundlagen des Historismus in der deutschen Nationalökonomie.* Stuttgart: F. Enke.

Ellickson, Robert C. 1989. "Bringing Culture and Human Frailty to Rational Actors: A Critique of Classical Law & Economics." *Chicago-Kent Law Review* 65:23–55.

Ely, Richard T. 1903. *Studies in the Evolution of Industrial Society.* New York: Macmillan.

———. 1914. *Property and Contract in Their Relations to the Distribution of Wealth,* 2 vols. New York: Macmillan.

Engels, Friedrich. 1884. *Der Ursprung der Familie, des Privateigentums, und des Staates.* Translated *The Origin of the Family, Private Property and the State.* New York: International Publishers, 1972.

Englard, Izhak. 1990. "Victor Mataja's *Liability for Damages from an Economic Viewpoint:* A Centennial to an Ignored Economic Analysis of Tort." *International Review of Law and Economics* 10:173–91.

Eschenmayer, P. C. H. 1809. *Lehrbuch über das Staats-Oekonomie Recht.* Frankfurt a.M.: F. Esslinger.

Eucken, Walter. 1940. *Grundlagen der Nationalökonomie.* Translated *Foundations of Economics.* London: W. Hodge, 1950.

Faucci, Ricardo. 1976–7. "Revisione del marxismo e teoria economica della proprietà in Italia, 1880–1900: Achille Loria (e gli altri)." *Quaderni Fiorentini per la Storia del Pensiero Giuridico Moderno* 5:587–680.

———. 1986. "Note su positivismo e pensiero economico in Italia tra otte e novecento." *Rivista Internazionale di Scienze Economiche e Commerciali* 33:75–94.

Faucher, Léon. 1853. "Propriété." In *Dictionnaire de l'économie politique,* ed. C. Coquelin et al., 2:460–72. Paris: Guillaumin.

Fawcett, Henry. 1863. *Manual of Political Economy.* London: Macmillan.

Felix, Ludwig. 1883. *Entwicklungsgeschichte des Eigenthums unter kulturgeschichtlichem und wirtschaftlichem Gesichtspunkte.* Leipzig: Duncker and Humblot.

Fenoaltea, Stefano. 1988. "Transaction Costs, Whig History, and the Open Fields." *Politics and Society* 16:171–240.

Field, Alexander J. 1979. "On the Explanation of Rules Using Rational Choice Models." *Journal of Economic Issues* 13:49–72.

Forbes, Duncan. 1954. "Scientific Whiggism: Adam Smith and John Millar." *Cambridge Journal* 7:643–70.

Frey, Bruno S., and Rene L. Frey. 1973. "The Economic Theory of Politics: A Survey of German Contributions." *Public Choice* 1:81–89.

Fuchs, Albert. 1949. *Geistige Strömungen in Österreich, 1867–1918.* Vienna: Globus.

Fuchs, Carl Johannes. 1898a. "Bauernbefreiung." In *Wörterbuch der Volkswirtschaft,* ed. Ludwig Elster, 1:297–311. Jena: G. Fischer.

———. 1898b. *Die Epochen der deutschen Agrargeschichte und Agrarpolitik.* Jena: G. Fischer.

Fustel de Coulanges, Numa Denis. 1889. "Le problème des origines de la propriété foncière." *Revue des Questions Historiques.* Translated *The Origin of Property in Land.* London: S. Sonnenschein, 1891.

Garnier, (Clément) Joseph. 1846. *Élements de l'économie politique.* 3d ed.; Paris: Guillaumin, 1856.

Gay, David E. R. 1975. "Adam Smith and Property Rights Analysis." *Review of Social Economy* 32:177–79.

George, Henry. 1879. *Progress and Poverty: An Inquiry into the Cause of Industrial Depressions and of Increase of Want with Increase of Wealth. The Remedy.* San Francisco: W. M. Hilton.

———. 1898. *The Science of Political Economy.* New York: Doubleday.

Gide, Charles, and Charles Rist. 1909. *Histoire des doctrines économiques.* 7th ed., translated *A History of Economic Doctrines.* Boston: Heath, 1948.

Gierke, Otto von. 1895–1917. *Deutsches Privatrecht,* 3 vols. Leipzig: Duncker and Humblot.

Gottl-Ottlilienfeld, Friedrich von. 1928. *Bedarf und Deckung. Ein Vorgriff in der Theorie der Wirtschaft als Leben.* Jena: G. Fischer.

———. 1936. *Volk, Staat, Wirtschaft und Recht.* Berlin: Duncker and Humblot.

Gray, Howard Levi. 1915. *English Field Systems.* Cambridge, Mass.: Harvard University Press.

Graziani, Augusto. 1893. *Il fondamento economico del diritto.* Siena: L. Lazzeri, 1894.

———. 1904. *Istituzioni di economia politica.* Turin: Bocca.

Gregory, David. 1983. "What Marx and Engels Knew of French Socialism." *Historical Reflections* 10:143–93.

Greif, Avner. 1994. "Cultural Beliefs and the Organization of Society: A Historical and Theoretical Reflection on Collectivist and Individualist Societies." *Journal of Political Economy* 102:912–50.

Grünberg, Karl. 1901. "Unfreiheit." In *Handwörterbuch der Staatswissenschaften,* 2d ed., 7:317–37. Jena: G. Fischer.

Grupp, Georg. 1897. "Die Anfänge der Geldwirtschaft." *Zeitschrift für Kulturgeschichte* 4:241–9.

Hadley, Arthur Twining. 1896. *Economics: An Account of the Relations Between Private Property and Public Welfare.* New York: Putnam.

Hahn, Eduard. 1905. *Das Alter der wirtschaftlichen Kultur der Menschheit: Ein Rückblick und ein Ausblick.* Heidelberg: C. Winter.

———. 1908. *Die Entstehung der wirtschaftlichen Arbeit.* Heidelberg: C. Winter.

Hahn, F. H. 1991. "The Next 100 Years." *Economic Journal* 101:47–50.

Hamilton, Walton Hale. 1919. "The Institutional Approach to Economic Theory." *American Economic Review* 9, Supplement: 309–18.

———. 1929. "Law and Economics." *American Economic Review* 19, Supplement: 56–60.

———. 1937. "Institutions." In *Encyclopaedia of the Social Sciences,* 8:84–89. New York: Macmillan.

Hammerstein, Notker. 1972. *Jus und Historie. Ein Beitrag zur Geschichte des historischen Denkens an deutschen Universitäten im späten 17. und im 18. Jahrhundert.* Göttingen: Vandenhoeck and Ruprecht.

Hanssen, Georg. 1835–7. "Ansichten über das Agrarwesen der Vorzeit." Reprinted in *Agrarhistorische Abhandlungen,* 1:1–76. Leipzig: S. Hirzel, 1880.

———. 1863. "Die Gehöferschaften im Regierungsbezirk Trier." Reprinted in *Agrarhistorische Abhandlungen,* 1:99–122. Leipzig: S. Hirzel, 1880.

———. 1870. "Die mittelalterliche Feldgemeinschaft in England nach Nasse im Zusammenhalt mit der skandinavisch-germanischen." *Göttingische Gelehrten Anzeigen.* Reprinted in *Agrarhistorische Abhandlungen,* 1:484–512. Leipzig: S. Hirzel, 1880.

———. 1878. "Wechsel der Wohnsitze und Feldmarken in germanischer Urzeit." Reprinted in *Agrarhistorische Abhandlungen,* 1:77–92. Leipzig: S. Hirzel, 1880.

Hasbach, Wilhelm. 1912. *Die moderne Demokratie. Eine politische Beschreibung.* Jena: G. Fischer.

Haxthausen, August von. 1866. *Die ländliche Verfassung Rußlands.* Leipzig: F. A. Brockhaus.

Hayek, Friedrich A. 1967. "Notes on the Evolution of Systems of Rules of Conduct." In *Studies in Philosophy, Politics and Economics,* 66–81. Chicago: University of Chicago Press.

———. 1973–9. *Law, Legislation and Liberty,* 3 vols. Chicago: University of Chicago Press.

Helferich, Johann A. 1864. Zusatz zu Kawelin, "Einiges über die russische Dorfgemeinde." *Zeitschrift für die gesamte Staatswissenschaft* 20:40–53.

Hennings, Klaus. 1988. "Aspekte der Institutionalisierung der Ökonomie an deutschen Universitäten." In *Die Institutionalisierung der Nationalökonomie an deutschen Universitäten*, ed. Norbert Waszek, 42–54. St. Katarinen: Scripta Mercaturae.

Hennis, Wilhelm. 1987. "A Science of Man: M. Weber and the Political Economy of the German Historical School." In *Max Weber and His Contemporaries*, ed. Wolfgang J. Mommsen and Jürgen Osterhammel, 25–58. London: Allen and Unwin.

Hentschel, Volker. 1978. "Die Staatswissenschaften an den deutschen Universitäten im 18. und frühen 19. Jahrhundert." *Berichte zur Wissenschaftsgeschichte* 1:181–200.

———. 1982. "Zwecksetzungen und Zielvorstellungen in den Wirtschafts- und Soziallehren des 18. und 19. Jahrhunderts." *Berichte zur Wissenschaftsgeschichte* 5:107–30.

Hess, Günter. 1980. "Der Property-Rights-Ansatz – Eine ökonomische Theorie oder Veränderung des Rechtes?" *Jahrbücher für Nationalökonomie und Statistik* 195: 481–95.

Hildebrand, Bruno. 1848. *Die Nationalökonomie der Gegenwart und Zukunft.* Frankfurt a.M.: J. Rutten.

———. 1869. "Die sociale Frage der Vertheilung des Grundeigenthums im klassischen Althertum." *Jahrbücher für Nationalökonomie und Statistik* 12:1–25, 139–55.

Hildebrand, Richard. 1894. *Ueber das Problem einer Allgemeinen Entwicklungsgeschichte des Rechts und der Sitte.* Graz: Leuschner and Lubensky.

———. 1896. *Recht und Sitte auf den primitiveren wirtschaftlichen Kulturstufen.* 2d ed.; Jena: G. Fischer, 1907.

Hirschman, Albert. 1977. *The Passions and the Interests: Political Arguments for Capitalism before Its Triumph.* Princeton, N.J.: Princeton University Press.

———. 1982. "Rival Interpretations of Market Society: Civilizing, Destructive, or Feeble?" *Journal of Economic Literature* 20:1463–84.

Hirt, Hermann. 1898. "Die wirtschaftlichen Zustände der Indogermanen." *Jahrbücher für Nationalökonomie und Statistik* 70:456–63.

Hodgson, Geoffrey. 1993. "Institutional Economics: Surveying the 'Old' and the 'New'." *Review of Political Economy* 1:249–69.

Hodgskin, Thomas. 1827. *Popular Political Economy: Four Lectures Delivered at the London Mechanics' Institution.* London: Tait.

Hont, Istvan, and Michael Ignatieff. 1983. "Needs and Justice in the *Wealth of Nations:* An Introductory Essay." In *Wealth and Virtue: The Shaping of Political Economy in the Scottish Enlightenment,* ed. I. Hont and M. Ignatieff. Cambridge: Cambridge University Press.

Hoselitz, Bert F. 1960. "Theories of Stages of Economic Growth." In *Theories of Economic Growth,* ed. B. Hoselitz. Glencoe, Ill.: Free Press.

Hovenkamp, Herbert. 1990. "The First Great Law & Economics Movement." *Stanford Law Review* 42:993–1058.

Hoyt, Homer. 1918. "The Economic Functions of the Common Law." *Journal of Political Economy* 26:167–99.

Hughes, H. Stuart. 1958. *Consciousness and Society: The Reorientation of European Social Thought, 1890–1930.* Revised ed.; New York: Random House, 1961.

Hutchison, Terence. 1990. *Before Adam Smith: The Emergence of Political Economy, 1662–1776.* Oxford: Blackwell.

Hutter, M. 1982. "Early Contributions to Law and Economics: Adolph Wagner's *Grundlegung.*" *Journal of Economic Issues* 16:131–47.

Iggers, Georg. 1968. *The German Conception of History: The National Tradition of Historical Thought from Herder to the Present.* Revised ed.; Middletown, Conn.: Wesleyan University Press, 1983.

———. 1986. "The European Context of Eighteenth-Century German Enlightenment Historiography." In *Aufklärung und Geschichte,* ed. H. E. Bödeker et al., Göttingen: Vandenhoeck and Ruprecht.

Inama-Sternegg, Karl Theodor von. 1879–99. *Deutsche Wirthschaftsgeschichte,* 3 vols. Leipzig: Duncker and Humblot.

———. 1885. "Nationalökonomische Vorstellungen bei Naturvölkern." *Mitteilungen der Anthropologischen Gesellschaft in Wien. Verhandlungen* 15:14–20.

———. 1896. Review of Meitzen 1895. *Jahrbücher für Nationalökonomie und Statistik* 67:751–60.

Ingram, John Kells. 1878. *The Present Position and Prospects of Political Economy.* London: Longmans.

Jakob, Ludwig Heinrich von. 1805. *Grundsätze der National-Oekonomie oder Theorie des National-Reichthums.* 3d ed.; Halle: F. Ruff, 1825.

James, Harold. 1989. *A German Identity, 1770–1990.* New York: Routledge.

Janssen, Albert. 1974. *Otto von Gierkes Methode der geschichtlichen Rechtswissenschaft.* Göttingen: Musterschmidt.

Jellinek, Georg. 1900. *Allgemeine Staatslehre.* 2d ed.; Berlin: O. Haring, 1905.

Jevons, William Stanley. 1905. *Principles of Economics. A Fragment of a Treatise on the Industrial Mechanism of Society.* London: Macmillan. [Published posthumously.]

Jhering, Rudolph. 1865. *Geist des römischen Rechts auf den verschiedenen Stufen seiner Entwicklung.* Leipzig: Breitkopf and Hartel.

———. 1872. *Der Kampf ums Recht.* Vienna: Manz.

———. 1877–83. *Der Zweck im Recht.* Leipzig: Breitkopf and Hartel.

———. 1889. *Der Besitzwille.* Jena: G. Fischer.

Johnson, Roger D. 1990. "Adam Smith's Radical Views on Property, Distributive Justice and the Market." *Review of Social Economy* 48:247–71.

Jones, Richard. 1859. *Literary Remains: Consisting of Lectures and Tracts on Political Economy.* London: J. Murray. [Published posthumously.]

Kautz, Gyula. 1858. *Die National-Oekonomik als Wissenschaft.* Vienna: C. Gerold's Sohn.

Kelley, Donald R. 1990. *The Human Measure: Social Thought in the Western Legal Tradition.* Cambridge: Harvard University Press.

Keussler, Johannes von. 1876. *Zur Geschichte und Kritik des bäuerlichen Gemeindebesitzes in Russland.* Riga, Moscow, and Odessa: J. Deubner.

Kitch, Edmund W., ed. 1983. "The Fire of Truth: A Remembrance of Law and Economics at Chicago, 1932–1970." *Journal of Law and Economics* 26:163–234.

Knapp, Georg Friedrich. 1872. "Darwin und die Sozialwissenschaften." *Jahrbücher für Nationalökonomie und Statistik* 18:233–47.

Knapp, Georg Friedrich. 1889. "Der Ursprung der Sklaverei in den Kolonien." *Archiv für soziale Gesetzgebung und Statistik* 2:129–45.

———. 1891. "Die Erbunterthänigkeit und die kapitalistische Wirtschaft." *Jahrbücher für Nationalökonomie und Statistik* 55:339–54.

———. 1894. "Die Bauernbefreiung in Österreich und in Preußen." [*Schmoller's*] *Jahrbuch für Gesetzgebung, Verwaltung und Volkswirtschaft* 18:409–31.

———. 1896. Review of Meitzen 1895. *Beilage zur Allgemeinen Zeitung,* 27 October: 1–6.

Knies, Karl. 1852. "Niccolò Machiavelli als volkswirthschaftlicher Schriftsteller." *Zeitschrift für die gesamte Staatswissenschaft* 8:251–96.

———. 1853. *Die politische Oekonomie vom Standpuncte der geschichtlichen Methode.* 2d ed., retitled *Die politische Oekonomie vom geschichtlichen Standpuncte.* Braunschweig: C. A. Schwetschke, 1883.

Knight, Frank. 1924. "Some Fallacies in the Interpretation of Social Cost." *Quarterly Journal of Economics* 38:582–606.

Knight, Jack. 1992. *Institutions and Social Conflict.* Cambridge: Cambridge University Press.

Knudsen, Jonathan B. 1986. *Justus Möser and the German Enlightenment.* Cambridge: Cambridge University Press.

Kocourek, Albert, and H. Wigmore, eds. 1915–18. *Evolution of Law: Select Readings on the Origin and Development of Legal Institutions,* 3 vols. Boston: Little, Brown.

Koehne, Carl. 1928. *Die Streitfragen über den Agrarkommunismus der germanischen Urzeit.* Berlin: Weldman.

Kohler, Josef. 1902. Review of Nieboer 1900. *Zeitschrift für Vergleichende Rechtswissenschaft* 15:314–15.

———. 1907–8. "Wesen und Ziele der Rechtsphilosophie." *Archiv für Rechts- und Wirtschaftsphilosophie* 1:3–16.

———. 1908. Review of Hildebrand [1896] 1907. *Deutsche Literatur-Zeitung,* pp. 3190–2.

———. 1909–10. "Vom Positivismus zum Neuhegelianismus." *Archiv für Rechts- und Wirtschaftsphilosophie* 3:167–72.

———. 1910–11. "Soziologie und Rechtsphilosophie." *Archiv für Rechts- und Wirtschaftsphilosophie* 4:167–72.

Kohler, Josef, and Fritz Berolzheimer. 1908–9. "Die Begründung einer Internationalen Vereinigung für Rechts- und Wirtschaftsphilosophie." *Archiv für Rechts- und Wirtschaftsphilosophie* 2:435–7.

Koot, Gerard M. 1987. *English Historical Economics, 1870–1926.* Cambridge: Cambridge University Press.

Kovalevskii, Maksim M. (Maxim Kovalevsky). 1901–14. *Die ökonomische Entwicklung Europas bis zum Beginn der kapitalistischen Wirtschaftsform,* 7 vols. Berlin: R. L. Präger. [An expansion of his 1898 Russian edition.]

Kroeschell, Karl. 1977. "Zur Lehre vom 'germanischen' Eigentumsbegriff." In *Rechtshistorische Studien: Hans Thieme zum 70. Geburtstag.* Cologne and Vienna: Bohlau.

Kruse, Volker. 1990. "Von der historischen Nationalökonomie zur historischen Soziologie." *Zeitschrift für Soziologie* 19:149–65.

Kulischer, J. 1899. "Aus der Wirtschaft der Naturvölker." *Zeitschrift für Sozialwissenschaft* 2:835–7.

Lafargue, Paul. 1890. *The Evolution of Property from Savagery to Civilization.* London: S. Sonnenschein.

Lampertico, Fedele. 1876. *La proprietà.* Milan: Treves.

Lamprecht, Karl. 1885–6. *Deutsches Wirtschaftsleben im Mittelalter.* Leipzig: A. Dürr.

———. 1889. *Zur Socialgeschichte der deutschen Urzeit.* Tübingen: H. Laupp.

———. 1910. "Geschichte des Grundbesitzes." In *Handwörterbuch der Staatswissenschaften,* 3d ed., 3:107–34. Jena: G. Fischer.

Landsberg, Ernst. 1910. *Geschichte der deutschen Rechtswissenschaft.* Munich: R. Oldenbourg. [Vol. 3 of Roderich von Stintzing's *Geschichte der deutschen Rechtswissenschaft* (1880–1910).]

Langlois, Richard. 1986. "The New Institutional Economics: An Introductory Essay." In *Economics as a Process: Essays in the New Institutional Economics,* ed. Richard Langlois, 1–26. Cambridge: Cambridge University Press.

Lapsley, Gaillard Thomas. 1903. "The Origin of Property in Land." *American Historical Review* 8:426–48.

Laveleye, Émile de. 1874. *De la propriété et de ses formes primitives.* 2d ed., translated *Primitive Property* by T. E. C. Leslie. London: Macmillan, 1878.

———. 1882. *Éléments d'économie politique.* 7th ed.; Paris: Hachette, 1902.

Le Hardy de Beaulieu, Charles. 1868. *La propriété et sa rente dans leurs rapports avec l'économie politique et le droit publique.* Liège: T. Sazonoff.

Leist, Burkard Wilhelm. 1859. *Über die Natur des Eigentums.* Jena: F. Frommann.

Leroy-Beaulieu, Paul. 1881. *Essai sur la répartition des richesses.* 3d ed.; Paris: Guillaumin, 1888.

———. 1888. *Précis d'économie politique.* 13th ed.; Paris: C. Delagrave, 1910.

———. 1895. *Traité theorique et pratique d'économie politique.* 3d ed.; Paris: Guillaumin, 1900.

Leslie, T. E. Cliffe. 1863. "The Wealth of Nations and the Slave Power." *Macmillan's Magazine.* Reprinted in *Essays in Political and Moral Philosophy.* Dublin: Hodges, Foster and Figris, 1879.

———. 1866. "Political Economy and the Tenure of Land." *Fortnightly Review.* Reprinted in *Land Systems and Industrial Economy of Ireland, England and Continental Countries.* London: Macmillan, 1870.

———. 1875. Review of Henry Sumner Maine, *Lectures on the Early History of Institutions* (1875). *Fortnightly Review,* pp. 448–68.

———. 1876. "On the Philosophical Method of Political Economy." *Hermathena.* Reprinted in *Essays in Political and Moral Philosophy.* Dublin: Hodges, Foster and Figris, 1879.

———. 1879. "Political Economy and Sociology." *Fortnightly Review* 31:25–46.

Levine, Norman. 1987. "The German Historical School of Law and the Origins of Historical Materialism." *Journal of the History of Ideas* 48:431–51.

Lewinski, Jan Stanislaw. 1913. *The Origin of Property and the Formation of the Village Community: A Course of Lectures Delivered at the London School of Economics.* London: Constable.

Libecap, Gary D. 1989. *Contracting for Property Rights.* Cambridge: Cambridge University Press.

———. 1992. Review of North 1990. *Journal of Economic Literature* 30:221–3.

Liebe, G. 1900. Review of Hildebrand 1896. *Zeitschrift für Kulturgeschichte* 7:285–6.

List, Friedrich. 1837. *Le système naturel d'économie politique.* Reprinted in *Schriften/Reden/Briefe,* vol. 6. Berlin: R. Hobbing, 1930.

———. 1841. *Das nationale System der politischen Ökonomie.* Reprinted in *Schriften/Reden/Briefe,* vol. 6. Berlin: R. Hobbing, 1930.

Loria, Achille. 1886. *La teoria economica della costituzione politica.* Rome: Bocca. [A much-expanded 2d edition appeared as Loria 1893.]

———. 1893. *Les bases économiques de la constitution sociale.* Translated *The Economic Foundations of Society.* London: S. Sonnenschein, 1910.

McCloskey, Donald. 1989. "English Open-Fields as Behavior Towards Risk." In *Markets in History,* ed. D. W. Galenson. Cambridge: Cambridge University Press.

M'Culloch, J. R. 1825. *The Principles of Political Economy.* Edinburgh: Tait.

Madrazo, Santiago Diego. 1874–6. *Lecciones de economía política,* 3 vols. Madrid: P. Calleja.

Maier, Hans. 1985. *Politische Wissenschaft in Deutschland.* Munich: Piper.

———. 1990. "Staatswissenschaft." In *Staatslexikon: Recht, Wirtschaft, Gesellschaft,* 5:226–7. Freiburg: Herder.

Maine, Henry Sumner. 1861. *Ancient Law: Its Connection with the Early History of Society and Its Relation to Modern Ideas.* Reprint; Boston: Beacon, 1963.

———. 1871. *Village-Communities in the East and West.* 3d ed.; London: J. Murray, 1876.

———. 1875. "The Effects of Observation of India on Modern European Thought." Lecture. Reprinted in Maine [1871] 1876: 203–39.

Mangoldt, Hans K. E. von. 1863. *Grundriß der Volkswirthschaftslehre.* 2d ed.; Stuttgart: J. Maier, 1871.

Marechal, Henry. 1919. *Les conceptions économiques d'A. Comte.* Bar-sur-Seine: Saillard.

Marshall, Alfred. 1890. *Principles of Economics.* 3d ed.; London: Macmillan, 1895.

Marx, Karl. 1842. "Philosophische Manifest der historischen Rechtsschule." *Rheinische Zeitung* 221. Translated "The Philosophical Manifesto of the Historical School of Law," in *Karl Marx, Frederick Engels: Collected Works,* 1:203–10. London: Lawrence and Wishart, 1975.

———. 1844. *Economic and Philosophic Manuscripts of 1844. Karl Marx, Frederick Engels: Collected Works,* vol. 3. London: Lawrence and Wishart, 1975.

———. 1847. *Das Elend der Philosophie.* Translated *The Poverty of Philosophy. Karl Marx, Frederick Engels: Collected Works,* vol. 6. London: Lawrence and Wishart, 1976.

———. 1857–8. *Grundrisse der Kritik der politischen Ökonomie.* [First published Moscow, 1939–41.]

———. 1859. *Zur Kritik der politischen Ökonomie.* Translated *A Contribution to the Critique of Political Economy. Karl Marx, Frederick Engels: Collected Works,* vol. 29. London: Lawrence and Wishart, 1987.

————. 1867. *Das Kapital,* vol. 1. Translated *Capital.* New York: Vintage, 1977.

Marx, Karl, and Engels, Friedrich. 1845. *Die heilige Familie.* Translated *The Holy Family. Karl Marx, Frederick Engels, Collected Works,* vol. 4. London: Lawrence and Wishart, 1975.

————. 1845–6. *Die deutsche Ideologie.* Translated *The German Ideology. Karl Marx, Frederick Engels, Collected Works,* vol. 5. London: Lawrence and Wishart, 1976.

Mauduit, Roger. 1929. *Auguste Comte et la science économique.* Paris: Alcan.

Mayr, Georg von. 1906. *Begriff und Gliederung der Staatswissenschaften.* 4th ed.; Tübingen: H. Laupp, 1921.

Meek, Ronald L. 1971. "Smith, Turgot and the 'Four Stages' Theory." *History of Political Economy* 3:9–27.

Meitzen, August. 1895. *Siedelung und Agrarwesen der Westgermanen und Ostgermanen, der Kelten, Römer, Finnen und Slawen,* 3 vols. Berlin: W. Hertz.

————. 1900. "Feldgemeinschaft." In *Handwörterbuch der Staatswissenschaften,* ed. J. Conrad et al., 2d ed., 3:831–45. Jena: G. Fischer.

Menger, Carl. 1871. *Grundsätze der Volkswirtschaftslehre.* Translated *Principles of Economics.* New York: New York University Press, 1981.

————. 1883. *Untersuchungen über die Methode der Sozialwissenschaften und der politischen Ökonomie insbesondere.* Translated *Investigations into the Method of the Social Sciences with Special Reference to Economics.* New York: New York University Press, 1985.

Mercier de la Rivière. 1767. *L'Ordre naturel et essentiel des sociétés politiques.* Reprinted in *Physiocrates,* ed. E. Daire. Paris: Guillaumin, 1846.

Meyer, Eduard. 1895. "Die wirtschaftliche Entwicklung des Altertums." *Jahrbücher für Nationalökonomie und Statistik.* Reprinted in *Kleine Schriften zur Geschichtstheorie und zur wirtschaftlichen und politischen Geschichte des Altertums,* 79–168. Halle: Niemeyer, 1910.

————. 1899. *Die Sklaverei im Altertum.* Reprinted in *Kleine Schriften zur Geschichtstheorie und zur wirtschaftlichen und politischen Geschichte des Altertums,* 169–212. Halle: Niemeyer, 1910.

Miaskowski, August von. 1879. Review of Bücher 1879. *Jahrbücher für Nationalökonomie und Statistik* 33:460–69.

————. 1890. *Das Problem der Grundbesitzverteilung in geschichtlicher Entwicklung.* Leipzig: Duncker and Humblot.

Milgate, Murray, and Shannon Stimson. 1991. *Ricardian Politics.* Princeton, N.J.: Princeton University Press.

Mill, John Stuart. 1848. *Principles of Political Economy.* Boston: Little, Brown.

Minghetti, Marco. 1859. *Dell'economia pubblica e delle sue attinenze colla morale e col diritto.* Translated *Des rapports de l'économie publique avec la morale et le droit.* Paris: Guillaumin, 1863.

Miraglia, Luigi. 1885. *Filosofia del diritto.* 3d ed.; Naples: Tip. della Regia Universita, 1903.

Molinari, Gustave de. 1853a. "Esclavage." In *Dictionnaire de l'économie politique,* ed. C. Coquelin et al., 1:712–31. Brussels: Méline.

————. 1853b. "Servage." In *Dictionnaire de l'économie politique,* ed. C. Coquelin et al., 2:610–13. Brussels: Méline.

Molinari, Gustave de. 1855. *Cours d'économie politique.* 2d ed., 2 vols.; Brussels: A. Lacroix, 1863.

———. 1891. *Notions fondamentales d'économie politique et programme économique.* Paris: Guillaumin.

Montague, F. C. 1899. "Property." In *Dictionary of Political Economy,* ed. R. H. I. Palgrave, 3:229–32. London: Macmillan.

Mood, Fulmer. 1943. "The Development of Frederick Jackson Turner as an Historical Thinker." *Publications of the Colonial Society of Massachusetts* 34:282–352.

Morgan, Lewis Henry. 1877. *Ancient Society.* Reprint; Chicago: Kerr, 1910.

Moszkowski, Max. 1911. *Vom Wirtschaftsleben der primitiven Völker. (Probleme der Weltwirtschaft,* 5.) Jena: G. Fischer.

Mourant, John A. 1943. *The Physiocratic Conception of Natural Law.* Chicago: University of Chicago Press.

Müller, Adam. ca. 1808. "Welches sind die Erfordernisse eines zureichenden Staatswirtschaftlichen Systems?" First published in *Jahrbücher für Nationalökonomie und Statistik* 134 (1931): 1–6.

Mueller, Dennis. 1979. *Public Choice.* Cambridge: Cambridge University Press.

Nardi-Greco, C. 1907. *La sociologia giuridica.* Turin: Bocca.

Navratil, Akos von. 1905. "Wirtschaft und Recht: Ein Beitrag zur Theorie der secundären wirthschaftlichen Erscheinungen" [first part]. *Zeitschrift für Ungarisches Öffentliches und Privatrecht* 11:273–305.

Nelson, Richard R., and Sidney G. Winter. 1982. *An Evolutionary Theory of Economic Change.* Cambridge, Mass.: Harvard University Press.

Neukamp, Ernst. 1895. *Einleitung in einer Entwicklungsgeschichte des Rechts.* Berlin: C. Heymann.

Neumann, Karl Johannes. 1900. *Die Grundherrschaft der römischen Republik, die Bauernbefreiung und die Entstehung der servianischen Verfassung.* Strassburg: Heitz and Mundel.

Neurath, Otto. 1909. *Antike Wirtschaftsgeschichte.* Leipzig: B. G. Teubner.

Newman, Samuel Philipps. 1835. *Elements of Political Economy.* Andover, Mass.: Gould and Newman.

Nicholson, J. Shield. 1893–1901. *Principles of Political Economy.* 2d ed., 3 vols.; London: Black, 1902–8.

———. 1903. *Elements of Political Economy.* London: Macmillan.

Nieboer, H. J. 1900. *Slavery as an Industrial System: Ethnological Researches.* The Hague: M. Nijhoff.

Normano, J. F. 1931. "Karl Bücher: An Isolated Economist." *Journal of Political Economy* 39:655–57.

North, Douglass C. 1981. *Structure and Change in Economic History.* New York: Norton.

———. 1990. *Institutions, Institutional Change and Economic Performance.* Cambridge: Cambridge University Press.

North, Douglass C., and Robert Paul Thomas. 1973. *The Rise of the Western World: A New Economic History.* Cambridge: Cambridge University Press.

———. 1977. "The First Economic Revolution." *Economic History Review.* [Reprinted with revisions in North 1981.]

Nyiri, J. C. 1986. "The Intellectual Foundations of Austrian Liberalism." In *Aus-*

*trian Economics: Historical and Philosophical Background,* ed. Wolfgang Grassl and Barry Smith. London: Croom Helm.

Oertmann, Paul. 1891. *Die Volkswirtschaftslehre des Corpus juris civilis.* Berlin: R. L. Präger.

Olson, Mancur. 1965. *The Logic of Collective Action.* Cambridge, Mass.: Harvard University Press.

———. 1982. *The Rise and Decline of Nations: Economic Growth, Stagflation and Social Rigidities.* New Haven, Conn.: Yale University Press.

Oppenheimer, Franz. 1900. "Nationalökonomie, Sociologie, Anthropologie." *Zeitschrift für Socialwissenschaft* 3:485–93, 621–33.

———. 1907. *Der Staat.* Translated *The State: Its History and Development Viewed Sociologically.* Indianapolis: Bobbs-Merrill, 1914.

———. 1921. *Die psychologischen Wurzel von Sittlichkeit und Recht.* Jena: G. Fischer.

Page, Thomas Walker. 1900. *The End of Villainage in England.* (Publications of the American Economic Association, 3d ser., vol. 1.) New York: Macmillan.

Pakhman (Pachman), Semen V. 1882. *Über die gegenwärtige Bewegung in der Rechtswissenschaft.* Reprint; Berlin: Duncker and Humblot, 1986.

Pareto, Vilfredo. 1896–7. *Cours d'économie politique,* 2 vols. Lausanne: F. Rouge.

Pascal, Roy. 1938. "Property and Society: The Scottish Historical School of the Eighteenth Century." *Modern Quarterly* (London) 1:167–179.

Peacock, Alan. 1992. *Public-Choice Analysis in Historical Perspective.* Cambridge: Cambridge University Press.

Pejovich, Steve. 1982. "Karl Marx, Property Rights School and the Process of Social Change." *Kyklos* 35:383–97.

Peter, Hans. 1949. *Wandlungen der Eigentumsordnung und der Eigentumslehre seit dem 19. Jahrhundert.* Aarau: H. R. Sauerlander.

Petrucci, Raphael. 1905. *Les origines naturelles de la propriété: Essai de sociologie comparée.* Brussels: Misch and Thron.

Philippovich von Philippsberg, Eugen. 1893. *Grundriß der politischen Oekonomie.* 15th ed.; Tübingen: J. C. B. Mohr, 1920.

Pöhlmann, Robert von. 1893–1901. *Geschichte des antiken Kommunismus und Sozialismus,* 2 vols. Munich: Beck.

Posner, Richard A. 1973. *The Economic Analysis of Law.* Boston: Little, Brown.

———. 1980. "A Theory of Primitive Society, with Special Reference to the Law." *Journal of Law and Economics* 23:1–53.

Pound, Roscoe. 1911–12. "The Scope and Purpose of Sociological Jurisprudence." *Harvard Law Review* 24:591–619, 25:140–68, 489–516.

Pribram, Karl. 1983. *A History of Economic Reasoning.* Baltimore: Johns Hopkins University Press.

Proudhon, Pierre-Joseph. 1840. *Qu'est-ce que la propriété? ou recherches sur le principe du droit et du gouvernement.* Translated *What Is Property? An Inquiry into the Principle of Right and of Government.* New York: Humboldt, 1890.

Pryor, Frederick L. 1977. *The Origins of the Economy: A Comparative Study of Distribution in Primitive and Peasant Societies.* New York: Academic Press.

Pyle, Kenneth B. 1974. "Advantages of Followership: German Economists and Japanese Bureaucrats, 1890–1925." *Journal of Japanese Studies* 1:127–64.

Quesnay, François. 1765–6. "Le droit naturel." *Journal de l'agriculture, du com-*

*merce et des finances.* Reprinted in *Oeuvres économiques et philosophiques de François Quesnay,* ed. A. Oncken. Frankfurt a.M.: J. Baer, 1888.

Rachfahl, Felix. 1900. "Zur Geschichte des Grundeigentums." *Jahrbücher für Nationalökonomie und Statistik* 74:1–33, 161–216.

Randa, Anton. 1884. *Das Eigenthumsrecht.* 2d ed.; Leipzig: Breitkopf and Hartel, 1893.

Rau, Karl Heinrich. 1826. *Grundsätze der Volkswirthschaftslehre.* (*Lehrbuch der politischen Oekonomie,* vol. 1.) 5th ed.; Heidelberg: C. F. Winter, 1847.

Reill, Hans Peter. 1975. *The German Enlightenment and the Rise of Historicism.* Berkeley: University of California Press.

Remer, Justus. 1935. *Die geistigen Grundlagen der historischen Schule der Nationalökonomie.* Leipzig: H. Buske.

Rioult de Neuville, R. 1891. Review of Laveleye [1874] 1878. *Revue des Questions Historiques* 50:214–27.

Rodbertus, Johann Karl. 1864. "Zur Geschichte der agrarischen Entwicklung Roms unter den Kaisern oder die Askriptitier, Inquilinen und Kolonen." *Jahrbücher für Nationalökonomie und Statistik* 2:206–67.

Roesler, Hermann. 1878. *Vorlesungen über Volkswirthschaft.* Erlangen: A. Deichert.

Rogers, James Edwin Thorold. 1889. *The Economic Interpretation of History.* London: T. F. Unwin.

Roscher, Wilhelm. 1843. *Grundriß zu Vorlesungen über die Staatswirthschaft. Nach geschichtlicher Methode.* Göttingen: Dieter.

———. ca. 1851. *Grundzüge einer nationalökonomischen Erklärung des Privateigenthums.* n.p., n.d.

———. 1854. *Grundlagen der Nationalökonomie.* (*System der Volkswirtschaft,* vol. 1.) 24th ed.; Stuttgart and Berlin: B. G. Teubner, 1906.

———. 1859. *Die Nationalökonomik des Ackerbaus und der verwandten Urproduktionen.* (*System der Volkswirtschaft,* vol. 2.) 13th ed.; Stuttgart and Berlin: J. G. Cotta, 1903.

———. 1861. *Ansichten der Volkswirtschaft aus dem geschichtlichen Standpunkt.* Leipzig: C. F. Winter.

———. 1862. Preface to Dankwardt 1862.

———. 1874. *Geschichte der National-Oekonomik in Deutschland.* Munich: R. Oldenbourg.

———. 1892. *Politik: Geschichtliche Naturlehre der Monarchie, Aristokratie und Demokratie.* Stuttgart: J. G. Cotta.

Rudmin, F. W. 1992. "Cross-Cultural Correlates of the Ownership of Private Property." *Social Science Research* 21:57–83.

Rutherford, M. 1983. "J. R. Commons's Institutional Economics." *Journal of Economic Issues* 17:721–44.

Samter, Adolph. 1878. "Der Eigenthumsbegriff." *Jahrbücher für Nationalökonomie und Statistik* 30:269–303.

———. 1879. *Das Eigenthum in seiner sozialen Bedeutung.* Jena: G. Fischer.

Samuelson, Paul. 1947. *Foundations of Economic Analysis.* Cambridge, Mass.: Harvard University Press.

Sartorius, Georg. 1806. "Von der Mitwirkung der obersten Gewalt im Staate zur Beförderung des National-Reichthums." In *Abhandlungen, die Elemente des*

*National-Reichthums und die Staatswirthschaft betreffend:* 199–519. Göttingen: J. F. Rower.

Sax, Emil. 1887. *Grundlegung der theoretischen Staatswirtschaft.* Vienna: A. Holder.

Say, Jean-Baptiste. 1803. *Traité d'économie politique. ou simple exposition de la manière dont se forment, se distribuent et se consomment les richness.* Translated *A Treatise on Political Economy.* Philadelphia: Claxtion, 1880.

———. 1815. *Catéchisme d'économie politique.* 2d ed; Paris: Bossange, 1821.

———. 1828–9. *Cours complet d'économie politique pratique.* 2d ed.; Brussels: Société Belge de Libraire, 1840.

Schäffle, Albert E. F. 1858. *Das gesellschaftliche System der menschlichen Wirthschaft: ein Lehr- und Handbuch der ganzen politischen Oekonomie einschließlich der Volkswirthschaftspolitik und Staatswissenschaft.* 3d ed.; Tübingen: H. Laupp, 1873.

———. 1875–8. *Bau und Leben des socialen Körpers,* 4 vols. Tübingen: H. Laupp.

Scheel, Hans von. 1865. Review of Friedrich Bitzer's *Die Genesis der Volkswirtschaft* (1866). *Jahrbücher für Nationalökonomie und Statistik* 4:355–9.

———. 1866. "Die wirtschaftlichen Grundbegriffe im Corpus juris Civilis." *Jahrbücher für Nationalökonomie und Statistik* 6:324–44.

———. 1877. *Eigentum und Erbrecht.* Berlin: C. Habel.

Schlatter, Richard. 1951. *Private Property: The History of an Idea.* New Brunswick, N.J: Rutgers University Press.

Schleicher, August. 1863. "Der wirthschaftliche Culturzustand des indogermanischen Urvolkes." *Jahrbücher für Nationalökonomie und Statistik* 1:401–11.

Schmidt, Wilhelm. 1937–42. *Das Eigentum auf den ältesten Stufen der Menschheit,* 3 vols. Münster i.W.: Aschendorff.

Schmoller, Gustav. 1874–5. "Über einige Grundfragen des Rechts und der Volkswirtschaft." *Jahrbücher für Nationalökonomie und Statistik* 24. Reprinted in *Über einige Grundfragen des Rechts und der Volkswirtschaft,* 1–211. Leipzig: Duncker and Humblot, 1898.

———. 1888a. "Der Kampf des preußischen Königthums um die Erhaltung des Bauernstands." [*Schmoller's*] *Jahrbuch für Gesetzgebung, Verwaltung und Volkswirtschaft* 12:645–55.

———. 1888b. "Die soziale Entwickelung Deutschlands und Englands hauptsächlich auf dem platten Lande des Mittelalters." [*Schmoller's*] *Jahrbuch für Gesetzgebung, Verwaltung und Volkswirtschaft* 12:203–18.

———. 1901–4. *Grundriß der allgemeinen Volkswirtschaftslehre,* 2 vols. Leipzig: Duncker and Humblot.

———. 1912. "Demokratie und soziale Zukunft." Reprinted in *Zwanzig Jahre deutscher Politik (1897–1917). Aufsätze und Vorträge von Gustav Schmoller,* 103–12. Munich and Leipzig: Duncker and Humblot, 1920.

Schön, Johann. 1835. *Neue Untersuchungen der Nationalökonomie und der natürlichen Volkswirthschaftsordnung.* Stuttgart and Tübingen: J. G. Cotta.

Schotter, Andrew. 1981. *The Economic Theory of Social Institutions.* Cambridge: Cambridge University Press.

Schreuer, H. 1898. Review of Hildebrand 1896. *Zeitschrift der Savigny-Stiftung, G.A.* 19:167–74.

Schüz, Carl Wolfgang Christoph. 1836. *Ueber den Einfluß der Vertheilung des Grun-*

*deigenthums auf das Volks- und Staatsleben.* Reprint; Berlin: Zentralantiquäriat der DDR, 1976.

Schumpeter, Joseph A. 1954. *History of Economic Analysis.* New York: Oxford University Press.

Schurtz, Heinrich. 1900. "Anfänge des Landbesitzes." *Zeitschrift für Sozialwissenschaft* 3:245–55, 532–61.

Schwiedland, Eugen Peter. 1912. "Allgemeine Volkswirtschaftslehre." In *Wirtschaft und Recht der Gegenwart,* ed. Leopold M. W. von Wiese und Kaiserswaldau, 1:12–95. Tübingen: J. C. B. Mohr.

Seckler, David W. 1975. *Thorstein Veblen and the Institutionalists.* London: Macmillan.

Sedgwick, Theodore. 1836. *Public and Private Economy.* New York: Harper.

Sée, Henri. 1929. *The Economic Interpretation of History.* New York: Adelphi.

Seebohm, Frederic. 1883. *The English Village Community Examined in Its Relations to the Manorial and Tribal Systems and to the Common or Open Field System of Husbandry: An Essay in Economic History.* London: Longmans, Green.

Seligman, Edwin R. A. 1902. *The Economic Interpretation of History.* 2d ed.; New York: Columbia University Press, 1907.

———. 1904. *Social Aspects of Economic Law.* (Publications of the American Economic Association, no. 5.) New York: Macmillan.

Sen, Amartya. 1970. "The Impossibility of a Paretian Liberal." *Journal of Political Economy* 78:152–7.

Sering, Max, et al. 1908. *Die Vererbung des ländlichen Grundbesitzes im Königreich Preußen.* Berlin: Parey.

Simkovich, Vladimir G. 1909. "Die Bauernbefreiung in Russland." In *Handwörterbuch der Staatswissenschaften,* ed. J. Conrad et al., 3d ed., 2:601–19. Jena: G. Fischer.

Sismondi, J.-C.-L. Simonde de. 1819. *Nouveaux principes d'économie politique.* Translated *New Principles of Political Economy.* New Brunswick, N.J.: Transaction, 1991.

———. 1833. "Lessons of Experience on the Emancipation of Slaves." *New Monthly Magazine,* 2d ser., no. 38: 257–71.

Skinner, Quentin. 1984. "The Idea of Negative Liberty: Philosophical and Historical Perspectives." In *Philosophy in History: Essays on the Historiography of Philosophy,* ed. Richard Rorty et al., 193–221. Cambridge: Cambridge University Press.

Smith, Adam. 1762–4. *Lectures on Jurisprudence.* New edition by R. L. Meek et al.; Oxford: Clarendon, 1978.

———. 1776. *An Inquiry into the Nature and Causes of the Wealth of Nations.* Chicago: University of Chicago Press, 1976.

Smith, Woodruff D. 1991. *Politics and the Sciences of Culture in Germany, 1840–1920.* Oxford: Oxford University Press.

Société d'Économie Politique. 1855. "Des fondaments du droit de propriété." *Journal des Économistes,* 2d ser., no. 5: 141–55.

Sombart, Werner. 1902. *Der moderne Kapitalismus,* 2 vols. Leipzig: Duncker and Humblot.

———. 1924. *Die Ordnung des Wirtschaftslebens.* 2d ed.; Berlin: J. Springer, 1927.

———. 1928. *Der moderne Kapitalismus,* 6th ed., 6 vols. Munich: Duncker and Humblot.

Sommer, Louise. 1920–5. *Die österreichischen Kameralisten in dogmengeschicht-licher Darstellung,* 2 vols. Vienna: C. Konegen.

Spiegel, Henry William. 1991. *The Growth of Economic Thought.* Durham, N.C.: Duke University Press.

Stammler, Rudolf. 1896. *Wirtschaft und Recht nach der materialistischen Geschicht-sauffassung.* Leipzig: Veit.

———. 1901. Review of R. Hildebrand 1894. *Archiv für Systematische Philosophie* 7:414.

Stein, Lorenz von. 1881. *Die drei Fragen des Grundbesitzes und seiner Zukunft.* Stuttgart: J. G. Cotta.

Stein, Peter. 1980. *Legal Evolution: The Story of an Idea.* Cambridge: Cambridge University Press.

Storch, Henri (Heinrich von). 1815. *Cours d'économie politique, ou exposition des principes qui déterminent la prospérité des nations.* Reprint, 4 vols.; Paris: J. P. Aillaud, 1823.

Sugden, Robert. 1986. *The Economics of Rights, Co-operation and Welfare.* Oxford: Blackwell.

Tarde, Gabriel de. 1893. *Les transformations du droit: Étude sociologique.* 2d ed.; Paris, 1909.

Tribe, Keith. 1983. "Prussian Agriculture—German Politics: Max Weber 1892–97." *Economy & Society* 12:181–226.

———. 1988. *Governing Economy: The Reformation of German Economic Discourse, 1750–1840.* Cambridge: Cambridge University Press.

Trinchera, Francesco. 1854. *Corso di economia politica.* Turin: A. Pons.

Turgot, Anne-Robert-Jacques. 1753–4. *Plan d'un ouvrage sur le commerce, la circulation et l'interêt de l'argent, la richesse des états.* Reprinted in *Oeuvres,* ed. Gustave Schelle. Paris: F. Alcan, 1913–23.

———. 1769. *Réflexions sur la formation et la distribution des richesses.* Reprinted in *Oeuvres,* ed. Gustave Schelle. Paris: F. Alcan, 1913–23.

Turner, Frederick Jackson. 1938. *The Early Writings of Frederick Jackson Turner.* Madison: University of Wisconsin Press.

Umbeck, John R. 1981. *A Theory of Property Rights, with Applications to the California Gold Rush.* Ames: Iowa State University Press.

Vaccaro, Michele Angelo. 1893. *Le basi del diritto e dello stato.* New ed., translated *Les bases sociologiques du droit et de l'état.* Paris: V. Giard and E. Brière, 1898.

Vanberg, Viktor. 1986. "Spontaneous Market Order and Social Rules: A Critical Examination of F. A. Hayek's Theory of Cultural Evolution." *Economics and Philosophy* 2:75–180.

———. 1989. "Carl Menger's Evolutionary and John R. Commons' Collective Action Approach to Institutions: A Comparison." *Review of Political Economy* 1:334–60.

Vanni, Icilio. 1890. *Il problema della filosofia del diritto nella filosofia, nella scienza e nella vita ai tempi nostri.* Verona: V. Tedeschi.

Veblen, Thorstein. 1894. Review of Karl Kautsky, *Der Parlamentarismus, die*

*Volksgesetzgebung und die Socialdemokratie* (1893). *Journal of Political Economy* 2:312–14.

———. 1898a. "The Beginnings of Ownership." *American Journal of Sociology* 4:352–65.

———. 1898b. "Why Is Economics Not an Evolutionary Science?" *Quarterly Journal of Economics*. Reprinted in *The Place of Science in Modern Civilization and Other Essays*. New York: Russell and Russell, 1961.

———. 1899. *The Theory of the Leisure Class: An Economic Study of the Evolution of Institutions*. New York: Macmillan.

———. 1909. "The Limits of Marginal Utility." *Journal of Political Economy* 17. Reprinted in *The Place of Science in Modern Civilization and Other Essays*. New York: Russell and Russell, 1961.

———. 1914. *The Instinct of Workmanship and the State of the Industrial Arts*. New York: Macmillan.

———. 1917. *An Inquiry into the Nature of Peace and the Terms of Its Perpetuation*. New York: Macmillan.

Veljanovski, C. G. 1982. *The New Law-and-Economics: A Research Review*. Oxford: Centre for Socio-Legal Studies.

Vierkandt, Alfred. 1899. "Die wirtschaftlichen Verhältnisse der Naturvölker." *Zeitschrift für Socialwissenschaft* 2:81–97, 175–85.

Vinogradoff, Paul. 1892. *Villainage in England: Essays in English Medieval History*. Oxford: Clarendon.

———. 1920–2. *Outlines of Historical Jurisprudence,* 2 vols. London.

Voigt, Andreas. 1911. "Wirtschaft und Recht" [plus comments from floor]. *Verhandlungen des Deutschen Soziologentages* 1:249–74.

Wagner, Adolph H. G. 1876. *Grundlegung der politischen Oekonomie. (Lehr- und Handbuch der politischen Oekonomie,* vols. 1–2.) 3d ed.; Leipzig: C. F. Winter, 1892–4.

Walker, Donald A. 1977. "Thorstein Veblen's Economic System." *Economic Inquiry* 15:213–37.

Walker, Mack. 1978. "Rights and Functions: The Social Categories of Eighteenth-Century German Jurists and Cameralists." *Journal of Modern History* 50:234–51.

Walras, Léon. 1860. *L'économie politique et la justice: examen critique et réfutation des doctrines économiques de P. J. Proudhon*. Paris: Guillaumin.

———. 1874. *Éléments d'économie politique pure*. 1926 ed., translated *Elements of Pure Economics*. London: Allen and Unwin, 1954.

———. 1896. *Études d'économie sociale et théorie de la répartition de la richesse sociale*. Lausanne: F. Rouge.

Ward, Benjamin. 1972. *What's Wrong with Economics?* New York: Basic Books.

Waszek, Norbert. 1988. "Die Staatswissenschaften an der Universität Berlin im 19. Jahrhundert." In *Die Institutionalisierung der Nationalökonomie an deutschen Universitäten,* ed. N. Waszek. St. Katarinen: Scripta Mercaturae.

Weber, Max. 1891. *Die römische Agrargeschichte in ihrer Bedeutung für das Staats- und Privatrecht*. Stuttgart: F. Enke.

———. 1904. "Der Streit um den Charakter der altgermanischen Sozialverfassung in der deutschen Zeitschriftenliteratur des letzten Jahrzehnts." *Jahrbücher für Nationalökonomie und Statistik* 83:433–70.

————. 1922. *Wirtschaft und Gesellschaft: Grundriss der verstehenden Soziologie.* (*Grundriss der Sozialökonomik,* vol. 3.) Translated *Economy and Society: An Outline of Interpretive Sociology,* 3 vols. Berkeley: University of California Press, 1978. [Published posthumously.]

————. 1923. *Wirtschafts-Geschichte. Abriss der universalen Sozial- und Wirtschafts-Geschichte.* Reprint; Munich and Leipzig: Duncker and Humblot, 1924. [Published posthumously from Weber's academic lectures.]

Westermarck, Edward. 1906–8. *The Origin and Development of the Moral Ideas.* London: Macmillan.

Whitman, James Q. 1990. *The Legacy of Roman Law in the German Romantic Era.* Princeton, N.J.: Princeton University Press.

Wieser, Friedrich von. 1901. *Über die gesellschaftlichen Gewalten.* Reprinted in *Gesammelte Abhandlungen,* 346–76. Tübingen: J. C. B. Mohr, 1929.

————. 1905. *Über Vergangenheit und Zukunft der österreichischen Verfassung.* Vienna: C. Konegen.

————. 1910. *Recht und Macht: Sechs Vorträge.* Leipzig: Duncker and Humblot.

————. 1914. *Theorie der gesellschaftlichen Wirtschaft.* (*Grundriss der Sozialökonomik,* vol. 1.) 2d ed. (1923), translated *Social Economics.* London: Allen and Unwin, 1928.

Wilhelm, Walter. 1979. "Private Freiheit und gesellschaftliche Grenzen des Eigentums in der Theorie der Pandektenwissenschaft." In *Wissenschaft und Kodifikation des Privatrechts im 19. Jahrhundert,* ed. C. Coing and W. Wilhelm, 4:19–39. Frankfurt a.M.: Klostermann

Williamson, Oliver E. 1985. *The Economic Institutions of Capitalism.* New York: Free Press.

Willoweit, Dietmar. 1987. "Hermann Conring." In *Staatsdenker im 17. und 18. Jahrhundert,* ed Michael Stolleis, 2d ed. Frankfurt a.M.: A. Metzner.

Winkel, Harald. 1976. "Zur theoretischen Begründung der Bodenmobilisierung in der Volkswirtschaftslehre." In *Wissenschaft und Kodifikation des Privatrechts im 19. Jahrhundert,* ed. C. Coing and W. Wilhelm, 3:156–71. Frankfurt a.M.: Klostermann.

————. 1977. *Die deutsche Nationalökonomie im 19. Jahrhundert.* Darmstadt: Wissenschaftliche Gesellschaft.

Wirth, Max. 1856–9. *Grundzüge der National-Ökonomie.* 5th ed., 2 vols; Cologne: M. DuMont-Schauberg, 1873–83.

Wittich, Werner. 1896. *Die Grundherrschaft in Nordwestdeutschland.* Leipzig: Duncker and Humblot.

————. 1897. "Die wirthschaftliche Kultur der Deutschen zur Zeit Cäsars" [review of R. Hildebrand 1896]. *Historische Zeitschrift* 79:45–67.

————. 1898. "Gutsherrschaft." In *Handwörterbuch der Staatswissenschaften,* ed. J. Conrad et al., 2d ed., 4:930–37. Jena: G. Fischer.

————. 1901. "Die Frage der Freibauern. Untersuchungen über die soziale Gliederung des deutschen Volkes in altgermanischer und frühkarolingischer Zeit." *Zeitschrift der Savigny-Stiftung, G.A.* 22:235–353.

Wolf, Erik. 1963. *Grosse Rechtsdenker der deutschen Geistesgeschichte.* 4th ed.; Tübingen: J. C. B. Mohr.

Wopfner, Hermann. 1912–13. "Beiträge zur Geschichte der älteren Markgenossenschaft." *Mitteilungen des Instituts für österreichische Geschichtsforschungen* 33: 553ff.; 34: 1ff.

Worms, René. 1885. "La sociologie et le droit." *Revue Internationale de Sociologie* 3:35–53.

Zöpel, Ch. 1974. *Ökonomie und Recht. Ein wissenschaftshistorischer und wissenschaftstheoretischer Beitrag zum Verhältnis von Wirtschafts-und Rechtswissenschaften.* Stuttgart: Kohlhammer.

# Index